Human Rights Perspectives

Published by
Saurabh Publishing House

Human Rights Perspectives

Parmesh Kumar

Saurabh
Publishing House
4263/3, Ansari Road,
Darya Ganj, New Delhi-110002

Published by:
SAURABH PUBLISHING HOUSE

Distributed by:
LOTUS PRESS
4263/3, Ansari Road, Darya Ganj, New Delhi-110002
Ph.: 32903912, 23280047 • E-mail : lotus_press@sify.com

Saurabh Publishing is an imprint of
Lotus Press

Human Rights Perspectives

ISBN : 978-81-89005-71-9 (H/B)

Printed in India by Anand Sons, Delhi

Preface

Human rights refer to the "basic rights and freedoms to which all humans are entitled." Examples of rights and freedoms which have come to be commonly thought of as human rights include civil and political rights, such as the right to life and liberty, freedom of expression, and equality before the law; and economic, social and cultural rights, including the right to participate in culture, the right to food, the right to work, and the right to education. All human beings are born free and equal in dignity and rights. They are endowed with reason and conscience and should act towards one another in a spirit of brotherhood.

The Universal Declaration of Human Rights (UDHR) is a non-binding declaration adopted by the United Nations General Assembly in 1948, partly in response to the atrocities of World War II. Although the UDHR is a non-binding resolution, it is now considered to be a central component of international customary law which may be invoked under appropriate circumstances by national and other judiciaries. The UDHR urges member nations to promote a number of human, civil, economic and social rights, asserting these rights are part of the "foundation of freedom, justice and peace in the world." The declaration was the first international legal effort to limit the behaviour of states and press upon them duties to their citizens following the model of the rights-duty duality.

The major topics dealt in this bok are: *Introduction to Human Rights; Human Security; Human Trafficking; Customary International Laws; Discrimination; Public International Law; Universal Declaration of Human Rights; European Convention on Human*

Rights; American Convention on Human Rights; Self-determination; Economic Freedom; Freedom of Movement; Freedom of Religion; Human Rights in India; etc.

We express our gratitude to various scholars, teachers and friends for their assistance and guidance. Finally, we thank our publisher for bringing out this book in very limited time.

– Author

Contents

1
Introduction to Human Rights

Human rights refer to the "basic rights and freedoms to which all humans are entitled." Examples of rights and freedoms which have come to be commonly thought of as human rights include civil and political rights, such as the right to life and liberty, freedom of expression, and equality before the law; and economic, social and cultural rights, including the right to participate in culture, the right to food, the right to work, and the right to education.

> All human beings are born free and equal in dignity and rights. They are endowed with reason and conscience and should act towards one another in a spirit of brotherhood.
>
> —Article 1 of the United Nations Universal Declaration of Human Rights (UDHR)

Several ancient documents and later religions and philosophies included a variety of concepts that may be considered to be human rights.

Notable among such documents are the Edicts of Ashoka issued by Ashoka the Great of India between 272-231 BC; and the Constitution of Medina of 622 AD, drafted by prophet Muhammad to mark a formal agreement between all of the significant tribes and families of Yathrib (later known as Medina), including Muslims, Jews and Pagans. The English Magna Carta of 1215 is particularly significant in the history of English law, and is hence significant in international law and constitutional law today.

Much of modern human rights law and the basis of most modern interpretations of human rights can be traced back to relatively recent history. The Twelve Articles of the Black Forest (1525) are considered to be the first record of human rights in Europe. They were part of the peasants' demands raised towards the Swabian League in the Peasants' War in Germany. The British Bill of Rights (or "An Act Declaring the Rights and Liberties of the Subject and Settling the Succession of the Crown") of 1689 made illegal a range of oppressive governmental actions in the United Kingdom. Two major revolutions occurred during the 18th century, in the United States (1776) and in France (1789), leading to the adoption of the United States Declaration of Independence and the French Declaration of the Rights of Man and of the Citizen respectively, both of which established certain legal rights. Additionally, the Virginia Declaration of Rights of 1776 encoded a number of fundamental rights and freedoms into law.

Declaration of the Rights of Man and of the Citizen approved by the National Assembly of France, August 26, 1789.

> We hold these truths to be self-evident, that all men are created equal, that they are endowed by their Creator with certain unalienable Rights, that among these are Life, Liberty and the pursuit of Happiness.
>
> —United States Declaration of Independence, 1776

These were followed by developments in philosophy of human rights by philosophers such as Thomas Paine, John Stuart Mill and G. W. F. Hegel during the 18th and 19th centuries. The term *human rights* probably came into use sometime between Paine's *The Rights of Man* and William Lloyd Garrison's 1831 writings in *The Liberator* saying he was trying to enlist his readers in "the great cause of human rights."

Many groups and movements have managed to achieve profound social changes over the course of the 20th century in the name of human rights. In Western Europe and North America, labour unions brought about laws granting workers the right to strike, establishing minimum work conditions and forbidding or regulating child labour.

The women's rights movement succeeded in gaining for many women the right to vote. National liberation movements in many countries succeeded in driving out colonial powers. One of the most influential was Mahatma Gandhi's movement to free his native India from British rule. Movements by long-oppressed racial and religious minorities succeeded in many parts of the world, among them the civil rights movement, and more recent diverse identity politics movements, on behalf of women and minorities in the United States.

The establishment of the International Committee of the Red Cross, the 1864 Lieber Code and the first of the Geneva Conventions in 1864 laid the foundations of International humanitarian law, to be further developed following the two World Wars.

The World Wars, and the huge losses of life and gross abuses of human rights that took place during the wars were a driving force behind the development of modern human rights instruments. The League of Nations was established in 1919 at the negotiations over the Treaty of Versailles following the end of World War I. The League's goals included disarmament, preventing war through collective security, settling disputes between countries through negotiation, diplomacy and improving global welfare. Enshrined in its Charter was a mandate to promote many of the rights which were later included in the Universal Declaration of Human Rights.

At the 1945 Yalta Conference, the Allied Powers agreed to create a new body to supplant the League's role. This body was to be the United Nations. The United Nations has played an important role in international human rights law since its creation. Following the World Wars the United Nations and its members developed much of the discourse and the bodies of law which now make up international humanitarian law and international human rights law.

INTERNATIONAL NORMS

Humanitarian Law

The Geneva Conventions came into being between 1864 and 1949 as a result of efforts by Henry Dunant, the founder of the

International Committee of the Red Cross. The conventions safeguard the human rights of individuals involved in armed conflict, and build on the 1899 and 1907 Hague Conventions, the international community's first attempt to formalise the laws of war and war crimes in the nascent body of secular international law. The conventions were revised as a result of World War II and readopted by the international community in 1949.

The Geneva Conventions define what is today referred to as humanitarian law. The International Committee of the Red Cross is the controlling body of the Geneva conventions.

Universal Declaration of Human Rights

"It is not a treaty...[In the future, it] may well become the international Magna Carta." Eleanor Roosevelt with the Spanish text of the Universal Declaration in 1949.

The Universal Declaration of Human Rights (UDHR) is a non-binding declaration adopted by the United Nations General Assembly in 1948, partly in response to the atrocities of World War II. Although the UDHR is a non-binding resolution, it is now considered to be a central component of international customary law which may be invoked under appropriate circumstances by national and other judiciaries. The UDHR urges member nations to promote a number of human, civil, economic and social rights, asserting these rights are part of the "foundation of freedom, justice and peace in the world." The declaration was the first international legal effort to limit the behaviour of states and press upon them duties to their citizens following the model of the rights-duty duality.

> ...recognition of the inherent dignity and of the equal and inalienable rights of all members of the human family is the foundation of freedom, justice and peace in the world.
>
> —Preamble to the Universal Declaration of Human Rights, 1948

The UDHR was framed by members of the Human Rights Commission, with former First Lady Eleanor Roosevelt as Chair, who began to discuss an *International Bill of Rights* in 1947. The members of the Commission did not immediately agree on the form of such a bill of rights, and whether, or how, it should be enforced. The Commission proceeded to frame the UDHR and accompanying treaties, but the UDHR quickly became the priority. Canadian law professor John Humprey and French lawyer René Cassin were responsible for much of the cross-national research and the structure of the document respectively, where the articles of the declaration were interpretative of the general principle of the preamble. The document was structured by Cassin to include the basic principles of dignity, liberty, equality and brotherhood in the first two articles, followed successively by rights pertaining to individuals; rights of individuals in relation to each other and to groups; spiritual, public and political rights; and economic, social and cultural rights. The final three articles place, according to Cassin, rights in the context of limits, duties and the social and political order in which they are to be realized. Humphrey and Cassin intended the rights in the UDHR to be legally enforceable through some means, as is reflected in the third clause of the preamble:

> Whereas it is essential, if man is not to be compelled to have recourse, as a last resort, to rebellion against tyranny and oppression, that human rights should be protected by the rule of law.
>
> —Preamble to the Universal Declaration of Human Rights, 1948

Some of the UDHR was researched and written by a committee of international experts on human rights, including representatives from all continents and all major religions, and drawing on consultation with leaders such as Mahatma Gandhi. The inclusion of both civil and political rights and economic, social and cultural rights was predicated on the assumption that basic human rights are indivisible and that the different types of rights listed are inextricably linked. This principle was not then opposed by any member states (the declaration was adopted unanimously, with the abstention of the Eastern Bloc,

Apartheid South Africa and Saudi Arabia), however this principle was later subject to significant challenges.

The Universal Declaration was bifurcated into two distinct and different covenants, a covenant on Civil and Political Rights and another covenant on Economic, Social and Cultural Rights. Over the objection of the more developed states [Capitalist], which questioned the relevance and propriety of such provisions in covenants on human rights, both begin with the right of people to self-determination and to sovereignty over their natural resources. Then the two covenants go different ways (see, Louis Henkin, The International Bill of Rights: The Universal Declaration and the Covenants, in International Enforcement of Human Rights 6-9, Bernhardt and Jolowicz, eds, (1987))

The drafters of the covenants initially intended only one instrument. The original drafts included only political and civil rights, but economic and social rights were added early. Western States then fought for, and obtained, a division into two covenants. They insisted that economic and social rights were essentially aspirations or plans, not rights, since their realisation depend on availability of resources and on controversial economic theory and ideology. These, they said, were not appropriate subjects for binding obligations and should not be allowed to dilute the legal character of provisions hononring political-civil rights; states prepared to assume obligations to respect political-civil rights should not be mitments. There was wide agreement and clear recognition that the means required to enforce or induce compliance with socio-economic undertakings were different from the means required for civil-political rights.

Because of the divisions over which rights to include, and because some states declined to ratify any treaties including certain specific interpretations of human rights, and despite the Soviet bloc and a number of developing countries arguing strongly for the inclusion of all rights in a so-called *Unity Resolution*, the rights enshrined in the UDHR were split into two separate covenants, allowing states to adopt some rights and derogate others. Though this allowed the covenants to be created, one commentator has written that it denied the proposed principle that all rights are linked which was central to some interpretations of the UDHR.

Human Rights Law

In 1966, the International Covenant on Civil and Political Rights (ICCPR) and the International Covenant on Economic, Social and Cultural Rights (ICESCR) were adopted by the United Nations, between them making the rights contained in the UDHR binding on all states that have signed this treaty, creating human rights law.

Since then numerous other treaties (pieces of legislation) have been offered at the international level. They are generally known as *human rights instruments*. Some of the most significant are:

- Convention on the Elimination of All Forms of Racial Discrimination (CERD) (adopted 1966, entry into force: 1969)
- Convention on the Elimination of All Forms of Discrimination Against Women (CEDAW) (entry into force: 1981)
- United Nations Convention Against Torture (CAT) (adopted 1984, entry into force: 1984)
- Convention on the Rights of the Child (CRC) (adopted 1989, entry into force: 1989)
- International Convention on the Protection of the Rights of All Migrant Workers and Members of their Families (ICRMW) (adopted 1990, entry into force: 2003)

Enforcement of Law

The enforcement of international human rights law is the responsibility of the Nation State, and its the primary responsibility of the State to make human rights a reality. There is currently no international court that upholds human rights law (the International Criminal Court deals with crimes against humanity, war crimes and genocide), although the Council of Europe is responsible for both the European Convention on Human Rights, and the European Court of

Human Rights that acts as a court of last appeal for human rights issues in member states.

In practice, many human rights are very difficult to legally enforce due to the absence of consensus on the application of certain rights, the lack of relevant national legislation or of bodies empowered to take legal action to enforce them.

Universal Jurisdiction

Universal jurisdiction is a controversial principle in international law whereby states claim criminal jurisdiction over persons whose alleged crimes were committed outside the boundaries of the prosecuting state, regardless of nationality, country of residence, or any other relation with the prosecuting country. The state backs its claim on the grounds that the crime committed is considered a crime against all, which any state is authorised to punish. The concept of universal jurisdiction is therefore closely linked to the idea that certain international norms are erga omnes, or owed to the entire world community, as well as the concept of jus cogens.

United Nations

The United Nations (UN) is the only multilateral governmental agency with universally accepted international jurisdiction for universal human rights legislation. Human rights are primarily governed by the United Nations Security Council and the United Nations Human Rights Council, and there are numerous committees within the UN with responsibilities for safeguarding different human rights treaties. The most senior body of the UN with regard to human rights is the Office of the High Commissioner for Human Rights. The United Nations has an international mandate to:

> ...achieve international co-operation in solving international problems of an economic, social, cultural, or humanitarian character, and in promoting and encouraging respect for human rights and for fundamental freedoms for all without distinction as to race, sex, language, or religion.
>
> —Article 1-3 of the United Nations Charter

HUMAN RIGHTS COUNCIL

The United Nations Human Rights Council, created at the 2005 World Summit to replace the United Nations Commission on Human Rights, has a mandate to investigate violations of human rights. The Human Rights Council is a subsidiary body of the General Assembly and reports directly to it. It ranks below the Security Council, which is the final authority for the interpretation of the United Nations Charter. Forty-seven of the one hundred ninety-one member states sit on the council, elected by simple majority in a secret ballot of the United Nations General Assembly. Members serve a maximum of six years and may have their membership suspended for gross human rights abuses. The Council is based in Geneva, and meets three times a year; with additional meetings to respond to urgent situations.

Independent experts (*rapporteurs*) are retained by the Council to investigate alleged human rights abuses and to provide the Council with reports.

The Human Rights Council may request that the Security Council take action when human rights violations occur. This action may be direct actions, may involve sanctions, and the Security Council may also refer cases to the International Criminal Court (ICC) even if the issue being referred is outside the normal jurisdiction of the ICC.

Security Council

The United Nations Security Council has the primary responsibility for maintaining international peace and security and is the only body of the UN that can authorise the use of force (including in the context of peace-keeping operations), or override member nations sovereignty by issuing binding Security Council resolutions. Created by the UN Charter, it is classed as a *Charter Body* of the United Nations. The UN Charter gives the Security Council the power to:

- Investigate any situation threatening international peace;
- Recommend procedures for peaceful resolution of a dispute;

- Call upon other member nations to completely or partially interrupt economic relations as well as sea, air, postal, and radio communications, or to sever diplomatic relations; and
- Enforce its decisions militarily, if necessary.

The Security Council hears reports from all organs of the United Nations, and can take action over any issue which it feels threatens peace and security, including human rights issues. It has at times been criticised for failing to take action to prevent human rights abuses, including the Darfur crisis, the Srebrenica massacre and the Rwandan Genocide.

The Rome Statute of the International Criminal Court recognises the Security Council the power to refer cases to the Court, where the Court could not otherwise exercise jurisdiction.

Other UN Treaty Bodies

A modern interpretation of the original Declaration of Human Rights was made in the Vienna Declaration and Programme of Action adopted by the World Conference on Human Rights in 1993. The degree of unanimity over these conventions, in terms of how many and which countries have ratified them varies, as does the degree to which they are respected by various states. The UN has setup a number of *treaty-based* bodies to monitor and study human rights, under the leadership of the UN High Commissioner for Human Rights (UNHCHR). The bodies are committees of independent experts that monitor implementation of the core international human rights treaties. They are created by the treaty that they monitor.

- The *Human Rights Committee* promotes participation with the standards of the ICCPR. The eighteen members of the committee express opinions on member countries and make judgements on individual complaints against countries which have ratified the treaty. The judgements are not legally binding.
- The *Committee on Economic, Social and Cultural Rights* monitors the ICESCR and makes general comments on

ratifying countries performance. It does not have the power to receive complaints.

- The *Committee on the Elimination of Racial Discrimination* monitors the CERD and conducts regular reviews of countries' performance. It can make judgements on complaints, but these are not legally binding. It issues warnings to attempt to prevent serious contraventions of the convention.

- The *Committee on the Elimination of Discrimination against Women* monitors the CEDAW. It receives states' reports on their performance and comments on them, and can make judgements on complaints against countries which have opted into the 1999 Optional Protocol.

- The *Committee Against Torture* monitors the CAT and receives states' reports on their performance every four years and comments on them. It may visit and inspect individual countries with their consent.

- The *Committee on the Rights of the Child* monitors the CRC and makes comments on reports submitted by states every five years. It does not have the power to receive complaints.

- The *Committee on Migrant Workers* was established in 2004 and monitors the ICRMW and makes comments on reports submitted by states every five years. It will have the power to receive complaints of specific violations only once ten member states allow it.

- The *Committee on the Rights of Persons with Disabilities* was established in 2008 to monitor the Convention on the Rights of Persons with Disabilities.

Each treaty body receives secretariat support from the Treaties and Commission Branch of Office of the High Commissioner on Human Rights (OHCHR) in Geneva except CEDAW, which is supported by the Division for the Advancement of Women (DAW).

CEDAW meets at United Nations headquarters in New York; the other treaty bodies generally meet at the United Nations Office in Geneva. The Human Rights Committee usually holds its March session in New York City.

REGIONAL HUMAN RIGHTS

The three principal regional human rights instruments are the African Charter on Human and Peoples' Rights, the American Convention on Human Rights (the Americas) and the European Convention on Human Rights.

Africa

The African Union (AU) is a supranational union consisting of fifty-three African states. Established in 2001, the AU's purpose is to help secure Africa's democracy, human rights, and a sustainable economy, especially by bringing an end to intra-African conflict and creating an effective common market.

The African Charter on Human and Peoples' Rights is the regions principal human rights instrument and emerged under the aegis of the Organisation of African Unity (OAU) (since replaced by the African Union). The intention to draw up the African Charter on Human and Peoples' Rights was announced in 1979 and the Charter was unanimously approved at the OAU's 1981 Assembly. Pursuant to its Article 63 (whereby it was to "come into force three months after the reception by the Secretary General of the instruments of ratification or adherence of a simple majority" of the OAU's member states), the African Charter on Human and Peoples' Rights came into effect on 21 October 1986 – in honour of which 21st of October was declared "African Human Rights Day".

The African Commission on Human and Peoples' Rights (ACHPR) is a quasi-judicial organ of the African Union tasked with promoting and protecting human rights and collective (peoples') rights throughout the African continent as well as interpreting the African Charter on Human and Peoples' Rights and considering individual complaints of violations of the Charter. The Commission has three broad areas of responsibility:

- Promoting human and peoples' rights
- Protecting human and peoples' rights
- Interpreting the African Charter on Human and Peoples' Rights

In pursuit of these goals, the Commission is mandated to "collect documents, undertake studies and researches on African problems in the field of human and peoples, rights, organise seminars, symposia and conferences, disseminate information, encourage national and local institutions concerned with human and peoples' rights and, should the case arise, give its views or make recommendations to governments" (Charter, Art. 45).

With the creation of the African Court on Human and Peoples' Rights (under a protocol to the Charter which was adopted in 1998 and entered into force in January 2004), the Commission will have the additional task of preparing cases for submission to the Court's jurisdiction. In a July 2004 decision, the AU Assembly resolved that the future Court on Human and Peoples' Rights would be integrated with the African Court of Justice.

The Court of Justice of the African Union is intended to be the "principal judicial organ of the Union" (Protocol of the Court of Justice of the African Union, Article 2.2). Although it has not yet been established, it is intended to take over the duties of the African Commission on Human and Peoples' Rights, as well as act as the supreme court of the African Union, interpreting all necessary laws and treaties. The Protocol establishing the African Court on Human and Peoples' Rights entered into force in January 2004 but its merging with the Court of Justice has delayed its establishment. The Protocol establishing the Court of Justice will come into force when ratified by 15 countries.

There are many countries in Africa accused of human rights violations by the international community and NGOs.

Americas

The Organisation of American States (OAS) is an international organisation, headquartered in Washington, D.C., United States. Its members are the thirty-five independent states of the Americas. Over the course of the 1990s, with the end of the Cold War, the return to democracy in Latin America, and the thrust toward globalisation, the OAS made major efforts to reinvent itself to fit the new context. Its stated priorities now include the following:

- Strengthening democracy
- Working for peace
- Protecting human rights
- Combating corruption
- The rights of Indigenous Peoples
- Promoting sustainable development

The Inter-American Commission on Human Rights (the IACHR) is an autonomous organ of the Organisation of American States, also based in Washington, D.C. Along with the Inter-American Court of Human Rights, based in San José, Costa Rica, it is one of the bodies that comprise the inter-American system for the promotion and protection of human rights. The IACHR is a permanent body which meets in regular and special sessions several times a year to examine allegations of human rights violations in the hemisphere. Its human rights duties stem from three documents:

- the OAS Charter
- the American Declaration of the Rights and Duties of Man
- the American Convention on Human Rights

The Inter-American Court of Human Rights was established in 1979 with the purpose of enforcing and interpreting the provisions of the American Convention on Human Rights. Its two main functions are thus adjudicatory and advisory. Under the former, it hears and rules on the specific cases of human rights violations referred to it.

Under the latter, it issues opinions on matters of legal interpretation brought to its attention by other OAS bodies or member states.

Many countries in the Americas, such as Colombia, Canada, Cuba, Mexico, The United States, and Venezuela have been accused of human rights violations.

Asia

There are no Asia-wide organisations or conventions to promote or protect human rights. Countries vary widely in their approach to human rights and their record of human rights protection.

The Association of Southeast Asian Nations (ASEAN) is a geo-political and economic organisation of ten countries located in Southeast Asia, which was formed in 1967 by Indonesia, Malaysia, the Philippines, Singapore and Thailand. The organisation now also includes Brunei, Vietnam, Laos, Myanmar and Cambodia. Its aims include the acceleration of economic growth, social progress, cultural development among its members, and the promotion of regional peace.

The South Asian Association for Regional Cooperation (SAARC) is an economic and political organisation of eight countries in Southern Asia, representing almost 1.5 billion people. It was established in 1985 by India, Pakistan, Bangladesh, Sri Lanka, Nepal, Maldives and Bhutan. In April 2007, at the Association's 14th summit, Afghanistan became its eighth member.

The Cooperation Council for the Arab States of the Gulf (CCASG) is a trade bloc involving the seven Arab states of the Persian Gulf, with many economic and social objectives. Created in 1981, the Council comprises the Persian Gulf states of Yemen Bahrain, Kuwait, Oman, Qatar, Saudi Arabia and the United Arab Emirates.

The Asia Cooperation Dialogue (ACD) is a body created in 2002 to promote Asian cooperation at a continental level, helping to integrate the previously separate regional organisations of political or economical cooperation. The main objectives of the ACD are as follows:

- To promote interdependence among Asian countries in all areas of cooperation by identifying Asia's common strengths and opportunities which will help reduce poverty and improve the quality of life for Asian people whilst developing a knowledge-based society within Asia and enhancing community and people empowerment;
- To expand the trade and financial market within Asia and increase the bargaining power of Asian countries in lieu of competition and, in turn, enhance Asia's economic competitiveness in the global market;
- To serve as the missing link in Asian cooperation by building upon Asia's potentials and strengths through supplementing and complementing existing cooperative frameworks so as to become a viable partner for other regions;
- To ultimately transform the Asian continent into an Asian Community, capable of interacting with the rest of the world on a more equal footing and contributing more positively towards mutual peace and prosperity.

None of the above organisations have a specific mandate to promote or protect human rights, but each has some human rights related economic, social and cultural objectives.

A number of Asian countries are accused of serious human rights abuses by the international community and human rights organisations.

Europe

The Council of Europe, founded in 1949, is the oldest organisation working for European integration. It is an international organisation with legal personality recognised under public international law and has observer status with the United Nations. The seat of the Council of Europe is in Strasbourg in France. The Council of Europe is responsible for both the European Convention on Human Rights and the European Court of Human Rights. These institutions bind the Council's members to a code of human rights which, though strict, are more lenient than those of the United Nations charter on human rights. The Council also promotes the European Charter for Regional or Minority Languages and the European Social Charter. Membership is open to all European states which seek European integration, accept the principle of the rule of law and are able and willing to guarantee democracy, fundamental human rights and freedoms.

The Council of Europe is separate from the European Union, but the latter is expected to accede to the European Convention and potentially the Council itself. The EU also has a separate human rights document; the Charter of Fundamental Rights of the European Union.

The European Convention on Human Rights defines and guarantees since 1950 human rights and fundamental freedoms in Europe. All 47 member states of the Council of Europe have signed this Convention and are therefore under the jurisdiction of the European Court of Human Rights in Strasbourg. In order to prevent torture and inhuman or degrading treatment (Article 3 of the Convention), the Committee for the Prevention of Torture was established.

The European Court of Human Rights is the only international court with jurisdiction to deal with cases brought by individuals (rather than states).

Oceania

There are no regional approaches or agreements on human rights for Oceania, but most countries have a well-regarded human rights record.

Australia is the only western democracy with no constitutional or legislative bill of rights, but a number of laws have been enacted to protect human rights and the Constitution of Australia has been found to contain certain implied rights by the High Court. However, Australia has been criticised at various times for its immigration policies, treatment of asylum seekers, treatment of its indigenous population, and foreign policy.

Philosophies

Several theoretical approaches have been advanced to explain how and why human rights become part of social expectations.

One of the oldest Western philosophies on human rights is that they are a product of a natural law, stemming from different philosophical or religious grounds.

Other theories hold that human rights codify moral behavior which is a human social product developed by a process of biological and social evolution (associated with Hume). Human rights are also described as a sociological pattern of rule setting (as in the sociological theory of law and the work of Weber). These approaches include the notion that individuals in a society accept rules from legitimate authority in exchange for security and economic advantage (as in Rawls) - a social contract.

NATURAL RIGHTS

Natural law theories base human rights on a "natural" moral, religious or even biological order that is independent of transitory human laws or traditions.

Socrates and his philosophic heirs, Plato and Aristotle, posited the existence of natural justice or natural right. Of these, Aristotle is often said to be the father of natural law, although evidence for this is due largely to the interpretations of his work by Thomas Aquinas.

The development of this tradition of natural justice into one of natural law is usually attributed to the Stoics.

Some of the early Church Fathers sought to incorporate the until then pagan concept of natural law into Christianity. Natural law theories have featured greatly in the philosophies of Thomas Aquinas, Francisco Suárez, Richard Hooker, Thomas Hobbes, Hugo Grotius, Samuel von Pufendorf, and John Locke.

In the Seventeenth century Thomas Hobbes founded a contractualist theory of legal positivism on what all men could agree upon: what they sought (happiness) was subject to contention, but a broad consensus could form around what they feared (violent death at the hands of another). The natural law was how a rational human being, seeking to survive and prosper, would act. It was discovered by considering humankind's natural rights, whereas previously it could be said that natural rights were discovered by considering the natural law. In Hobbes' opinion, the only way natural law could prevail was for men to submit to the commands of the sovereign. In this lay the foundations of the theory of a social contract between the governed and the governor.

Hugo Grotius based his philosophy of international law on natural law. He wrote that "even the will of an omnipotent being cannot change or abrogate" natural law, which "would maintain its objective validity even if we should assume the impossible, that there is no God or that he does not care for human affairs." (*De iure belli ac pacis*, Prolegomeni XI). This is the famous argument *etiamsi daremus* (*non esse Deum*), that made natural law no longer dependent on theology.

John Locke incorporated natural law into many of his theories and philosophy, especially in *Two Treatises of Government*. Locke turned Hobbes' prescription around, saying that if the ruler went against natural law and failed to protect "life, liberty, and property," people could justifiably overthrow the existing state and create a new one.

The Belgian philosopher of law Frank Van Dun is one among those who are elaborating a secular conception of natural law in the liberal tradition. There are also emerging and secular forms of natural law theory that define human rights as derivative of the notion of universal human dignity.

The term "human rights" has replaced the term "natural rights" in popularity, because the rights are less and less frequently seen as requiring natural law for their existence.

Social Contract

The English philosopher Thomas Hobbes suggested the existence of a hypothetical *social contract* where a group of free individuals agree for the sake of the common good to form institutions to govern themselves. They give up some liberties in exchange for protection from the Sovereign. This led to John Locke's theory that a failure of the government to secure rights is a failure which justifies the removal of the government, and was mirrored in later postulation by Jean-Jacques Rousseau in his "Du Contrat Social" (The Social Contract).

International equity expert Paul Finn has echoed this view:

> The most fundamental fiduciary relationship in our society is manifestly that which exists between the community (the people) and the state, its agencies and officials.
>
> —Paul Finn

The relationship between government and the governed in countries which follow the English law tradition is a fiduciary one. In equity law, a politician's fiduciary obligations are not only the duties of good faith and loyalty, but also include duties of skill and competence in managing a country and its people. Originating from within the Courts of Equity, the fiduciary concept exists to prevent those holding positions of power from abusing their authority. The fiduciary relationship between government and the governed arises from the governments ability to control people with the exercise of its power. In effect, if a government has the power to abolish any rights, it is equally burdened with the fiduciary duty to protect such an interest because it would benefit from the exercise of its own discretion to extinguish rights which it alone had the power to dispose of.

Reciprocity

The Golden Rule, or the *ethic of reciprocity* states that one must do unto others as one would be treated themselves; the principle being that reciprocal recognition and respect of rights ensures that one's own rights will be protected. This principle can be found in all the world's major religions in only slightly differing forms, and was enshrined in the "Declaration Toward a Global Ethic" by the Parliament of the World's Religions in 1993.

Other Theories of Human Rights

The philosopher John Finnis argues that human rights are justifiable on the grounds of their instrumental value in creating the necessary conditions for human well-being. Interest theories highlight the duty to respect the rights of other individuals on grounds of self-interest:

> Human rights law, applied to a State's own citizens serves the interest of states, by, for example, minimising the risk of violent resistance and protest and by keeping the level of dissatisfaction with the government manageable
>
> —Niraj Nathwani in *Rethinking refugee law*

The biological theory considers the comparative reproductive advantage of human social behaviour based on empathy and altruism in the context of natural selection.

Human Security

Human security is an emerging school of thought which challenges the traditional, state-based conception of security and argues that a people-focused approach to security is more appropriate in the modern interdependent world and would be more effective in advancing the security of individuals and societies across the globe.

Philosopher Friedrich Nietzsche has argued to the effect that those who speak most vehemently about their rights, doubt at the bottom of their soul if they truly have any.

Critiques of Human Rights

Philosophers who have criticised the concept of human rights include Jeremy Bentham, Edmund Burke, Friedrich Nietzsche and

Karl Marx. A recent critique has been advanced by Charles Blattberg in his essay "The Ironic Tragedy of Human Rights." Blattberg argues that rights talk, being abstract, demotivates people from upholding the values that rights are meant to assert. In his book After Virtue Alisdair McIntyre claimed the concept that all human beings have certain rights simply by virtue of being human was illogical, stated "the best reason for asserting so bluntly that there are no such rights is indeed of precisely the same type as the best reason which we possess for asserting that there are no witches and the best reason which we possess for asserting that there are no unicorns: every attempt to give good reasons for believing there *are* such rights has failed."

INDIVISIBILITY AND CATEGORISATION

The most common categorisation of human rights is to split them into civil and political rights, and economic, social and cultural rights.

Civil and political rights are enshrined in articles 3 to 21 of the Universal Declaration of Human Rights (UDHR) and in the International Covenant on Civil and Political Rights (ICCPR). Economic, social and cultural rights are enshrined in articles 22 to 28 of the Universal Declaration of Human Rights (UDHR) and in the International Covenant on Economic, Social and Cultural Rights (ICESCR).

Indivisibility

The UDHR included both economic, social and cultural rights and civil and political rights because it was based on the principle that the different rights could only successfully exist in combination:

> The ideal of free human beings enjoying civil and political freedom and freedom from fear and want can only be achieved if conditions are created whereby everyone may enjoy his civil and political rights, as well as his social, economic and cultural rights
>
> —International Covenant on Civil and Political Rights and the International Covenant on Economic Social and Cultural Rights, 1966

This is held to be true because without civil and political rights the public cannot assert their economic, social and cultural rights. Similarly, without livelihoods and a working society, the public cannot assert or make use of civil or political rights (known as the *full belly thesis*).

The indivisibility and interdependence of all human rights has been confirmed by the 1993 Vienna Declaration and Programme of Action:

> All human rights are universal, indivisible and interdependent and related. The international community must treat human rights globally in a fair and equal manner, on the same footing, and with the same emphasis
>
> —Vienna Declaration and Programme of Action, World Conference on Human Rights, 1993

This statement was again endorsed at the 2005 World Summit in New York (paragraph 121).

Although accepted by the signatories to the UDHR, most do not in practice give equal weight to the different types of rights. Some Western cultures have often given priority to civil and political rights, sometimes at the expense of economic and social rights such as the right to work, to education, health and housing. For example, in the United States there is no universal access to healthcare free at the point of use. That is not to say that Western cultures have overlooked these rights entirely (the welfare states that exist in Western Europe are evidence of this). Similarly the ex Soviet bloc countries and Asian countries have tended to give priority to economic, social and cultural rights, but have often failed to provide civil and political rights.

Categorisation

Opponents of the indivisibility of human rights argue that economic, social and cultural rights are fundamentally different from civil and political rights and require completely different approaches.

Economic, social and cultural rights are argued to be:

- *positive*, meaning that they require active provision of entitlements by the state (as opposed to the state being required only to prevent the breach of rights)
- *resource-intensive*, meaning that they are expensive and difficult to provide
- *progressive*, meaning that they will take significant time to implement
- *vague*, meaning they cannot be quantitatively measured, and whether they are adequately provided or not is difficult to judge
- *ideologically divisive/political*, meaning that there is no consensus on what should and shouldn't be provided as a right
- *socialist*, as opposed to capitalist
- *non-justiciable*, meaning that their provision, or the breach of them, cannot be judged in a court of law
- *aspirations or goals*, as opposed to real 'legal' rights

Similarly civil and political rights are categorised as:

- *negative*, meaning the state can protect them simply by taking no action
- *cost-free*
- *immediate*, meaning they can be immediately provided if the state decides to
- *precise*, meaning their provision is easy to judge and measure
- *non-ideological/non-political*
- *capitalist*
- *justiciable*
- *real 'legal' rights*

In *The No-Nonsense Guide to Human Rights* Olivia Ball and Paul Gready argue that for both civil and political rights and economic, social and cultural rights it is easy to find examples which do not fit into the above categorisation. Amongst several others, they highlight the fact that maintaining a judicial system, a fundamental requirement of the civil right to due process before the law and other rights relating to judicial process, is positive, resource-intensive, progressive and vague, while the social right to housing is precise, justiciable and can be a real 'legal' right.

Another categorisation, offered by Karel Vasak, is that there are *three generations of human rights*: first-generation civil and political rights (right to life and political participation), second-generation economic, social and cultural rights (right to subsistence) and third-generation solidarity rights (right to peace, right to clean environment). Out of these generations, the third generation is the most debated and lacks both legal and political recognition. This categorisation is at odds with the indivisibility of rights, as it implicitly states that some rights can exist without others. Prioritisation of rights for pragmatic reasons is however a widely accepted necessity. Human rights expert Philip Alston argues:

> If every possible human rights element is deemed to be essential or necessary, then nothing will be treated as though it is truly important.
>
> —Philip Alston

He, and others, urge caution with prioritisation of rights:

> ...the call for prioritising is not to suggest that any obvious violations of rights can be ignored.
>
> —Philip Alston

> Priorities, where necessary, should adhere to core concepts (such as reasonable attempts at progressive realisation) and principles (such as non-discrimination, equality and participation.
>
> —Olivia Ball, Paul Gready

Some human rights are said to be "inalienable rights." The term inalienable rights (or unalienable rights) refers to "a set of human rights that are fundamental, are not awarded by human power, and cannot be surrendered."

Universalism *vs.* Cultural Relativism

The UDHR enshrines universal rights that apply to all humans equally, whichever geographical location, state, race or culture they belong to.

Proponents of cultural relativism argue for acceptance of different cultures, which may have practices conflicting with human rights.

For example, female genital mutilation occurs in different cultures in Africa, Asia and South America. It is not mandated by any religion, but has become a tradition in many cultures. It is considered a violation of women's and girl's rights by much of the international community, and is outlawed in some countries.

Universalism has been described by some as cultural, economic or political imperialism. In particular, the concept of human rights is often claimed to be fundamentally rooted in a politically liberal outlook which, although generally accepted in Europe, Japan or North America, is not necessarily taken as standard elsewhere.

For example, in 1981, the Iranian representative to the United Nations, Said Rajaie-Khorassani, articulated the position of his country regarding the Universal Declaration of Human Rights by saying that the UDHR was "a secular understanding of the Judeo-Christian tradition", which could not be implemented by Muslims without trespassing the Islamic law. The former Prime Ministers of Singapore, Lee Kuan Yew, and of Malaysia, Mahathir bin Mohamad both claimed in the 1990s that *Asian values* were significantly different from western values and included a sense of loyalty and foregoing personal freedoms for the sake of social stability and prosperity, and therefore authoritarian government is more appropriate in Asia than democracy. This view is countered by Mahathir's former deputy:

> To say that freedom is Western or un-Asian is to offend our traditions as well as our forefathers, who gave their lives in the struggle against tyranny and injustices.
>
> —A Ibrahim in his keynote speech to the Asian Press Forum title *Media and Society in Asia*, 2 December 1994

and also by Singapore's opposition leader Chee Soon Juan who states that it is racist to assert that Asians do not want human rights.

An appeal is often made to the fact that influential human rights thinkers, such as John Locke and John Stuart Mill, have all been Western and indeed that some were involved in the running of Empires themselves.

Cultural relativism is a self-detonating position; if cultural relativism is true, then universalism must also be true. Relativistic arguments also tend to neglect the fact that modern human rights are new to all cultures, dating back no further than the UDHR in 1948. They also don't account for the fact that the UDHR was drafted by people from many different cultures and traditions, including a US Roman Catholic, a Chinese Confucian philosopher, a French zionist and a representative from the Arab League, amongst others, and drew upon advice from thinkers such as Mahatma Gandhi.

Michael Ignatieff has argued that cultural relativism is almost exclusively an argument used by those who wield power in cultures which commit human rights abuses, and that those whose human rights are compromised are the powerless. This reflects the fact that the difficulty in judging universalism versus relativism lies in who is claiming to represent a particular culture.

Although the argument between universalism and relativism is far from complete, it is an academic discussion in that all international human rights instruments adhere to the principle that human rights are universally applicable. The 2005 World Summit reaffirmed the international community's adherence to this principle:

> The universal nature of human rights and freedoms is beyond question.
>
> —2005 World Summit, paragraph 120

State and Non-state Actors

Companies, NGOs, political parties, informal groups, and individuals are known as *non-State actors*. Non-state actors can also commit human rights abuses, but are not generally subject to human rights law other than under International Humanitarian Law, which applies to individuals. Also, certain national instruments such as the Human Rights Act 1998 (UK), impose human rights obligations on certain entities which are not traditionally considered as part of government ("public authorities").

Multinational companies play an increasingly large role in the world, and are responsible for a large number of human rights abuses. Although the legal and moral environment surrounding the actions of governments is reasonably well developed, that surrounding multinational companies is both controversial and ill-defined. Multinational companies' primary responsibility is to their shareholders, not to those affected by their actions. Such companies may be larger than the economies of some the states within which they operate, and can wield significant economic and political power. No international treaties exist to specifically cover the behavior of companies with regard to human rights, and national legislation is very variable. Jean Ziegler, Special Rapporteur of the UN Commission on Human Rights on the right to food stated in a report in 2003:

> the growing power of transnational corporations and their extension of power through privatization, deregulation and the rolling back of the State also mean that it is now time to develop binding legal norms that hold corporations to human rights standards and circumscribe potential abuses of their position of power.
>
> —Jean Ziegler

In August 2003 the Human Rights Commission's Sub-Commission on the Promotion and Protection of Human Rights produced draft *Norms on the responsibilities of transnational corporations and other business enterprises with regard to human rights*. These were considered by the Human Rights Commission in 2004, but have no binding status on corporations and are not monitored.

Theory of Value and Property

Henry of Ghent articulated the theory that every person has a property interest in their own body. John Locke uses the word property in both broad and narrow senses. In a broad sense, it covers a wide range of human interests and aspirations; more narrowly, it refers to material goods. He argues that property is a natural right and it is derived from labour." In addition, property precedes government and government cannot "dispose of the estates of the subjects arbitrarily." To deny valid property rights according to Locke is to deny human rights. The British philosopher had significant impacts upon the development of the Government of the UK and was central to the fundamental founding philosophy of the United States. Karl Marx later critiqued Locke's theory of property in his *Theories of Surplus Value*, seeing the beginnings of a theory of surplus value in Locke's works. In Locke's *Second Treatise* he argued that the right to own private property was unlimited as long as nobody took more than they could use without allowing any of their property to go to waste and that there were enough common resources of comparable quality available for others to create their own property. Locke did believe that some would be more "industrious and rational" than others and would amass more property, but believed this would not cause shortages. Though this system could work before the introduction of money, Marx argued in *Theories of Surplus Value* that Locke's system would break down and claimed money was a contradiction of the law of nature on which private property was founded.

Reproductive Rights

Reproductive rights are rights relating to reproduction and reproductive health. The World Health Organisation defines reproductive rights as follows:

> Reproductive rights rest on the recognition of the basic right of all couples and individuals to decide freely and responsibly the number, spacing and timing of their children and to have the information and means to do so, and the right to attain the highest standard of sexual and reproductive health. They also include the right of all to make decisions concerning reproduction free of discrimination, coercion and violence.
>
> —World Health Organisation

Reproductive rights were first established as a subset of human rights at the United Nation's 1968 International Conference on Human Rights. The sixteenth article of the resulting Proclamation of Teheran states, "Parents have a basic human right to determine freely and responsibly the number and the spacing of their children."

Reproductive rights may include some or all of the following rights: the right to legal or safe abortion, the right to control one's reproductive functions, the right to quality reproductive healthcare, and the right to education and access in order to make reproductive choices free from coercion, discrimination, and violence. Reproductive rights may also be understood to include education about contraception and sexually transmitted infections, and freedom from coerced sterilisation and contraception, protection from gender-based practices such as female genital cutting (FGC) and male genital mutilation (MGM).

LEGAL ISSUES

Human Rights *vs.* National Security

With the exception of non-derogable human rights (international conventions class the right to life, the right to be free from slavery, the right to be free from torture and the right to be free from retroactive application of penal laws as non-derogable), the UN recognises that human rights can be limited or even pushed aside during times of national emergency – although

> the emergency must be actual, affect the whole population and the threat must be to the very existence of the nation. The declaration of emergency must also be a last resort and a temporary measure
>
> —United Nations. *The Resource*

Rights that cannot be derogated for reasons of national security in any circumstances are known as peremptory norms or *jus cogens*. Such United Nations Charter obligations are binding on all states and cannot be modified by treaty.

Examples of national security being used to justify human rights violations include the Japanese American internment during World War II, Stalin's Great Purge, and the actual and alleged modern-day abuses of terror suspects rights by some western countries, often in the name of the War on Terror.

Human Rights Violations

Human rights violations occur when any state or non-state actor breaches any part of the UDHR treaty or other international human rights or humanitarian law. In regard to human rights violations of United Nations laws. Article 39 of the United Nations Charter designates the UN Security Council (or an appointed authority) as the only tribunal that may determine UN human rights violations.

Human rights abuses are monitored by United Nations committees, national institutions and governments and by many independent non-governmental organisations, such as Amnesty International, International Federation of Human Rights, Human Rights Watch, World Organisation Against Torture, Freedom House, International Freedom of Expression Exchange and Anti-slavery International. These organisations collect evidence and documentation of alleged human rights abuses and apply pressure to enforce human rights laws.

Only a very few countries do not commit significant human rights violations, according to Amnesty International. In their 2004 human rights report (covering 2003), the Netherlands, Norway, Denmark, Iceland and Costa Rica are the only (mappable) countries that did not (in their opinion) violate at least some human rights significantly.

There are a wide variety of databases available which attempt to measure, in a rigorous fashion, exactly what violations governments commit against those within their territorial jurisdiction. An example of this is the list created and maintained by Prof. Christian Davenport at the University of Maryland.

Wars of aggression, war crimes and crimes against humanity, including genocide, are breaches of International humanitarian law and represent the most serious of human rights violations.

When a government closes a geographical region to journalists, it raises suspicions of human rights violations. Seven regions are currently closed to foreign journalists:

- Chechnya, Russia
- Jaffna, Sri Lanka
- Myanmar (Burma)
- North Korea
- Papua, Indonesia
- Peshawar, Pakistan
- Tibet, People's Republic of China
- Medellin, Colombia

Currently Debated Rights

Events and new possibilities can affect existing rights or require new ones. Advances of technology, medicine, and philosophy constantly challenge the status quo of human rights thinking.

Environmental Rights

There are two basic conceptions of environmental human rights in the current human rights system. The first is that the right to a healthy or adequate environment is itself a human right (as seen in the both Article 21 of the African Charter of Human and People's Rights, and Article 11 of the San Salvador Protocol to the American Charter of Human Rights). The second conception is the idea that environmental human rights can be derived from other human rights, usually – the right to life, the right to health, the right to private family life and the right to property (among many others). This second theory enjoys much more widespread use in human rights courts around the world, as those rights are contained in many human rights documents.

The onset of various environmental issues, especially climate change, has created potential conflicts between different human rights. Human rights ultimately require a working ecosystem and healthy environment, but the granting of certain rights to individuals may damage these. Such as the conflict between right to decide number of offspring and the common need for a healthy environment, as noted in the tragedy of the commons. In the area of environmental rights, the responsibilities of multinational corporations, so far relatively unaddressed by human rights legislation, is of paramount consideration.

Environmental Rights revolve largely around the idea of a right to a livable environment both for the present and the future generations.

Future Generations

In 1997 UNESCO adopted the Declaration on the Responsibilities of the Present Generation Towards the Future Generation. The Declaration opens with the words:

> Mindful of the will of the peoples, set out solemnly in the Charter of the United Nations, to 'save succeeding generations from the scourge of war' and to safeguard the values and

principles enshrined in the Universal Declaration of Human Rights, and all other relevant instruments of international law.

—Declaration on the Responsibilities of the Present Generation Towards the Future Generation

Article 1 of the declaration states "the present generations have the responsibility of ensuring that the needs and interests of present and future generations are fully safeguarded." The preamble to the declaration states that "at this point in history, the very existence of humankind and its environment are threatened" and the declaration covers a variety of issues including protection of the environment, the human genome, biodiversity, cultural heritage, peace, development, and education. The preamble recalls that the responsibilities of the present generations towards future generations has been referred to in various international instruments, including the Convention for the Protection of the World Cultural and Natural Heritage (UNESCO 1972), the United Nations Framework Convention on Climate Change and the Convention on Biological Diversity (Rio de Janeiro, 1992), the Rio Declaration on Environment and Development (UN Conference on Environment and Development, 1992), the Vienna Declaration and Programme of Action (World Conference on Human Rights, 1993) and a number of UN General Assembly resolutions relating to the protection of the global climate for present and future generations adopted since 1990.

Lesbian, Gay, Bisexual, Transgender (LGBT) Rights

Some organisations argue that LGBT issues, such as same-sex marriage, gay adoption rights, and protection from discrimination should be considered human rights.Canadian courts have recognized certain rights under section fifteen of the Canadian Charter of Rights and Freedoms. Current campaigns, such as the Human Rights Campaign, specifically focus on the rights of the LGBT community.

Part of this debate includes a proposed UN declaration on LGBT rights which would for the first time condemn "discrimination based on sexual orientation and gender identity." While receiving widespread global support, including signatures from the member states of the European Union, opposition has come from several UN member nations, as well as the Vatican, where the Vatican's permanent observer at the UN, indicated his belief that the declaration would discriminate against states which support traditional marriage.

Trade

Although both the Universal Declaration of Human Rights and the International Covenant on Economic, Social and Cultural Rights emphasize the importance of a right to work, neither of these documents explicitly mention trade as a mechanism for ensuring this fundamental right. And yet trade plays a key role in providing jobs.

Some experts argue that trade is inherent to human nature and that when governments inhibit international trade they directly inhibit the right to work and the other indirect benefits, like the right to education, that increased work and investment help accrue. Others have argued that the ability to trade doesn't affect everyone equally — often groups like the rural poor, indigenous groups and women are less likely to access the benefits of increased trade.

On the other hand, others think that it is no longer primarily individuals but companies that trade, and therefore it cannot be guaranteed as a human right. Additionally, trying to fit too many concepts under the umbrella of what qualifies as a human right has the potential to dilute their importance. Finally, it is difficult to define a right to trade as either "fair" or "just" in that all trade regimes create winners and losers, and changing the rules only creates different losers, not necessarily fewer.

Water

There is no current universal human right to water, binding or not, enshrined by the United Nations or any other multilateral body. In November 2002, the United Nations Committee on Economic, Social and Cultural Rights issued a non-binding comment affirming that access to water was a human right:

the human right to water is indispensable for leading a life in human dignity. It is a prerequisite for the realisation of other human rights.

—United Nations Committee on Economic, Social and Cultural Rights

This principle was reaffirmed at the 3rd and 4th World Water Councils in 2003 and 2006. This marks a departure from the conclusions of the 2nd World Water Forum in The Hague in 2000, which stated that water was a commodity to be bought and sold, not a right. There are calls from many NGOs and politicians to enshrine access to water as a binding human right, and not as a commodity.

CRIME AND PUNISHMENT

The Universal Declaration of Human Rights states that everyone has the "right to life". According to many Human Rights activists, the death penalty violates these rights. The United Nations also called on retentionist states to establish a moratorium on Capital Punishment with a view to abolition.States which do not face considerable moral and political pressure. The Universal Declaration of Human Rights also prohibits torture and other cruel, inhuman, and degrading punishment. Countries have argued that "enhanced interrogation methods", which amount to torture, are needed for national security. Human rights activists have also criticized some methods used to punish criminal offenders. For example, Corporal Punishment is also an issue. One example is Caning, used in Malaysia, Brunei, and Singapore is considered to be cruel, inhuman, and degrading punishment. In Mexico, Life Imprisonment without parole is also considered to be cruel and unusual punishment. Other issues, such as Police Brutality and impunity for Human Rights violators are also serious issues.

Medicine

In Canada several legal medical marijuana patients have filed human rights complaints over their discrimination and treatment. ◆

2
Human Security

Human security is an emerging paradigm for understanding global vulnerabilities whose proponents challenge the traditional notion of national security by arguing that the proper referent for security should be the individual rather than the state. Human security holds that a people-centred view of security is necessary for national, regional and global stability.

The concept emerged from a post-Cold War, multi-disciplinary understanding of security involving a number of research fields, including development studies, international relations, strategic studies, and human rights. The United Nations Development Programme's 1994 Human Development Report is considered a milestone publication in the field of human security, with its argument that insuring "freedom from want" and "freedom from fear" for all persons is the best path to tackle the problem of global insecurity. Frequently referred to in a wide variety of global policy discussions and scholarly journals, human security is often taught in universities as part of international relations, globalization, or human rights studies.

Critics of the concept argue that its vagueness undermines its effectiveness; that it has become little more than a vehicle for activists wishing to promote certain causes; and that it does not help the research community understand what security means or help decision makers to formulate good policies.

UNDP's 1994 Definition

Dr. Mahbub ul Haq first drew global attention to the concept of human security in the United Nations Development Programme's

1994 *Human Development Report* and sought to influence the UN's 1995 World Summit on Social Development in Copenhagen. The UNDP's 1994 Human Development Report's definition of human security argues that the scope of global security should be expanded to include *threats in seven areas*:

- **Economic security** — Economic security requires an assured basic income for individuals, usually from productive and remunerative work or, as a last resort, from a publicly financed safety net. In this sense, only about a quarter of the world's people are presently economically secure. While the economic security problem may be more serious in developing countries, concern also arises in developed countries as well. Unemployment problems constitute an important factor underlying political tensions and ethnic violence.
- **Food security** — Food security requires that all people at all times have both physical and economic access to basic food. According to the United Nations, the overall availability of food is not a problem, rather the problem often is the poor distribution of food and a lack of purchasing power. In the past, food security problems have been dealt with at both national and global levels. However, their impacts are limited. According to UN, the key is to tackle the problems relating to access to assets, work and assured income (related to economic security).
- **Health security** — Health security aims to guarantee a minimum protection from diseases and unhealthy lifestyles. In developing countries, the major causes of death are infectious and parasitic diseases, which kill 17 million people annually. In industrialised countries, the major killers are diseases of the circulatory system, killing 5.5 million every year. According to the United Nations, in both developing and industrial countries, threats to health security are usually greater for poor people in rural areas, particularly children. This is mainly due to malnutrition and insufficient supply of medicine, clean water or other necessity for healthcare.

- **Environmental security** — Environmental security aims to protect people from the short- and long-term ravages of nature, man-made threats in nature, and deterioration of the natural environment. In developing countries, lack of access to clean water resources is one of the greatest environmental threats. In industrial countries, one of the major threats is air pollution. Global warming, caused by the emission of greenhouse gases, is another environmental security issue.
- **Personal security** — Personal security aims to protect people from physical violence, whether from the state or external states, from violent individuals and sub-state actors, from domestic abuse, or from predatory adults. For many people, the greatest source of anxiety is crime, particularly violent crime.
- **Community security** — Community security aims to protect people from the loss of traditional relationships and values and from sectarian and ethnic violence. Traditional communities, particularly minority ethnic groups are often threatened. About half of the world's states have experienced some inter-ethnic strife. The United Nations declared 1993 the Year of Indigenous People to highlight the continuing vulnerability of the 300 million aboriginal people in 70 countries as they face a widening spiral of violence.
- **Political security** — Political security is concerned with whether people live in a society that honors their basic human rights. According to a survey conducted by Amnesty International, political repression, systematic torture, ill treatment or disappearance was still practised in 110 countries. Human rights violations are most frequent during periods of political unrest. Along with repressing individuals and groups, governments may try to exercise control over ideas and information.

Since then, human security has been receiving more attention from the key global development institutions, such as the World

Bank. Tadjbakhsh, among others, traces the evolution of human security in international organisations, concluding that the concept has been manipulated and transformed considerably since 1994 to fit organisational interests.

Freedom from Fear *vs* Freedom from Want and Beyond

In an ideal world, each of the UNDP's seven categories of threats would receive adequate global attention and resources. Yet attempts to implement this human security agenda have led to the emergence of two major schools of thought on how to best practice human security — '"*Freedom from Fear*"' and '"*Freedom from Want*"'. While the UNDP 1994 report originally argued that human security requires attention to both *freedom from fear* and *freedom from want,* divisions have gradually emerged over the proper scope of that protection (e.g. over what threats individuals should be protected from) and over the appropriate mechanisms for responding to these threats.

- **Freedom from Fear** — This school seeks to limit the practice of Human Security to protecting individuals from violent conflicts while recognising that these violent threats are strongly associated with poverty, lack of state capacity and other forms of inequities. This approach argues that limiting the focus to violence is a realistic and manageable approach towards Human Security. Emergency assistance, conflict prevention and resolution, peace-building are the main concerns of this approach. Canada, for example, was a critical player in the efforts to ban landmines and has incorporated the "Freedom from Fear" agenda as a primary component in its own foreign policy. However, whether such "narrow" approach can truly serve its purpose in guaranteeing more fruitful results remains to be an issue. For instance, the conflicts in Darfur are often used in questioning the effectiveness of the "Responsibility to Protect", a key component of the Freedom from Fear agenda.

- **Freedom from Want** — The school advocates a holistic approach in achieving human security and argues that the threat agenda should be broadened to include hunger, disease and natural disasters because they are inseparable concepts in addressing the root of human insecurity and they kill far more people than war, genocide and terrorism combined. Different from "Freedom from Fear", it expands the focus beyond violence with emphasis on development and security goals.

Despite their differences, these two approaches to human security can be considered complementary rather than contradictory. Expressions to this effect include:

- Franklin D. Roosevelt's famous Four Freedoms speech of 1941, in which "Freedom from Want" is characterized as the third and "Freedom from Fear" is the fourth such fundamental, universal, freedom.
- The Government of Japan considers Freedom from Fear and Freedom from Want to be equal in developing Japan's foreign policy. Moreover, the UNDP 1994 called for the world's attention to both agendas.
- Surin Pitsuwan, current Secretary-General of ASEAN cites theorists such as Hobbes, Locke, Rousseau and Houme to conclude that "human security is the primary purpose of organising a state in the beginning.". He goes on to observe that the 1994 Human Development Report states that it is "reviving this concept" and suggests that the authors of the 1994 HDR may be alluding to Franklin Roosevelt's Four Freedoms speech without literally citing that presentation.

Although "freedom from fear" and "freedom from want" are the most commonly referred to categories of human security practice, an increasing number of alternative ideas continue to emerge on how to best practice human security. Among them:

- **G. King and C. Murray.** King and Murray try to narrow down the human security definition to one's "expectation of years of life without experiencing the state of generalised poverty". In their definition, the "generalized poverty" means "falling below critical thresholds in any domain of well-being"; and it is in the same article, they give brief review and categories of "Domains of Well-being". This set of definition is similar with "freedom from want" but more concretely focused on some value system.

- **Caroline Thomas.** She regards human security as describing "a condition of existence" which entails basic material needs, human dignity, including meaningful participation in the life of the community, and an active and substantive notion of democracy from the local to the global.
- **Roland Paris.** He argues that many ways to define "human security" are related with certain set of value and lose the neutral position. So he suggests to take human security as a category of research. As such, he gives a 2*2 matrix to illustrate the security studies field.

Security for Whom?	*What is the Source of the Security Threat?*	
	Military	*Military, Non-military, or Both*
States	National security (conventional realist approach to security studies)	Redefined security (e.g., environmental and economic [cooperative or comprehensive] security)
Societies, Groups, and Individuals	Intrastate security (e.g., civil war, ethnic conflict, and democide)	Human security (e.g., environmental and economic threats to the survival of societies, groups, and individuals)

- **Sabina Alkire.** Different with those approaches seek to narrow down and specify the objective of human security, Sabina Alkire pushes the idea a step further as "to safeguard the vital core of all human lives from critical pervasive threats, without impeding long-term human fulfilment". In a concept as such, she suggests the "vital core" cover a minimal or basic or fundamental set of functions related to survival, livelihood and dignity; and all institutions should at least and necessarily protect the core from any intervention.

RELATIONSHIP WITH TRADITIONAL SECURITY

Human security emerged as a challenge to ideas of traditional security, but human and traditional or national security are not mutually exclusive concepts. Without human security, traditional state security cannot be attained and vice-versa.

Traditional security is about a state's ability to defend itself against external threats. Traditional security (often referred to as national security or state security) describes the philosophy of international security predominance since the Peace of Westphalia in 1648 and the rise of the nation-states. While international relations theory includes many variants of traditional security, from realism to idealism, the fundamental trait that these schools share is their focus on the primacy of the nation-state.

The following table contrasts four differences between the two perspectives:

	Traditional Security	*Human Security*
Referent	Traditional security policies are designed to promote demands ascribed to the state. Other interests are subordinated to those of the state. Traditional security protects a state's boundaries, people, institutions and values.	Human security is people-centred. Its focus shifts to protecting individuals. The important dimensions are to entail the well-being of individuals and respond to ordinary people's needs in dealing with sources of threats.

	Traditional Security	*Human Security*
Scope	Traditional security seeks to defend states from external aggression.Walter Lippmann explained that state security is about a state's ability to deter or defeat an attack. It makes uses of deterrence strategies to maintain the integrity of the state and protect the territory from external threats.	In addition to protecting the state from external aggression, human security would expand the scope of protection to include a broader range of threats, including environmental pollution, infectious diseases, and economic deprivation.
Actor(s)	The state is the sole actor, to ensure its own survival. Decision making power is centralised in the government, and the execution of strategies rarely involves the public. Traditional security assumes that a sovereign state is operating in an anarchical international environment, in which there is no world governing body to enforce international rules of conduct.	The realisation of human security involves not only governments, but a broader participation of different actors, viz. regional and international organisations, non-governmental organisations and local communities.
Means	Traditional security relies upon building up national power and military defence. The common forms it takes are armament races, alliances, strategic boundaries etc.	Human security not only protects, but also empowers people and societies as a means of security. People contribute by identifying and implementing solutions to insecurity.

Relationship with Development

Human security also challenged and drew from the practice of international development.

Traditionally, embracing liberal market economics was considered to be the universal path for economic growth, and thus development for all humanity. Yet, continuing conflict and human rights abuses following the end of the Cold War and the fact that two-thirds of the global population seemed to have gained little from the economic gains of globalization, led to fundamental questions about the way development was practiced. Accordingly, human development has emerged in 1990s to challenge the dominant paradigm of liberal economy in the development community. Human development proponents argue that economic growth is insufficient to expand people's choice or capabilities, areas such as health, education, technology, the environment, and employment should not be neglected.

Human security could be said to further enlarge the scope for examining the causes and consequences of underdevelopment, by seeking to bridge the divide between development and security. Too often, militaries didn't address or factor in the underlying causes of violence and insecurity while development workers often underplayed the vulnerability of development models to violent conflict . Human security springs from a growing consensus these two fields need to be more fully integrated in order to enhance security for all.

The paper *Development and Security* by Frances Stewart argues that security and development are deeply interconnected.

- *Human security forms an important part of people's well-being, and is therefore an objective of development.*

  An objective of development is "the enlargement of human choices". Insecurity cuts life short and thwarts the use of human potential, thereby affecting the reaching of this objective.

- *Lack of human security has adverse consequences on economic growth, and therefore development.*

  Some development costs are obvious. For example, in wars, people who join the army or flee can no longer work productively. Also, destroying infrastructure reduces the productive capacity of the economy.

- *Imbalanced development that involves horizontal inequalities is an important source of conflict.*

  Therefore, vicious cycles of lack of development which leads to conflict, then to lack of development, can readily emerge. Likewise, virtuous cycles are possible, with high levels of security leading to development, which further promotes security in return.

Further, it could also be said that the practice of human development and human security share three fundamental elements:

- First, human security and human development are both people-centered. They challenge the orthodox approach to security and development i.e. state security and liberal economic growth respectively. Both emphasise people are be the ultimate ends but not means. Both treat human as agents and should be empowered to participate in the course.
- Second, both perspectives are multidimensional. Both address people's dignity as well as their material and physical concerns.
- Third, both schools of thought consider poverty and inequality as the root causes of individual vulnerability.

Despite these similarities, the relationship with development is one of the most contested areas of human security . "Freedom from fear" advocates, such as Andrew Mack argue that human security should focus on the achievable goals of decreasing individual vulnerability to violent conflict, rather than broadly defined goals of economic and social development. Others, such as Tadjbakhsh and Chenoy, argue that human development and human security are inextricably linked since progress in one enhances the chances of progress in another while failure in one increases risk of failure of another.

The following table is adopted from Tadjbakhsh to help clarify the relationship between these two concepts.

Variables	*Human Development*	*Human Security*
Values	Well-being.	Security, stability, sustainability of development gains
Orientation	Moves forward, is progressive and aggregate: "Together we rise."	Looks at who was left behind at the individual level: "Divided we fall."
Time Frame	Long-term	Combines short-term measures to deal with risks with long-term prevention efforts.
General objectives	Growth with equity. Expanding the choices and opportunities of people to lead lives they value.	"Insuring" downturns with security. Identification of risks, prevention to avoid them through dealing with root causes, preparation to mitigate them, and cushioning when disaster strikes.
Policy goals	Empowerment, sustainability, equity and productivity.	Protection and promotion of human survival (freedom from fear), daily life (freedom from want), and the avoidance of indignities (life of dignity).

RELATIONSHIP WITH HUMAN RIGHTS

Human security is indebted to the human rights tradition (the ideas of natural law and natural rights). The development of the human security model can be seen to have drawn upon ideas and concepts fundamental to the human rights tradition. Both approaches use the individual as the main referent and both argue that a wide range of issues (i.e. civil rights, cultural identity, access to education and healthcare) are fundamental to human dignity. A major difference between the two models is in their approach to addressing threats to human dignity and survival. Whilst the human rights framework takes a legalistic approach, the human security framework, by utilising a diverse range of actors, adopts flexible and issue-specific approaches, which can operate at local, national or international levels.

The nature of the relationship between human security and human rights is contested among human security advocates. Some human security advocates argue that the goal of human security should be to build upon and strengthen the existing global human rights legal framework . However, other advocates view the human rights legal framework as part of the global insecurity problem and believe that a human security approach should propel us to move above and beyond this legalistic approach to get at the underlying sources of inequality and violence which are the root causes of insecurity in today's world.

Gender and Human Security

Human security focuses on the serious neglect of gender concerns under the traditional security model. Traditional security's focus on external military threats to the state has meant that the majority of threats women face have been overlooked. By focusing on the individual, the human security model aims to address the security concerns of both women and men equally. Women are often the worst victims of violence and conflict: they form the majority of civilian deaths; the majority of refugees; and, are often the victims of cruel and degrading practices, such as rape. Women's security is also threatened by unequal access to resources, services and opportunities. Human security seeks to empower women, through education, participation and access, as gender equality is seen as a necessary precondition for peace, security and a prosperous society.

Prevent, React, and Rebuild

Human security seeks to address underlying causes and long-term implications of conflicts instead of simply reacting to problems, as the traditional security approach is often accused of doing. "The basic point of preventive efforts is, of course, to reduce, and hopefully eliminate, the need for intervention altogether," while an investment in rehabilitation or rebuilding seeks to ensure that former conflicts do not breed future violence. The concepts of prevention and rebuilding are clearly embraced as the "responsibility to prevent" and well elaborated in "The Responsibility to protect report of the International Commission on Intervention and State Sovereignty."

Practice

While there are numerous examples of the human security approach in action, two notable global political events with direct ties to the human security agenda include the development of Responsibility to Protect (R2P) principles guiding humanitarian intervention and the passage of the Ottawa Treaty banning anti-personnel landmines.

Humanitarian Intervention

The application of human security is highly relevant within the area of humanitarian intervention, as it focuses on addressing the deep rooted and multi-factorial problems inherent in humanitarian crises, and offers more long-term resolutions. In general, the term humanitarian intervention generally applies to when a state uses force against another state in order to alleviate suffering in the latter state.

Under the traditional security paradigm humanitarian intervention is contentious. As discussed above, the traditional security paradigm places emphasis on the notion of states. Hence, the principles of state sovereignty and non-intervention that are paramount in the traditional security paradigm make it difficult to justify the intervention of other states in internal disputes. Through the development of clear principles based on the human security concept, there has been a step forward in the development of clear rules of when humanitarian intervention can occur and the obligations of states that intervene in the internal disputes of a state.

These principles on humanitarian intervention are the product of a debate pushed by the then United Nations Secretary General Kofi Annan. He posed a challenge to the international community to find a new approach to humanitarian intervention that responded to its inherent problems. In 2001, the International Commission on Intervention and State Sovereignty (ICISS) produced the "The Responsibility to protect", a comprehensive report detailing how the "right of humanitarian intervention" could be exercised. It was considered a triumph for the human security approach as it emphasised and gathered much needed attention to some of its main principles:

- The protection of individual welfare is more important than the state. If the security of individuals is threatened internally by the state or externally by other states, state authority can be overridden.
- Addressing the root causes of humanitarian crises (e.g. economic, political or social instability) is a more effective way to solve problems and protect the long-term security of individuals.
- Prevention is the best solution. A collective understanding of the deeper social issues along with a desire to work together is necessary to prevent humanitarian crises, thereby preventing a widespread absence of human security within a population (which may mean investing more in development projects).

The report illustrates the usefulness of the human security approach, particularly its ability to examine the cause of conflicts that explain and justify humanitarian intervention. In addition, it could also act as a paradigm for identifying, prioritising and resolving large transnational problems, one of the fundamental factors that act as a stimulus for humanitarian intervention in the first place. However, human security still faces difficulties concerning the scope of its applicability, as large problems requiring humanitarian intervention usually are built up from an array of socio-political, cultural and economic problems that may be beyond the limitations of humanitarian projects. On the other hand, successful examples of the use of human security principles within interventions can be found.

The success of humanitarian intervention in international affairs is varied. As discussed above, humanitarian intervention is a contentious issue. Examples of humanitarian intervention illustrate, that in some cases intervention can lead to disastrous results, as in Srebrenica and Somalia. In other cases, a lack of clarity as to the rules of when intervention can occur has resulted in tragic inaction, as was witnessed during the Rwandan genocide.) One example is of a successful humanitarian intervention and also of humanitarian principles being applied is East Timor which, prior to its independence, was plagued with massive human rights abuses by pro-Indonesian militias and an insurgency war led by indigenous East Timorese against Indonesian forces. A peacekeeping mission was deployed to safeguard the move to independence and the UN established the United Nations Transitional Administration in East Timor (UNTAET). This not only dealt with traditional security priorities, but also helped in nation building projects, coordinated humanitarian aid and civil rehabilitation, illustrating not only a successful humanitarian intervention but also a effective application of human security principles.

Anti-personnel Landmines

In contrast to the traditional security discourse which sees security as focused on protecting state interests, human security proponents believe that Anti-personnel mines could not be viable weapons of war due to the massive collateral damage they cause, their indiscriminate nature and persistence after conflict. In particular, they argue that Anti-personnel mines differ from most weapons, which have to be aimed and fired since they have the potential to kill and maim long after the warring parties have ceased fighting. The United Nations has reckoned that landmines are at least ten times more likely to kill or injure a civilian after a conflict than a combatant during hostilities.The effects are also long-lasting. The ICBL estimates that anti-personnel mines were the cause of 5,751 casualties in 2006. Whereas traditionally, states would justify these negative impacts of mines due to the advantage they give on the battlefield, under the human security lens, this is untenable as the wide-ranging post-conflict impact on the day-to-day experience of individuals outweighs the military advantage.

The Ottawa Convention, which led to the banning of anti-personnel landmines, is seen as a victory for the Human Security agenda. The Ottawa Convention has proved to be a huge step forward in the 'Freedom from Fear' approach. In Ottawa, the negotiations were moved outside traditional disarmament forums, thus avoiding the entrenched logic of traditional arms control measures. According to Don Hubert an advocate of Human Security from the Canadian Department of Foreign Affairs, the main reason for its success was a multilateral focus. While INGO's like the UN and the ICRC remain the key players along with middle power states like Norway and Canada, its actual power and push comes from the involvement of a host of civil society actors (NGOs) and the general public.Human Security proponents believe that this treaty has set new standards in humanitarian advocacy and has acted as a landmark in international lawmaking for a more secure world.

Critics of the treaty, however, caution against complacency on its success. Many states, they point out, have neither signed nor ratified this convention. They include China, Russia and the United States who are major contributors to the global weapons trade. Second, even though there were a diverse group of civil society actors, the real influence on the treaty came from the ones in the 'global north'. Third, cynics may argue that the success of this campaign stems from the fact that these weapons were outdated and of limited military value and this treaty just helped to accelerate a process that would have happened anyway.

Criticisms

Tadjbakhsh introduced seven challenging questions on the concept of human security on September 13, 2005 at the "Human Security: 60 minutes to Convince" discussion held at UNESCO:

(1) **Can there be an agreement on definitions?** Without a consensus on the definition of human security, it will be difficult to implement and decide on a common human security programme. Today, there is an agreement that human security should be taken from a people-centred more than a state-centred approach, but as mentioned above, the definition or scope of human security is still vague.

(2) **Is the rise of "National Security" disrupting the process of expanding human security?** Since the September 11 attacks, the attention on security has become more on national security rather than human security. According to a study by Christian Aid, "the year 2004 saw $1 billion in aid was diverted to the war on terrorism at the expense of poverty and MDGs." As the focus has shifted from a bottom-up approach to a top-down approach, this has also meant that the investments made are strategically long-term plans rather than short-term, and this has been reflected in the amount of spending. Military expenditures as of 2004 were apparently "twenty times larger than aid outlays," as stated by the SIRPI Yearbook 2004. The question now is, is it too late to revive the focus of state and national security to human security?

(3) **Who is responsible for implementation?** Much discussion today has been in regards to the approach of human security, but with little emphasis on who is in charge of implementing it. Many states have "adopted it as a foreign policy tool" but it has mostly been disregarded "as a domestic policy on development and human rights." Also, people seem to be absent in the process of human security; "people are not passive recipient of security," or victims of its absence, but active subjects who should contribute directly to

identifying and implementing solutions to security problems." There also lies the lack of mandate for IGO's to act in times of need. The genocide in Rwanda and to a certain degree the acts which are currently occurring in Darfur seem to point to this direction. The lack of the strong political will to act in times of dire need has been cited by former UN-Secretary General Kofi Annan as a major speedbump to eliminating immediate security threats.

(4) **What are the priorities and trade-offs?** "Which of the many threats that exist deserves the most attention?" There is no prioritization or "hierarchy" today on which issues are more important than others. This can cause difficulties in establishing goals and directing resources on specific solutions to immediate problems. Specifically under the current context of the world, where there are so many growing problems, including increasing food prices, scarce fresh water sources and the ever-prevalent threat of regional instability in "hotzones" around the world; it seems necessary to have some sort of an agenda as to what threat must be contained first.

(5) **Can a "true inter-sectoral agenda" be implemented?** Are we ready or able to create "inter, or better yet, intra-sectoral interventions?" There needs to be more focus on "relationships," how an intervention can positively or negatively affect other areas and how these effects can improve the human security intervention approach. However, as idealistic as this sounds, the question is how we will implement this when there is a "lack of interdisciplinary approaches among donors and governments"? Once again this also raises the issue of the scope of security. Under current status quo it is primarily states and IGO's that are the primary actors in any security crisis, whereas it is the individuals of the states that are actually at harm. While NGO's and other humanitarian organisations do raise efforts to focus on individuals, there is still a massive gap between the two.

(6) **How can we better understand conflicts?** It is important to understand conflicts in order to resolve and prevent them, and it is easiest to understand conflict during times of conflict, "both to

address conflict prevention and for rebuilding and reconstruction in post conflict-stages." Today, we question how well do we really understand conflict? How can we improve our understanding of it?

(7) **How can we best implement human security and not do harm?** In the past, when human intervention was taken in countries such as the former Yugoslavia, Somalia and Rwanda, some have argued that more harm was done than benefit. Interventions must be better "targeted, implemented, monitored, and coordinated" to decrease "dependency, power and patronage of certain groups." Something must be done to ensure that future interventions do not cause harm, but the question now is how.

NATIONAL SECURITY

National security refers to the requirement to maintain the survival of the nation-state through the use of economic, military and political power and the exercise of diplomacy.

Measures taken to ensure national security include:

- using diplomacy to rally allies and isolate threats
- marshalling economic power to facilitate or compel cooperation
- maintaining effective armed forces
- implementing civil defense and emergency preparedness measures (including anti-terrorism legislation)
- ensuring the resilience and redundancy of critical infrastructure
- using intelligence services to detect and defeat or avoid threats and espionage, and to protect classified information
- using counterintelligence services or secret police to protect the nation from internal threats.

History of the National Security Concept

The relatively new concept of national security was first introduced in the United States after World War II, and has to some degree replaced other concepts that describe the struggle of states to overcome various external and internal threats.

The concept of national security became an official guiding principle of foreign policy in the United States when the National Security Act of 1947 was signed on July 26, 1947 by U.S. President Harry S. Truman.

The majority of the provisions of the Act took effect on 18 September 1947, the day after the Senate confirmed James V. Forrestal as the first Secretary of Defense. Together with its 1949 amendment, this act:

- created the National Military Establishment (NME) which became known as the Department of Defense when the act was amended in 1949,
- created a separate Department of the Air Force from the existing United States Army Air Forces,
- subordinated the military branches to the new cabinet level position of the Secretary of Defense, and
- established the National Security Council, a central place of coordination for national security policy in the Executive Branch, as well as the Central Intelligence Agency, the United States' first peacetime intelligence agency.

During the Cold War's bipolar system, states were relying on the two superpowers to guarantee their national security.

But any system is not everlasting. Communism collapsed and sovereign states emerged without a guarantor. States had to build a nation, maintain national security and rely on themselves.

Following the terrorist September 11, 2001 attacks in the United States, and subsequent terrorist incidents around the world, national security has had to become a paramount concern for governments and societies.

National Security and Rights & Freedoms

The measures adopted to maintain national security in the face of threats to society has led to ongoing dialectic, particularly in liberal democracies, on the appropriate scale and role of authority in matters of civil and human rights.

Tension exists between the preservation of the state (by maintaining self-determination and sovereignty) and the rights and freedoms of individuals.

Although national security measures are imposed to protect society as a whole, such measures will necessarily tend to restrict the rights and freedoms of all individuals in society. The concern is that where the exercise of national security laws and powers is not subject to good governance, the rule of law, and strict checks and balances, there is a risk that "national security" may simply serve as a pretext for suppressing unfavourable political and social views. Taken to its logical conclusion, this view contends that measures which may ostensibly serve a national security purpose (such as mass surveillance, and censorship of mass media), could ultimately lead to an Orwellian dystopia.

In the United States, the politically controversial USA Patriot Act and other government action has brought some of these issues to the citizen's attention, raising two main questions – to what extent, for the sake of national security, should individual rights and freedoms be restricted and can the restriction of civil rights for the sake of national security be justified?

Technical Aspects of National Security

Because of the highly competitive nature of nation states, national security for countries with significant resources and value is based largely on technical measures and operational processes. This ranges from information protection related to state secrets to weaponry for militaries to negotiations strategies with other nation states. The national security aparatus depends largely on combinations of management practices, technical capabilities, the projection of images both internally and externally, and the capacity to gain enough of the will of the people to gather taxes and spend them on useful efforts. While some nation states use power to gain more power for their leadership, others provide quality of life improvements to their people, thus creating larger geopolitical conflicts between types of governments. These all have foudations in internal educaiton and communicaitons systems that serve to build the nation states on strategic and tactical bases and create the conditions for success and failure of the nation state. Increasingly the world is replacing transportaiton with communication and thus the ability to communicate effectively and convey messages in the informaiton environment is critical to national security for the Western nations. Issues like global warming and research priorities increasingly dominate the reality of competition between nation states. All of these lead to the need to have a clear understanding of the technical issues underlying national security in order to create and sustain the institutions that ultimately feed the future of the nation states.

HUMANITARIAN INTERVENTION

Humanitarian intervention refers to armed interference in one state by another state(s) with the objective of ending or reducing the suffering of the population within the first state.

That suffering may be the result of civil war, humanitarian crisis, or crimes committed by the occupied nation (such as genocide). The goal of humanitarian intervention is neither annexation nor interference with territorial integrity, but minimisation of the suffering of civilians in that state.

The claimed rationale behind such an intervention is the belief, embodied in international customary law, in a duty under certain circumstances to disregard a state's sovereignty to preserve our common humanity.

History

Intervening in the affairs of another state has been a subject of discussion in public international law for as long as laws of nations were developed. Attitudes have changed considerably since the end of World War II, the Allied discovery of the Holocaust, and the Nuremberg trials. One of the classic statements for intervention in the affairs of another country is found in John Stuart Mill's essay, *A Few Words on Non-Intervention* (1859)

> "There seems to be no little need that the whole doctrine of non-interference with foreign nations should be reconsidered, if it can be said to have as yet been considered as a really moral question at all... To go to war for an idea, if the war is aggressive, not defensive, is as criminal as to go to war for territory or revenue; for it is as little justifiable to force our ideas on other people, as to compel them to submit to our will in any other respect. But there assuredly are cases in which it is allowable to go to war, without having been ourselves attacked, or threatened with attack; and it is very important that nations should make up their minds in time, as to what these cases are... To suppose that the same international customs, and the same rules of international morality, can obtain between one civilised nation and another, and between civilized nations and barbarians, is a grave error..."

According to Mill's opinion (in 1859) barbarous peoples were found in Algeria and India where the French and British armies had been involved. Mill's justification of intervention was overt imperialism. First, he argued that with "barbarians" there is no hope for "reciprocity", an international fundamental. Second, barbarians are apt to benefit from civilised intervenors, said Mill, citing Roman conquests of Gaul, Spain, Numidia and Dacia. Barbarians,

> "have no rights as a nation, except a right to such treatment as may, at the earliest possible period, fit them for becoming one. The only moral laws for the relation between a civilised and a barbarous government, are the universal rules of morality between man and man."

While seeming wildly out of kilter with modern discourse, a similar approach can be found in theory on intervention in failed states. Of more widespread relevance, Mill discussed the position between "civilised peoples".

"The disputed question is that of interfering in the regulation of another country's internal concerns; the question whether a nation is justified in taking part, on either side, in the civil wars or party contests of another: and chiefly, whether it may justifiably aid the people of another country in struggling for liberty; or may impose on a country any particular government or institutions, either as being best for the country itself, or as necessary for the security of its neighbours.

Mill brushes over the situation of intervening on the side of governments who are trying to oppress an uprising of their own, saying "government which needs foreign support to enforce obedience from its own citizens, is one which ought not to exist". In the case however of a civil war, where both parties seem at fault, Mill argues that third parties are entitled to demand that the conflicts shall cease. He then moves to the more contentious situation of wars for liberation.

> "When the contest is only with native rulers, and with such native strength as those rulers can enlist in their defence, the answer I should give to the question of the legitimacy of intervention is, as a general rule, No. The reason is, that there can seldom be anything approaching to assurance that intervention, even if successful, would be for the good of the people themselves. The only test possessing any real value, of a people's having become fit for popular institutions, is that they, or a sufficient portion of them to prevail in the contest, are willing to brave labour and danger for their liberation. I know all that may be said, I know it may be urged that the virtues of freemen cannot be learnt in the school of slavery, and that if a people are not fit for freedom, to have any chance of becoming so they must first be free. And this would be conclusive, if the intervention recommended would really give them freedom. But the evil is, that if they have not sufficient

love of liberty to be able to wrest it from merely domestic oppressors, the liberty which is bestowed on them by other hands than their own, will have nothing real, nothing permanent. No people ever was and remained free, but because it was determined to be so..."

MODERN DOCTRINE

A modern, post World War II example of humanitarian intervention appeared during the Biafran War (1967-1970). The conflict lead to a famine which caused great suffering, widely covered in western press outlets but totally ignored by government leaders in the name of neutrality and non-intervention. This situation lead to the creation of NGOs like Médecins Sans Frontières, which defended the idea that certain public health situations might justify the extraordinary action of calling into question the sovereignty of states. The concept was developed theoretically at the end of the 1980s, notably by law professor Mario Bettati and French politician (and former president of Médecins Sans Frontières) Bernard Kouchner.

More recently, an alternative approach to humanitarian intervention known as 'Responsibility to Protect' (R2P) has emerged. Responsibility to Protect is the name of a report produced in 2001 by the International Commission on Intervention and State Sovereignty (ICISS) which was established by the Canadian government in response to the history of unsatisfactory humanitarian interventions. The report sought to establish a set of clear guidelines for determining when intervention is appropriate, what the appropriate channels for approving an intervention are and how the intervention itself should be carried out.

Responsibility to Protect seeks to establish a clearer code of conduct for humanitarian interventions and also advocates a greater reliance on non-military measures. The report also criticises and attempts to change the discourse and terminology surrounding the issue of humanitarian intervention. It argues that the notion of a 'right to intervene' is problematic and should be replaced with the 'responsibility to protect'. Under Responsibility to Protect doctrine, rather than having a right to intervene in the conduct of other states,

states are said to have a responsibility to intervene and protect the citizens of another state where that other state has failed in its obligation to protect its own citizens.

This responsibility is said to involve three stages: to prevent, to react and to rebuild. Responsibility to Protect has gained strong support in some circles, such as in Canada, a handful of European and African nations, and among proponents of human security, but has been criticised by others, with some Asian nations being among the chief dissenters.

Definitions

Defenders of humanitarian intervention justify it primarily in the name of a moral imperative: "we should not let people die." This idea is grounded in the Universal Declaration of Human Rights, written in 1948. For these defenders, intervention is only legitimate when it is motivated by a massive violation of human rights and when it is put in motion by an international body, typically the United Nations Security Council. In particular Article 28 announces a right to a social and international order in which human rights are realised.

Further, the Chapter Seven powers of the United Nations Security Council are often used to legitimate intervention for stopping any threats to international peace and security. From the 1990s the understanding of what constituted threats to international peace were radically broadened to include such things as the movement of refugees, to justify intervention into Somalia and Yugoslavia. These two countries were the first that the United Nations intervened without gaining permission from the States involved.

In practice, humanitarian intervention actions are often carried out by coalitions of nations, which can create two somewhat different situations:

The right to interfere, which constitutes jus ad bellum, a term coined by the philosopher Jean-François Revel in 1979, is the recognition of the right of one or many nations to violate the national sovereignty of another state, when a mandate has been granted by a supranational authority. In practice, because of humanitarian emergencies, it is common that the mandate is provided retroactively; for instance, France's intervention in Côte d'Ivoire was made initially without a UN mandate.

The duty to interfere is an obligation which falls to all nation-states to provide assistance at the request of the supranational authority, to the extent possible. Obviously, this notion is the closest to the original concept of humanitarian intervention, except that a right translates into a duty, and is managed by a supranational authority.

Examples of Humanitarian Intervention

Examples of past possible humanitarian interventions include:

- Greece (1824)
- Bulgaria (1877)
- Cuba (1898)
- Haiti (1915)
- Democratic Republic of the Congo (1964)
- Dominican Republic (1965)
- East Pakistan (Bangladesh) (1971)
- Cambodia (1978)
- Tanzania (1979)
- Operation Provide Comfort (Iraq, 1991)
- Unified Task Force (Somalia, 1992)
- Haiti (1994)
- UNAMIR (Rwanda, 1994)
- UNTAET (East Timor, 1999)
- NATO bombing of Yugoslavia (1999)

The above are only "possible" examples of humanitarian intervention due to the advancement of other reasons of intervention (such as self-defence) as justifications of the use of force. They are, however, academically accepted 'incidences' of humanitarian intervention.

Limitations

Despite the generous notions underlying the concept, which place emphasis on values like self-government and respect for human rights, this idea has been queried ever since it was first advanced.

When implemented, an intervention mission can contravene the fundamental objectives of the United Nations, such as maintaining peace, and is contravenes Article 2.7 of the Charter of the United Nations whenever a recognised state is subject to an intervention: "Nothing contained in the present Charter shall authorize the United Nations to intervene in matters which are essentially within the domestic jurisdiction of any state". However, the UN Charter also justifies interventions under Chapters VI and VII. Advocates of interventions argue that the creation of a new right is not necessary, but rather the simple application of rights which already exist.

More fundamentally than this legal problem are the contradictions inherent in the concept of humanitarian intervention, which are primarily due to the confusion created by the blurring of the right and the duty to interfere. It is difficult, when such confusion occurs, to separate the humanitarian motives from the political motives and be assured that the powers intervening are entirely disinterested.

Even though it is called universal, the declaration of human rights is strongly influenced by the work of Western philosophers from the Enlightenment and more generally by a Judeo-Christian tradition. Intervention has often been an action directed by Northern states toward Southern states. It is thus unlikely that a Rwandan contingent might one day be assigned a peacekeeping mission in Northern Ireland, or that the Lebanese might intervene in Basque country.

In reality, the powerful nation-states run little risk of becoming the target of a humanitarian intervention action. For example, the

Chechen population is probably in as much danger as of 2005 as the Kosovars were in previous years, but Russia is significantly more powerful in the realm of international relations than Serbia, and so an international action into Chechnya is much less likely.

It is thus logical that invoking the principles of humanitarian intervention in such an asymmetrical way is met with some considerable reticence. Thus, during the G-77 summit, which brought together the poorest nation-states, the "so-called right of humanitarian intervention" claimed by powerful states was condemned.

Even in the West, humanitarian intervention has opposition. Many believe it bears too much resemblance to the colonialism of the 19th century, and that it is little more than a propaganda term used to justify aggression against countries for other reasons. Others argue that the alleged rationale of advancing the values of Western-style liberal democracy in effect constitutes a dismissal of other cultures or alternative political systems as having negligible value. Others criticise the event-based nature of the concept; there is a tendency for the concept to be invoked in the heat of action, to give the appearance of propriety for Western television viewers, and to neglect the conflicts that are forgotten by the media or occur based on chronic distresses rather than sudden crises.

As is demonstrated by the criticism surrounding the American intervention in Iraq, the delicate balance between repressing bullies and respecting the equality of sovereign states is still one that must be found.

Forced Prostitution

Forced prostitution is a form of sexual slavery that is considered more profitable than the drug trade and arms trade. It is frequently linked to human trafficking.

The line between forced and voluntary prostitution is very thin, and prostitution in and on itself is seen by many as an abusive practice and a form of violence against women. In Sweden, Norway and in Iceland it is illegal to pay for sex (the client commits a crime, but not the prostitute), as these countries consider all forms of prostitution to be exploitive or *de facto* slavery, and place emphasis on suppressing the demand for sex services, by prosecuting the customers and the profiteers.

Many individuals and organisations believe that prostitution (or the activities which surround it) should be kept illegal; they insist that legalised prostitution does nothing to improve the situation of the prostitutes and leads only to an increase in criminal activities and human trafficking. Many feminists are also opposed to prostitution, see feminist objections to prostitution.

However, the criminalisation of voluntary prostitution is condemned by sex workers' rights advocates, who have issued numerous critiques of these laws as another form of prohibition and stigmatisation that serve mainly to marginalise sex workers. Sex workers' rights organisations argue that decriminalisation and extension of labor rights to sex workers is more effective in ensuring their economic, mental and medical health than any form of prohibition.

One form of forced prostitution is the officers or older service mates using conscripts as sex slaves. ◆

3
Human Trafficking

Human trafficking is the commerce and trade in the movement or migration of people, legal and illegal, including both legitimate labour activities as well as forced labour. The term is used in a more narrow sense by advocacy groups to mean the recruitment, transportation, harbouring, or receipt of people for the purposes of slavery, prostitution, forced labour (including bonded labour or debt bondage), and servitude. The UNODC, United Nations Office on Drugs and Crime, defines human trafficking according to Article 3, paragraph (a) of the Protocol to Prevent, Suppress and Punish Trafficking in Persons defines Trafficking in Persons as the recruitment, transportation, transfer, harbouring or receipt of persons, by means of the threat or use of force or other forms of coercion, of abduction, of fraud, of deception, of the abuse of power or of a position of vulnerability or of the giving or receiving of payments or benefits to achieve the consent of a person having control over another person, for the purpose of exploitation. The UNODC offers practical help to States, not only helping to draft laws and create comprehensive national anti-trafficking strategies but also assisting with resources to implement them. In March 2009, UNODC launched the Blue Heart Campaign to fight human trafficking, to raise awareness and to encourage involvement and inspire action. Human trafficking is the fastest growing criminal industry in the world, with the total annual revenue for trafficking in persons estimated to be between $5 billion and $9 billion. The Council of Europe states that "people trafficking has reached epidemic proportions over the past decade, with a global annual market of about $42.5 billion." Trafficking victims typically are recruited using coercion, deception, fraud, the abuse of power, or outright abduction.

Exploitation includes forcing people into prostitution or other forms of sexual exploitation, forced labour or services, slavery or practices similar to slavery and servitude. For children, exploitation may also include forced prostitution, illicit international adoption, trafficking for early marriage, or recruitment as child soldiers, beggars, for sports (such as child camel jockeys or football players), or within certain religious groups.

The OSCE (Organisation for Security and Co-operation in Europe) is one of the leading agencies fighting the problem of human trafficking. Human trafficking is by its very nature an international crime that requires a high level of co-operation and collaboration between States if it is to be tackled effectively. This means that the OSCE is ideally placed to provide a transnational framework against this modern day slavery all across its area of operation, which spans the North Atlantic, Europe, Russia and Central Asia.

Human trafficking differs from people smuggling. In the latter, people voluntarily request smuggler's service for fees and there may be no deception involved in the (illegal) agreement. On arrival at their destination, the smuggled person is usually freed. On the other hand, the trafficking victim is enslaved, or the terms of their debt bondage are highly exploitative. The trafficker takes away the basic human rights of the victim.

Victims are sometimes tricked and lured by false promises or physically forced. Some traffickers use coercive and manipulative tactics including deception, intimidation, feigned love, isolation, threat and use of physical force, debt bondage, or other abuse. People who are seeking entry to other countries may be picked up by traffickers, and misled into thinking that they will be free after being smuggled across the border. In some cases, they are captured through slave raiding, although this is increasingly rare.

Trafficking is a fairly lucrative industry. In some areas, like Russia, Eastern Europe, Hong Kong, Japan, and Colombia, trafficking is controlled by large criminal organisations. However, the majority of trafficking is done by networks of smaller groups that each specialise in a certain area, like recruitment, transportation, advertising, or retail. This is very profitable because little start up capital is needed, and prosecution is relatively rare.

Trafficked people are usually the most vulnerable and powerless minorities in a region. They often come from the poorer areas where opportunities are limited, they often are ethnic minorities, and they often are displaced persons such as runaways or refugees (though they may come from any social background, class or race).

Women are particularly at risk from sex trafficking. Criminals exploit lack of opportunities, promise good jobs or opportunities for study, and then force the victims to become prostitutes. Through agents and brokers who arrange the travel and job placements, women are escorted to their destinations and delivered to the employers. Upon reaching their destinations, some women learn that they have been deceived about the nature of the work they will do; most have been lied to about the financial arrangements and conditions of their employment; and find themselves in coercive or abusive situations from which escape is both difficult and dangerous.

Trafficking of children often involves exploitation of the parents' extreme poverty. The latter may sell children to traffickers in order to pay off debts or gain income or they may be deceived concerning the prospects of training and a better life for their children. In West Africa, trafficked children have often lost one or both parents to the African AIDS crisis. Thousands of male (and sometimes female) children have also been forced to be child soldiers.

The adoption process, legal and illegal, results in cases of trafficking of babies and pregnant women between the West and the developing world. In David M. Smolin's papers on child trafficking and adoption scandals between India and the United States, he cites there are systemic vulnerabilities in the inter-country adoption system that makes adoption scandals predictable.

Thousands of children from Asia, Africa, and South America are sold into the global sex trade every year. Often they are kidnapped or orphaned, and sometimes they are actually sold by their own families.

Men are also at risk of being trafficked for unskilled work predominantly involving forced labour which globally generates $31bn according to the International Labour Organisation. Other forms of trafficking include forced marriage, and domestic servitude.

The most common destinations for victims of human trafficking are Thailand, Japan, Israel, Belgium, the Netherlands, Germany, Italy, Turkey and the US, according to a report by the UNODC (United Nations Office on Drugs and Crime).

The major sources of trafficked persons include Thailand, China, Nigeria, Albania, Bulgaria, Belarus, Moldova and Ukraine.

Extent

Due to the illegal nature of trafficking and differences in methodology, the exact extent is unknown. According to United States State Department data, an "estimated 600,000 to 820,000 men, women, and children trafficked across international borders each year, approximately 70 percent are women and girls and up to 50 percent are minors. The data also illustrates that the majority of transnational victims are trafficked into commercial sexual exploitation." However, they go on to say that "the alarming enslavement of people for purposes of labour exploitation, often in their own countries, is a form of human trafficking that can be hard to track from afar." Thus the figures for persons trafficked for labour exploitation are likely to be greatly underestimated.

Reporters have witnessed a rapid increase in prostitution in Cambodia, Bosnia, and Kosovo after UN and, in the case of the latter two, NATO peacekeeping forces moved in. Peacekeeping forces have been linked to trafficking and forced prostitution. Proponents of peacekeeping argue that the actions of a few should not incriminate the many participants in the mission, yet NATO and the UN have come under criticism for not taking the issue of forced prostitution linked to peacekeeping missions seriously enough.

A common misconception is that trafficking only occurs in poor countries. But every country in the world is involved in the underground, lucrative system. A "source country" is a country that girls are trafficked from. Usually, these countries are destitute and may have been further weakened by war, corruption, natural disasters or climate. Some source countries are Nepal, Guatemala, the former Soviet territories, and Nigeria, but there are many more. A "transit country", like Mexico or Israel, is a temporary stop on trafficked victims' journey to the country where they will be enslaved. A "destination country" is where trafficked persons end up. These countries are generally affluent, since they must have citizens with enough "disposable income" to "buy the traffickers' 'products'". Japan, India, much of Western Europe, and the United States are all destination countries.

In a 2006 report the Future Group, a Canadian humanitarian organisation dedicated to combatting human trafficking and the child sex trade, ranked eight industrialised nations. In the report, titled "Falling Short of the Mark: An International Study on the Treatment of Human Trafficking Victims", Canada received an F rating, the United Kingdom received a D, while the United States received a B+ and Australia, Norway, Sweden, Germany and Italy all received grades of B or B-.

North America

According to the National Human Rights Center in Berkeley, California, there are currently about 10,000 forced labourers in the U.S., around one-third of whom are domestic servants and some portion of whom are children. The Associated Press reports, based on interviews in California and in Egypt, that trafficking of children for domestic labour in the U.S. is an extension of an illegal but common practice in Africa. Families in remote villages send their daughters to work in cities for extra money and the opportunity to escape a dead-end life. Some girls work for free on the understanding that they will at least be better fed in the home of their employer. This custom has led to the spread of trafficking, as well-to-do Africans accustomed to employing children immigrate to the U.S.

Research conducted by University of California at Berkeley on behalf of the anti-trafficking organisation Free the Slaves found that about 46% of people in slavery in the United States are forced into prostitution. Domestic servitude claims 27%, agriculture 10%, and other occupations 17%.

An estimated 14,000 people are trafficked into the United States each year, although again because trafficking is illegal, accurate statistics are difficult. According to the Massachusetts based Trafficking Victims Outreach and Services Network (project of the nonprofit MataHari: Eye of the Day) in Massachusetts alone, there were 55 documented cases of human trafficking in 2005 and the first half of 2006 in Massachusetts. In 2004, the Royal Canadian Mounted Police (RCMP) estimated that 600-800 persons are trafficked into Canada annually and that additional 1,500-2,200 persons are trafficked through Canada into the United States. In Canada, foreign trafficking for prostitution is estimated to be worth $400 million annually.

According to the Future Group report, Canada in particular has a major problem with modern-day sexual slavery, giving Canada an F for its "abysmal" record treating victims. The report concluded that Canada "is an international embarrassment" when it comes to combating this form of slavery.

The report's principal author Benjamin Perrin wrote, "Canada has ignored calls for reform and continues to re-traumatise trafficking victims, with few exceptions, by subjecting them to routine deportation and fails to provide even basic support services." The report criticises former Liberal Party of Canada cabinet ministers Irwin Cotler, Joe Volpe and Pierre Pettigrew for "passing the buck" on the issue.

Commenting on the report, the then Minister of Citizenship and Immigration, Monte Solberg told Sun Media Corporation, "It's very damning, and if there are obvious legislative or regulatory fixes that need to be done, those have to become priorities, given especially that we're talking about very vulnerable people."

The 2009 US Trafficking in Persons Report released by Secretary of State Hillary Clinton, lists Canada as a Tier One country. "The

Government of Canada fully complies with the minimum standards for the elimination of trafficking. During the past year, the Canadian government maintained strong victim protection and prevention efforts, and demonstrated modest progress in prosecuting and punishing trafficking offenders, securing five trafficking-specific convictions during the past year. Law enforcement personnel, however, reported difficulties with securing adequate punishments against offenders."

Asia

In Asia, Japan is the major destination country for trafficked women, especially from the Philippines and Thailand. The US State Department has rated Japan as either a 'Tier 2' or a 'Tier 2 Watchlist' country every year since 2001 in its annual *Trafficking in Persons* reports. Both these ratings implied that Japan was (to a greater or lesser extent) not fully compliant with minimum standards for the elimination of human trafficking trade. There are currently an estimated 300,000 women and children involved in the sex trade throughout Southeast Asia. It is common that Thai women are lured to Japan and sold to Yakuza-controlled brothels where they are forced to work off their price. By the late 1990s, UNICEF estimated that there are 60,000 child prostitutes in the Philippines, describing Angeles City brothels as "notorious" for offering sex with children. UNICEF estimates many of the 200 brothels in the notorious Angeles City offer children for sex.

Many of the Iraqi women fleeing the Iraq War are turning to prostitution, while others are trafficked abroad, to countries like Syria, Jordan, Qatar, the United Arab Emirates and Turkey. In Syria alone an estimated 50,000 Iraqi refugee girls and women, many of them widows, had been forced into prostitution as of 2007· Cheap Iraqi prostitutes have helped to make Syria a popular destination for sex tourists. The clients come from wealthier countries in the Middle East. High prices are offered for virgins.

As many as 200,000 Nepali girls, many under 14, have been sold into the sex slavery in India. Nepalese women and girls, especially virgins, are favoured in India because of their light skin.

Africa

In parts of Ghana, a family may be punished for an offense by having to turn over a virgin female to serve as a sex slave within the offended family. In this instance, the woman does not gain the title of "wife." In parts of Ghana, Togo, and Benin, shrine slavery persists, despite being illegal in Ghana since 1998. In this system of slavery of ritual servitude, sometimes called *trokosi* (in Ghana) or *voodoosi* in Togo and Benin, young virgin girls are given as slaves in traditional shrines and are used sexually by the priests in addition to providing free labour for the shrine.

Europe

Since the fall of the Iron Curtain, the impoverished former Eastern bloc countries such as Albania, Moldova, Romania, Bulgaria, Russia, Belarus and Ukraine have been identified as major trafficking source countries for women and children. Young women and girls are often lured to wealthier countries by the promises of money and work and then reduced to sexual slavery. It is estimated that 2/3 of women trafficked for prostitution worldwide annually come from Eastern Europe, three-quarters have never worked as prostitutes before. The major destinations are Western Europe (Germany, Italy, Netherlands, Spain, UK, Greece), the Middle East (Turkey, Israel, the United Arab Emirates), Asia, Russia and the United States. An estimated 500,000 women from Central and Eastern Europe are working in prostitution in the EU alone.

In the United Kingdom, the Home Office has stated that 71 women were trafficked into prostitution in 1998. They also suggest that the actual figure could be up to 1,420 women trafficked into the UK during the same period. However, the figures are problematic as the definition used in the UK to identify cases of sex trafficking – derived from the Sexual Offences Act 2003 – does not require that victims have been coerced or misled. Thus, any individual who moves to the UK for the purposes of sex work can be regarded as having been trafficked – even if they did so with their knowledge and consent. The Home Office do not appear to be keeping records of the number of people trafficked into the UK for purposes other than sexual exploitation.

In poverty-stricken Moldova, where the unemployment rate for women ranges as high as 68% and one-third of the workforce live and work abroad, experts estimate that since the collapse of the Soviet Union between 200,000 and 400,000 women have been sold into prostitution abroad—perhaps up to 10% of the female population. In Ukraine, a survey conducted by the NGO La Strada Ukraine in 2001–2003, based on a sample of 106 women being trafficked out of Ukraine found that 3% were under 18, and the U.S. State Department reported in 2004 that incidents of minors being trafficked was increasing. It is estimated that half a million Ukrainian women were trafficked abroad since 1991 (80% of all unemployed in Ukraine are women).

Russia is a source, transit, and destination country for men, women, and children trafficked for various forms of exploitation. Many women have been trafficked overseas for the purpose of sexual exploitation. Annually, thousands of trafficked Russian women end up as prostitutes in Western Europe, America, Canada, Israel and Asian countries. The ILO estimates that there may be up to one million illegal immigrants in Russia who are victims of forced labour, which is a form of trafficking. There have also been reports of child sex tourism in Russia; however, law enforcement authorities report a decrease in the number of cases of child sex tourism and attribute this to aggressive police investigations and Russian cooperation with foreign law enforcement agencies.

CAUSES OF TRAFFICKING

Trafficking in people has been facilitated by porous borders and advanced communication technologies, it has become increasingly transnational in scope and highly lucrative. Unlike drugs or arms, people can be "sold" many times. The opening up of Asian markets, porous borders, the end of the Soviet Union and the collapse of the former Yugoslavia have contributed to this globalisation.

Some causes and facilitators of trafficking include:

- Lack of employment opportunities
- Organised crime
- Regional imbalances
- Economic disparities
- Social discrimination
- Corruption in government
- Political instability
- Armed conflict
- Mass resettlement for large projects without proper Resettlement and Rehabilitation packages.
- Profitability
- Insufficient penalties against traffickers
- Minimal law enforcement on global sex tourism industry
- Legal processes that prosecute victims for prosecution instead of the traffickers.
- Poor international border defence.

Relation to Other Vulnerability Issues

Human trafficking is not a stand alone issue. It is closely related other issues that threaten security well-being of the victims. Victims are exposed to continuous threats of physical violence by traffickers to ensure compliance. Many are held in bondage and beaten to suppress resistance. Other threats include absolute poverty due to wage deprivation. They are unprotected by labour laws, and long working hours as well as lack of holiday is common. For example, 15 is the standard working hours per day among Chinese victims in France. In Japan, Thai trafficking victims also complained of breach of work contracts, non-payment of wages, mandatory night work and poor accommodation.

Human Trafficking and Sexual Exploitation

Human Trafficking is a wrong doing. There is no universally accepted definition of trafficking for sexual exploitation. The term encompasses the organised movement of people, usually women, between countries and within countries for sex work with the use of physical coercion, deception and bondage through forced debt. However, the issue becomes contentious when the element of coercion is removed from the definition to incorporate facilitating the willing involvement in prostitution. For example, in the United Kingdom, The Sexual Offenses Act, 2003 incorporated trafficking for sexual exploitation but did not require those committing the offense to use coercion, deception or force, so that it also includes any person who enters the UK to carry out sex work with consent as having been trafficked.

Save the Children stated "The issue gets mired in controversy and confusion when prostitution itself is considered as a violation of the basic human rights of both adult women and minors, and equal to sexual exploitation per se..... trafficking and prostitution become conflated with each other.... On account of the historical conflation of trafficking and prostitution both legally and in popular understanding, an overwhelming degree of effort and interventions of anti-trafficking groups are concentrated on trafficking into prostitution."

Sexual trafficking includes coercing a migrant into a sexual act as a condition of allowing or arranging the migration. Sexual trafficking uses physical coercion, deception and bondage incurred through forced debt. Trafficked women and children, for instance, are often promised work in the domestic or service industry, but instead are usually taken to brothels where their passports and other identification papers are confiscated. They may be beaten or locked up and promised their freedom only after earning – through prostitution – their purchase price, as well as their travel and visa costs.

The main motive of a woman (in some cases an underage girl) to accept an offer from a trafficker is better financial opportunities for herself or her family. In many cases traffickers initially offer 'legitimate' work or the promise of an opportunity to study. The main types of work offered are in the catering and hotel industry, in bars and clubs, modeling contracts, or au pair work. Traffickers sometimes use offers of marriage, threats, intimidation and kidnapping as means of obtaining victims. In the majority of cases, the women end up in prostitution. Also some (migrating) prostitutes become victims of human trafficking. Some women know they will be working as prostitutes, but they have an inaccurate view of the circumstances and the conditions of the work in their country of destination. In Japan the prosperous entertainment market had created huge demand for commercial sexual workers, and such demand is being met by trafficking women and children from the Philippines, Colombia and Thailand. Women are forced into street prostitution, based stripping and live sex acts. However, detainees or deportees from Japan said that about 80 percent of the women went there with the intention of working as prostitutes.

The Fundamentalist Church of Jesus Christ of Latter Day Saints, in the US and Canada, has also been implicated in the trafficking of underage women across state lines and international borders (US/Canada). In most cases, this is for the continuation of polygamous practices, in the form of plural marriage.

Trafficking victims are also exposed to different psychological problems. They suffer social alienation in the host and home countries. Stigmatization, social exclusion and intolerance make reintegration into local communities difficult. The governments offer little assistance and social services to trafficked victims upon their return. As the victims are also pushed into drug trafficking, many of them face criminal sanctions.

Efforts to Reduce Human Trafficking

Governments, international associations, and nongovernmental organisations have all tried to end human trafficking with various degrees of success.

INTERGOVERNMENTAL ORGANISATIONS

Organisation of State Council of Europe

In 2003 the OSCE established an anti-trafficking mechanism aimed at raising public awareness of the problem and building the political will within participating States to tackle it effectively.

The OSCE actions against human trafficking are coordinated by the Office of the Special Representative for Combating the Traffic of Human Beings Since 2006 this office has been headed by Eva Biaudet, a former Member of Parliament and Minister of Health and Social Services in her native Finland.

The activities of the Office of the Special Representative range from training law enforcement agencies to tackle human trafficking to promoting policies aimed at rooting out corruption and organised crime. The Special Representative also visits countries and can, on their request, support the formation and implementation of their anti-trafficking policies. In other cases the Special Representative provides advice regarding implementation of the decisions on human trafficking, and assists governments, ministers and officials to achieved their stated goals of tackling human trafficking.

Government Actions

Actions taken to combat human trafficking vary from government to government. Some have introduced legislation specifically aimed at making human trafficking illegal. Governments can also develop systems of co-operation between different nation's law enforcement agencies and with non-government organisations (NGOs). Many countries though have come under criticism for inaction, or ineffective action. Criticisms include failure of governments in not properly identifying and protecting trafficking victims, that immigration policies might re-victimise trafficking victims, or insufficient action in helping prevent vulnerable people becoming trafficking victims.

A particular criticism has been the reluctance of some countries to tackle trafficking for purposes other than sex.

Other actions governments could take is raise awareness. This can take on three forms. Firstly, in raising awareness amongst potential victims, in particular in countries where human traffickers are active. Secondly, raising awareness amongst police, social welfare workers and immigration officers. And in countries where prostitution is legal or semi-legal, raising awareness amongst the clients of prostitution, to look out for signs of a human trafficking victim.

Raising awareness can take on different forms. One method is through the use of awareness films or through posters.

International Law

In 2000 the United Nations adopted the Convention against Transnational Organised Crime, also called the Palermo Convention, and two Palermo protocols there to:

- Protocol to Prevent, Suppress and Punish Trafficking in Persons, especially Women and Children; and
- Protocol against the Smuggling of Migrants by Land, Sea and Air.

All of these instruments contain elements of the current international law on trafficking in human beings.

Council of Europe

The Council of Europe Convention on Action against Trafficking in Human Beings was adopted by the Council of Europe on 16 May 2005. The aim of the convention is to prevent and combat the trafficking in human beings. The Convention entered into force on 1 February 2008. Of the 47 member states of the Council of Europe, so far 21 have signed the convention and 17 have ratified it.

United Kingdom

In the United Kingdom, after intense pressure from Human Rights organisations, trafficking for labour exploitation was made illegal in 2004 (trafficking for sexual exploitation being criminalised many years previously). However, the 2004 law has been used very rarely and by mid-2007 there had not been a single conviction under these provisions.

United States Law

Laws against trafficking in the United States exist at the federal and state levels. Over half of the states now criminalise human trafficking though the penalties are not as tough as the federal laws. Related federal and state efforts focus on regulating the tourism industry to prevent the facilitation of sex tourism and regulate international marriage brokers to ensure criminal background checks and information on how to get help are given to the potential bride.

The United States federal government has taken a firm stance against human trafficking both within its borders and beyond. Domestically, human trafficking is a federal crime under Title 18 of the United States Code. Section 1584 makes it a crime to force a person to work against his will, whether the compulsion is effected by use of force, threat of force, threat of legal coercion or by "a climate of fear" (an environment wherein individuals believe they may be harmed by leaving or refusing to work); Section 1581 similarly makes it illegal to force a person to work through "debt servitude." Human trafficking as it relates to involuntary servitude and slavery is prohibited by the 13th Amendment. Federal laws on human trafficking are enforced by Immigration and Customs Enforcement as well as the United States Department of Justice Civil Rights Division, Criminal Section.

The Victims of Trafficking and Violence Protection Act of 2000 allowed for greater statutory maximum sentences for traffickers, provided resources for protection of and assistance for victims of trafficking and created avenues for interagency cooperation. It also allows many trafficking victims to remain in the United States and apply for permanent residency under a T-1 Visa. The Act also attempted to encourage efforts to prevent human trafficking internationally, by creating annual country reports on trafficking and tying financial non-humanitarian assistance to foreign countries to real efforts in addressing human trafficking.

The United States Department of State has a high-level official charged with combating human trafficking, the Director of the Office to Monitor and Combat Trafficking in Persons ("anti-trafficking czar"). The current director is Lou de Baca.

International NGOs such as Human Rights Watch and Amnesty International have called on the United States to improve its measures aimed at reducing trafficking.They recommend that the United States more fully implement the United Nations Convention against Transnational Organised Crime Protocol to Prevent, Suppress and Punish Trafficking in Persons, especially Women and Children and for immigration officers to improve their awareness of trafficking and support the victims of trafficking.

Several state governments have taken action to address human trafficking in their borders, either through legislation or prevention activities. For example, Florida state law prohibits forced labour, sex trafficking, and domestic servitude, and provides for mandatory law enforcement trainings and victim services. A 2006 Connecticut law prohibits coerced work and makes trafficking a violation of the Connecticut RICO Act.

NON-GOVERNMENTAL ORGANISATIONS

Human rights organisations, including Amnesty International, Anti-Slavery International and Human Rights Watch have campaigned against human trafficking. Several non-governmental organisations (NGOs) and human rights organisations have been formed to combat human trafficking. Some of these include:

Arizona League to End Regional Trafficking (ALERT) is a coalition representing partnerships with law enforcement, faith-based communities, non-profit organisations, social service agencies, attorneys and concerned citizens. ALERT helps victims of trafficking by providing: food and shelter; medical care; mental health counselling; immigration assistance; legal assistance; language interpretation; case management; and other culturally appropriate services throughout the state of Arizona. Through education, outreach and a variety of programmes and services, ALERT strives to end the suffering and dehumanisation of victims of human trafficking.

Coalition to Abolish Slavery and Trafficking (CAST) is a Los Angeles-based anti-human trafficking organisation. Founded in 1998, CAST helps rehabilitate survivors of trafficking, raises awareness, and affects legislation and public policy surrounding human trafficking, through social, advocacy and legal services. CAST defines human trafficking as "a modern-day form of slavery," in which victims are subjected to force, fraud or coercion for the purpose of forced labour or sexual exploitation. Victims of trafficking can work in domestic service, factories, farms, restaurants, construction sites, hotel housekeeping, servile marriage, forced prostitution, child prostitution and child pornography.

Chab Dai, ("joining hands" in Khmer) was founded in Cambodia in 2005, and now has international offices in the US, UK, and Canada. Chab Dai aims to bring an end to human trafficking and commercial sexual exploitation through coalition building, advocacy, research and education. In Cambodia, Chab Dai facilitates a coalition of over 40 NGOs all working against trafficking in areas such as prevention, aftercare and legal intervention. Chab Dai assists coalition members collaborate and improve capacity through training, advice clinics, and discussion forums; and works to build bridges between members, UN agencies and government. Chab Dai USA, located in California, is committed to encouraging collaboration amongst existing agencies while assisting organisations improve capacity, particularly according to international best practice models.

The SOLD Project, founded in 2007 is a grassroots organisation dedicated to inspiring and empowering individuals to stop child prostitution before it begins. The SOLD Project started as a film project to document the realities of child prostitution in Thailand with hopes to increase awareness and advocacy. However, SOLD became more than a film and is now a non-profit organisation focused on the prevention of child prostitution through education and community reform. The SOLD Project Prevention Programme is 4-fold

(1) Scholarships (2) Mentorship (3) After School Programs (4) Human Trafficking Awareness Programmes.

Alliance Anti-Traffic (AAT), founded in 2007 is a French non-governmental organisation created to fight against trafficking in Women and Children.The organisation intervenes to protect women and girls from these forms of abuse. AAT also works on suppression and the demand side. AAT assist targeted women and children through a full process: first it prevents at-risk groups, AAT protect victims found in exploitation places and after repatriate them back into their communities. Then AAT reintegrate women and girls based on their choice and the needs of their communities. AAT finally empowers targeted girls to develop alternatives and to prevent as well as to protect vulnerable women and children. www.Allianceantitrafic.org.

Somaly Mam Foundation, founded in 2007 at the United Nations with the support of UNICEF, UNIFEM, and IOM, the Somaly Mam Foundation is known for empowering victims of human trafficking to become activists and agents of change. With the leadership of world renowned Cambodian activist, Somaly Mam, the organisation has garnered support from influential leaders and celebrities such as Susan Sarandon, Daryl Hannah, Diane von Furstenberg, and Hillary Clinton. The foundation also runs activities to support Rescue and Rehabilitation of victims in Southeast Asia and works to increase global awareness to inspire action.

Redlight Children Campaign, founded in 2002 is a non-profit organisation created by New York lawyer and president of Priority Films Guy Jacobson and Israeli actress Adi Ezroni in 2002, to combat worldwide child sexual exploitation and human trafficking. Its mission is to decrease the demand side of the international sex trade through legislation and enforcement while raising awareness utilising mass media and grassroots outreach. Through its partnership with Priority Films, Redlight Children has recently launched the K11 Project—three films which attempt to expose real life experiences of the underage sex trade. K11 consists of two documentaries and a feature-length narrative, Holly (film), which were all filmed on location in Cambodia. RedLight also began working the Somaly Mam Foundation in 2003. A comprehensive blueprint outlines three phases of the attack on this crime against humanity: raising awareness, correcting, improving, and enforcing current legislation, followed by allocating the appropriate resources to mirror the size and scope of the epidemic. The hope is that utilising both film and mass media will put the issue on the international agenda, inciting action from the general public and policy makers, thereby leading to an allocation of appropriate resources and stricter enforcement that will effectively reduce demand.

Not For Sale Campaign, founded in 2007, equips and mobilizes Smart Activists to deploy innovative solutions to re-abolish slavery in their own backyards and across the globe. Headquartered in Montara, CA, the Not For Sale Campaign has more than 40 regional chapters across the United States and Canada. Through the innovation and implementation of 'open-source activism', the campaign identifies trafficking rings inside the United States and collaborates with local law enforcement and community groups to shut them down and provide support for the victims. Internationally, the campaign partners with poorly resourced abolitionist groups internationally to enhance their capacity.

Polaris Project, founded in 2002, is an international anti-human trafficking organisation with offices in Washington DC, New Jersey, Colorado, and Japan. Polaris Project's comprehensive approach includes operating local and national human trafficking hotlines, conducting direct outreach and victim identification, providing social services and housing to victims, advocating for stronger state and national anti-trafficking legislation, and engaging community members in grassroots efforts.

Tiny Stars. Using the Protect Act of 2003, Tiny Stars works closely with Federal Law enforcement agencies to build cases against American child predators. Founded by Jake Collins in 2001, Tiny Stars focuses on identifying and tracking pedophiles who victimise children under the age of 14 years old. To advance its mission, the organization has developed a network of undercover agents, often former government operatives.

National Human Trafficking Resource Center (NHTRC) is a program funded by the Department of Health and Human Services. The NHTRC operates the National Human Trafficking Resource Center Hotline 24-hours a day, 365 days a year.

Made By Survivors (MBS) is a division of The Emancipation Network (TEN) and is an organisation that uses economic empowerment to help survivors of trafficking and people at high risk to rebuild their lives. MBS's handicraft programmes offer these survivors a job that enables them to support themselves and live a meaningful, independent life. For those still living at the shelter, handicrafts programmes provide therapeutic benefits, job training, literacy, social interaction, and a stipend for part-time work. MBS partners with 18 anti-slavery organisations around the world, including Thailand, Cambodia, Nepal, India, Ukraine, Uganda, the Philippines, Tanzania, and the United States. MBS also runs volunteer trips to India as a way to educate people who can use the experience to get more involved and educate the public. The trips also help the survivors to trust people again and reintegrate them back into a normal life. In addition, MBS offers people the opportunity to host parties at their homes to sell the handicrafts and educate friends and family.

Criticisms

Lack of Accurate Data and Possible Overestimation or Underestimation

Distinguishing human trafficking from voluntary migration is crucial because the ability of people to purposefully and voluntarily migrate for work should be respected; in fact is required to be respected by Article 13 of the Universal Declaration of Human Rights.

Most controversy is centered around human trafficking for the purpose of prostitution, especially since prostitution in and on itself is seen by many as a form of exploitation. Estimates of the number of people trafficked for sexual purposes is contentious – problems of definition can be compounded by the willingness of victims to identify as being trafficked.

The United Nations Special Rapporteur on trafficking in persons reported that most prostitution that occurs today is connected to human trafficking: "For the most part, prostitution as actually practiced in the world usually does satisfy the elements of trafficking." Even most domestic prostitution satisfies the elements of trafficking as defined in the Trafficking Protocol. The Trafficking Protocol defines illegal trafficking as "the recruitment, transportation, transfer, harbouring or receipt of a person" if an existing vulnerability – such as economic vulnerability or sexual vulnerability – is exploited. For this reason, threat, coercion, or use of force is not necessary to constitute trafficking.

Much criticism of the recent publicity around sex trafficking, and the associated demands for legal sanction against prostitutes or their customers, has come from some sexual health – AIDS organisations. Their principal concern is that such measures hinder efforts to prevent the spread of HIV/AIDS. The epidemiologist Elizabeth Pisani, in her book *The Wisdom of Whores: Bureaucrats, Brothels, and the Business of AIDS*, examines the phenomenon of sex trafficking and its impact on HIV prevention in detail. She concludes that forced trafficking (as opposed to voluntary involvement in sex work) is wildly over-estimated.

Focus on "Sex Trafficking"

Whilst most mainstream human rights groups acknowledge all forms of trafficking, there is growing criticism of the focus on trafficking for sexual exploitation at the expense of tackling other forms such as domestic or agricultural trafficking. Ambassador Nancy Elly Raphael, the first director of the U.S. Federal Trafficking in Persons Office, resigned over what she saw as misrepresentation of the issue in order to provide support for the anti-prostitution lobby. She says "It was so ideological. Prostitution, that's what was driving the whole programme. They kept saying, 'If you didn't have prostitution, you wouldn't have trafficking.' I was happy to leave."

In many countries, particularly the United States and the United Kingdom, the overwhelming majority of interventions concentrate on sex trafficking. For example, on 8 July 2008, Fiona Mactaggart MP, a prominent UK government spokesperson on the issue, admitted that the UK government concentrated on disrupting sex trafficking. Quoting from Sigma Huda, UN special reporter on trafficking in persons, she said "For the most part, prostitution as actually practiced in the world usually does satisfy the elements of trafficking..."

Opponents of this criticism state that of the estimated 700, 000 people trafficked worldwide annually, 80% are female, and 70% of those women and girls are trafficked "for sexual exploitation" and therefore the focus of human trafficking groups on sex trafficking is necessary and justified.

In Popular Culture

- *Lilya 4-ever*, a film based loosely on the real life of Dangoule Rasalaite, portrays a young woman from the former Soviet Union who is deceived into being trafficked for exploitation in Sweden.
- Human trafficking has also been portrayed in the Canadian/ UK TV drama *Sex Traffic*.
- Based on true events, *Svetlana's Journey* by Michael Cory Davis depicts the trials of a 13-year-old who loses her family and is sold to human traffickers by her adoptive family. Drugged, raped, and forced to endure continuous abuse by her 'clients' and traffickers, she attempts to commit suicide, but survives.
- *River of Innocents* follows the 17-year-old Majlinda into the world of modern-day slavery, where she struggles to hold on to her humanity and to help the stolen children around her survive.

- Dimanasus Prophecy, a movie by Dzmitry Vasilyeu about human trafficking in Eastern Europe.
- David Mamet's 2004 film *Spartan* centres on the hunt for the daughter of a high ranking US official who has been kidnapped by an international sex slavery ring.
- *Holly* (2006) is a movie about a little girl, sold by her poor family and smuggled across the border to Cambodia to work as a prostitute in a red light village. *The Virgin Harvest* is a feature length documentary that was filmed at the same time.
- The 2007 film *Trade* deals with human trafficking out of Mexico and a brother's attempt to rescue his kidnapped and trafficked young sister. It is based on Peter Landesman's article about sex slaves, which was featured as the cover story in the January 24, 2004 issue of New York Times Magazine.
- *Human Trafficking* (2005) (TV) by Christian Duguay stars Mira Sorvino, Donald Sutherland, and Robert Carlyle. A sixteen-year-old girl from the Ukraine, a single mother from Russia, an orphaned seventeen-year-old girl from Romania, and a twelve-year-old American tourist become the victims of international sex slave traffickers. Sorvino and Sutherland are the Immigration and Customs Enforcement (ICE) agents who struggle to save them.
- *Ghosts*, a documentary by independent film maker Nick Broomfield, follows the story of the victims of the 2004 Morecambe Bay cockling disaster, in which smuggled immigrants are forced in to hard labour.
- *The Jammed*, an Australian film about human trafficking in Australia.
- The 2007 film *The Sugar Babies* by Amy Serrano is a documentary that highlights the plight of Haitian victims of human trafficking in the Dominican Republic. It was produced by Thor Halvorssen and funded by the Human Rights Foundation.

- The European series *Matroesjka's* deals with girls from ex-Soviet countries, who have been deceived into sex slavery in Belgium.
- The 2007 film *Eastern Promises* by David Cronenberg deals with a British midwife who unravels a gang of Russian slavers when she seeks relatives to a baby of a sex slave named Tatiana.
- The 2008 film *Taken (film)* by Pierre Morel, casting e.g. Liam Neeson, which is about foreign girls in Paris who are "trafficked" with the purpose of forcing them to prostitution.
- The 2008 documentary and concert film Call + Response combines contemporary musician performances with an investigative report on worldwide human trafficking including hidden camera footage from Thailand brothels.
- A 2006 *Punisher* story arc called The Slavers, written by Garth Ennis, dealt with the horrors of human trafficking and sex slavery.
- In the *CSI: NY* episode, "She's Not There", the episode showcases the horrors of human trafficking when a Russian tourist is murdered and a girl that went missing.
- The 2009 novel, *A False Dawn*, by Tom Lowe (St. Martins Press, ISBN 031237917X) depicts the horrors of human trafficking in the U.S.
- The 2009 film *Happy Endings?*, filmed in Rhode Island, chronicles the lives of the women in massage parlors in Rhode Island during a battle in the state legislature to make prostitution illegal, focusing on issues of human trafficking.

◆

4

Customary International Laws

Customary international laws are those aspects of international laws that derive from custom. Coupled with general principles of law and treaties, custom is considered by the International Court of Justice, jurists, the United Nations, and its member states to be among the primary sources of international law. For example, laws of war were a matter of customary law before they were codified in the Hague Conventions of 1899 and 1907, Geneva Conventions, and other treaties.

The vast majority of the world's governments accept in principle the existence of customary international law, although there are many differ opinions as to what rules are contained in it.

The Statute of the International Court of Justice acknowledges the existence of customary international law in Article 38(1)(b), incorporated into the United Nations Charter by Article 92: "The Court, whose function is to decide in accordance with international law such disputes as are submitted to it, shall apply...international custom, as evidence of a general practice accepted as law."

Customary international law "... consists of rules of law derived from the consistent conduct of States acting out of the belief that the law required them to act that way." It follows that customary international law can be discerned by a "widespread repetition by States of similar international acts over time (State practice); Acts must occur out of sense of obligation (*opinio juris*); Acts must be taken by a significant number of States and not be rejected by a significant number of States." A marker of customary international law is consensus among states exhibited both by widespread conduct and a discernible sense of obligation.

A peremptory norm (also called *jus cogens*, Latin for "compelling law") is a fundamental principle of international law which is accepted by the international community of states as a norm from which no derogation is ever permitted. Examples include various international crimes; a state which carries out or permits slavery, genocide, war of aggression, or crimes against humanity is always violating customary international law.

Other examples accepted or claimed as customary international law include the principle of non-refoulement, immunity of visiting foreign heads of state, and the right to humanitarian intervention.

CRIME AGAINST HUMANITY

Crimes against humanity, as defined by the Rome Statute of the International Criminal Court Explanatory Memorandum, "are particularly odious offences in that they constitute a serious attack on human dignity or grave humiliation or a degradation of one or more human beings. They are not isolated or sporadic events, but are part either of a government policy (although the perpetrators need not identify themselves with this policy) or of a wide practice of atrocities tolerated or condoned by a government or a de facto authority. Murder; extermination; torture; rape and political, racial, or religious persecution and other inhumane acts reach the threshold of crimes against humanity only if they are part of a widespread or systematic practice. Isolated inhumane acts of this nature may constitute grave infringements of human rights, or depending on the circumstances, war crimes, but may fall short of falling into the category of crimes under discussion."

Abolition of the Slave Trade

Although the phrase "crime against humanity" was not used in the *Declaration of the Powers, on the Abolition of the Slave Trade, of 8th of February 1815* (Which also formed ACT, No. XV. of the Final Act of the Congress of Vienna of the same year) the text of the declaration included in its first sentence the concept of the "principles of humanity and universal morality" as justification for ending a trade that was "odious in its continuance".

First Use

On May 24, 1915, the Allied Powers, Britain, France, and Russia, jointly issued a statement explicitly charging for the first time ever another government of committing "a crime against humanity". An excerpt from this joint statement reads:

In view of these new crimes of Turkey against humanity and civilisation, the Allied Governments announce publicly to the Sublime Porte that they will hold personally responsible for these crimes all members of the Ottoman Government, as well as those of their agents who are implicated in such massacres.

Nuremberg Trials

The London Charter of the International Military Tribunal was the decree that set down the laws and procedures by which the post-World War II Nuremberg trials were to be conducted. The charter defined that only crimes of the European Axis Powers could be tried. Article 6 stated that the Tribunal was established for the trial and punishment of the major war criminals of the European Axis countries; paragraph 6.a defined crimes against peace, 6.b war crimes and paragraph 6.c, Crimes Against Humanity defined as

"Murder, extermination, enslavement, deportation, and other inhumane acts committed against any civilian population, before or during the war, or persecutions on political, racial or religious grounds in execution of or in connection with any crime within the jurisdiction of the Tribunal, whether or not in violation of the domestic law of the country where perpetrated".

In the Judgement of the International Military Tribunal for the Trial of German Major War Criminals it was also stated:

The Tribunal therefore cannot make a general declaration that the acts before 1939 were crimes against humanity within the meaning of the Charter, but from the beginning of the war in 1939 war crimes were committed on a vast scale, which were also crimes against humanity; and insofar as the inhumane acts charged in the Indictment, and committed after the beginning of the war, did not constitute war crimes, they were all committed in execution of, or in connection with, the aggressive war, and therefore constituted crimes against humanity.

Tokyo Trials

The International Military Tribunal for the Far East (IMTFE), also known as the Tokyo Trial, was convened to try the leaders of the Empire of Japan for three types of crimes: "Class A" (crimes against peace), "Class B" (war crimes), and "Class C" (crimes against humanity), committed during World War II. The first refers to their joint conspiracy to start and wage the war, and the latter two refer to atrocities including the Nanking Massacre.

The legal basis for the trial was established by the Charter of the International Military Tribunal for the Far East (CIMTFE) that was proclaimed on 19 January 1946. The tribunal convened on May 3, 1946, and was adjourned on November 12, 1948.

A panel of eleven judges presided over the IMTFE, one each from victorious Allied powers (United States, Republic of China, Soviet Union, United Kingdom, the Netherlands, Provisional Government of the French Republic, Australia, New Zealand, Canada, British India, and the Philippines).

War crimes charges against more junior personnel were dealt with separately, in other cities throughout Far East Asia, such as the Nanjing War Crimes Tribunal and the Khabarovsk War Crimes Trials.

Apartheid

The systematic persecution of one racial group by another, such as occurred during the South African apartheid government, was recognized as a crime against humanity by the United Nations

General Assembly in 1976. The Charter of the United Nations (Article 13, 14, 15) makes actions of the General Assembly advisory to the Security Council. In regard to apartheid in particular, the UN General Assembly has not made any findings, nor have apartheid-related trials for crimes against humanity been conducted.

United Nations

The United Nations has been primarily responsible for the prosecution of crimes against humanity since it was chartered in 1948. The UN has been where all modern prosecutions for crimes against humanity have occurred. The International Criminal Court (ICC) was recently organised by the Rome Statute and the UN has delegated several crimes against humanity cases to the ICC. Because these cases were referred to the ICC by the UN, the ICC has broad authority and jurisdiction for these cases. The ICC acting without a UN referral lacks the broad jurisdiction to prosecute crimes against humanity, and cannot prosecute many cases, particularly if they occur outside of ICC-member nations. The most recent 2005 UN referral to the ICC of Darfur resulted in an indictment of Sudanese President Omar al-Bashir for genocide, crimes against humanity and war crimes in 2008. The first person to be handed over to the ICC was Thomas Lubanga. His trial has still has not been completed. The ICC still is seeking Joseph Kony. When the ICC President reported to the UN regarding its progress handling this crimes against humanity case, Judge Phillipe Kirsch said "The Court does not have the power to arrest these persons. That is the responsibility of States and other actors. Without arrests, there can be no trials. The UN has not referred any further crimes against humanity cases to the ICC since March 2005.

UN Security Council Responsibility

UN Security Council Resolution 1674, adopted by the United Nations Security Council on 28 April 2006, "reaffirms the provisions of paragraphs 138 and 139 of the 2005 World Summit Outcome Document regarding the responsibility to protect populations from genocide, war crimes, ethnic cleansing and crimes against humanity".

The resolution commits the Council to action to protect civilians in armed conflict.

International Criminal Court

In 2002, the International Criminal Court (ICC) was established in The Hague (Netherlands) and the Rome Statute provides for the ICC to have jurisdiction over genocide, crimes against humanity and war crimes. The definition of what is a "crime against humanity" for ICC proceedings has significantly broadened from its original legal definition or that used by the UN, and Article 7 of the treaty stated that:

> For the purpose of this Statute, "crime against humanity" means any of the following acts when committed as part of a widespread or systematic attack directed against any civilian population, with knowledge of the attack:
>
> *(a)* Murder;
>
> *(b)* Extermination;
>
> *(c)* Enslavement;
>
> *(d)* Deportation or forcible transfer of population;
>
> *(e)* Imprisonment or other severe deprivation of physical liberty in violation of fundamental rules of international law;
>
> *(f)* Torture;
>
> *(g)* Rape, sexual slavery, enforced prostitution, forced pregnancy, enforced sterilisation, or any other form of sexual violence of comparable gravity;
>
> *(h)* Persecution against any identifiable group or collectivity on political, racial, national, ethnic, cultural, religious, gender as defined in paragraph 3, or other grounds that are universally recognised as impermissible under international law, in connection with any act referred to in this paragraph or any crime within the jurisdiction of the Court;

(*i*) Enforced disappearance of persons;

(*j*) The crime of apartheid;

(*k*) Other inhumane acts of a similar character intentionally causing great suffering, or serious injury to body or to mental or physical health.

The Rome Statute Explanatory Memorandum states that crimes against humanity are particularly odious offenses in that they constitute a serious attack on human dignity or grave humiliation or a degradation of one or more human beings. They are not isolated or sporadic events, but are part either of a government policy (although the perpetrators need not identify themselves with this policy) or of a wide practice of atrocities tolerated or condoned by a government or a de facto authority. However, murder, extermination, torture, rape, political, racial, or religious persecution and other inhumane acts reach the threshold of crimes against humanity only if they are part of a widespread or systematic practice. Isolated inhumane acts of this nature may constitute grave infringements of human rights, or depending on the circumstances, war crimes, but may fall short of meriting the stigma attaching to the category of crimes under discussion. On the other hand, an individual may be guilty of crimes against humanity even if he perpetrates one or two of the offences mentioned above, or engages in one such offense against only a few civilians, provided those offenses are part of a consistent pattern of misbehavior by a number of persons linked to that offender (for example, because they engage in armed action on the same side or because they are parties to a common plan or for any similar reason.) Consequently when one or more individuals are not accused of planning or carrying out a policy of inhumanity, but simply of perpetrating specific atrocities or vicious acts, in order to determine whether the necessary threshold is met one should use the following test: one ought to look at these atrocities or acts in their context and verify whether they may be regarded as part of an overall policy or a consistent pattern of an inhumanity, or whether they instead constitute isolated or sporadic acts of cruelty and wickedness.

Council of Europe

The Committee of Ministers of the Council of Europe on 30 April 2002 issued a recommendation to the member states, on the protection of women against violence. In the section "Additional measures concerning violence in conflict and post-conflict situations", states in paragraph 69 that member states should: "penalise rape, sexual slavery, forced pregnancy, enforced sterilisation or any other form of sexual violence of comparable gravity as an intolerable violation of human rights, as crimes against humanity and, when committed in the context of an armed conflict, as war crimes."

In the Explanatory Memorandum on this recommendation when considering paragraph 69:

> Reference should be made to the Statute of the International Criminal Tribunal adopted in Rome in July 1998. Article 7 of the Statute defines rape, sexual slavery, enforced prostitution, forced pregnancy, enforced sterilisation or any other form of sexual violence of comparable gravity, as crimes against humanity. Furthermore, Article 8 of the Statute defines rape, sexual slavery, enforced prostitution, forced pregnancy, enforced sterilisation or any other form of sexual violence as a serious breach of the Geneva Conventions and as war crimes.

To fall under the Rome Statute, a crime against humanity which is defined in Article 7.1 must be "part of a widespread or systematic attack directed against any civilian population". Article 7.2.a states "For the purpose of paragraph 1: Attack directed against any civilian population means a course of conduct involving the multiple commission of acts referred to in paragraph 1 against any civilian population, pursuant to or in furtherance of a State or organizational policy to commit such attack." This means that an individual crime on its own, or even a number of such crimes, would not fall under the Rome Statute unless they were the result of a State policy or an organisational policy. This was confirmed by Luis Moreno-Ocampo in an open letter publishing his conclusions about allegations of crimes committed during the invasion of Iraq in March 2003 which might fall under the ICC. In a section entitled "Allegations concerning Genocide and Crimes against Humanity" he states that "the available information provided no reasonable indicator of the required elements for a crime against humanity," i.e. 'a widespread or systematic attack directed against any civilian population'". ◆

5
Discrimination

Discrimination is a sociological term that refers to treatment taken toward or against a person of a certain group that is taken in consideration based on class or category. The United Nations explains: "Discriminatory behaviours take many forms, but they all involve some form of exclusion or rejection." Discriminatory laws such as redlining have existed in many countries. In some countries, controversial attempts such as racial quotas have been used to redress negative effects of discrimination.

Race Discrimination

Racial discrimination differentiates between individuals on the basis of real and perceived racial differences, and has been official government policy in several countries, such as South Africa in the apartheid era, and the USA.

In the United States, racial profiling of minorities by law enforcement officials has been called racial discrimination. As early as 1865, the Civil Rights Act provided a remedy for intentional race discrimination in employment by private employers and state and local public employers. The Civil Rights Act of 1871 applies to public employment or employment involving state action prohibiting deprivation of rights secured by the federal constitution or federal laws through action under color of law. Title VII is the principal federal statute with regard to employment discrimination prohibiting unlawful employment discrimination by public and private employers, labor organisations, training programmes and employment agencies based on race or color, religion, gender, and national origin.

Title VII also prohibits retaliation against any person for opposing any practice forbidden by statute, or for making a charge, testifying, assisting, or participating in a proceeding under the statute. The Civil Rights Act of 1991 expanded the damages available in Title VII cases and granted Title VII plaintiffs the right to a jury trial. Title VII also provides that race and color discrimination against every race and color is prohibited.

In the UK the inquiry following the murder of Stephen Lawrence accused the police of institutional racism.

- Weaver *vs* NATFHE (now part of the UCU) Race/sex discrimination case. An Industrial (Employment) Tribunal in the UK in 1987 decided that a trade union was justified in not assisting a Black woman member, complaining of racist/sexist harassment, regardless of the merits of the case, because the accused male would lose his job. The Employment Appeal Tribunal upheld the decision, which still stands today as the definitive legal precedent in this field. Also known as the Bournville College Racial Harassment issue.

- Gingerism is a form of discrimination which is sometimes considered to be racism.

Within the criminal justice system in some Western countries, minorities are convicted and imprisoned disproportionately when compared with whites. In 1998, nearly one out of three black men between the ages of 20-29 were in prison or jail, on probation or parole on any given day in the United States. First Nations make up about 2% of Canada's population, but account for 18% of the federal prison population as of 2000. According to the Australian government's June 2006 publication of prison statistics, indigenous peoples make up 24% of the overall prison population in Australia. ("Indigenous" meaning those identifying themselves as being of Aboriginal or Torres Strait Islander origin) In 2004, Maori made up just 15% of the total population of New Zealand but 49.5% of prisoners. Maori were entering prison at 8 times the rate of non-Maori.

AGE DISCRIMINATION

Age discrimination is discrimination on the grounds of age. Although theoretically the word can refer to the discrimination against any age group, age discrimination usually comes in one of three forms: discrimination against youth (also called adultism), discrimination against those 40 years old or older , and discrimination against elderly people.

In the United States, the Age Discrimination in Employment Act prohibits employment discrimination nationwide based on age with respect to employees 40 years of age or older. The Age Discrimination in Employment Act also addresses the difficulty older workers face in obtaining new employment after being displaced from their jobs, arbitrary age limits.

In many countries, companies more or less openly refuse to hire people above a certain age despite the increasing lifespans and average age of the population. The reasons for this range from vague feelings younger people are more "dynamic" and create a positive image for the company, to more concrete concerns about regulations granting older employees higher salaries or other benefits without these expenses being fully justified by an older employees' greater experience.

Some people consider that teenagers and youth (around 15–25 years old) are victims of adultism, age discrimination framed as a paternalistic form of protection. In seeking social justice, they feel that it is necessary to remove the use of a false moral agenda in order to achieve agency and empowerment.

This perspective is based on the grounds that youth should be treated more respectfully by adults and not as second-class citizens. Some suggest that social stratification in age groups causes outsiders to incorrectly stereotype and generalize the group, for instance that all adolescents are equally immature, violent or rebellious, listen to rock tunes, and do drugs. Some have organized groups against age discrimination.

Ageism is the causal effect of a continuum of fears related to age. This continuum includes:

- Ephebiphobia: the fear of youth.
- Gerontophobia: the fear of elderly people.
- Pediaphobia: the fear of infants or small children.

Related terms include:

- **Adultism:** Also called adultarchy, adult privilege, and adultcentrism/adultocentrism, this is the wielding of authority over young people and the preference of adults before children and youth.
- **Jeunism:** Also called "youthism" is the holding of beliefs or actions taken that preference 'younger' people before adults.

GENDER DISCRIMINATION

Though gender discrimination and sexism refers to beliefs and attitudes in relation to the gender of a person, such beliefs and attitudes are of a social nature and do not, normally, carry any legal consequences. Sex discrimination, on the other hand, may have legal consequences.

Though what constitutes sex discrimination varies between countries, the essence is that it is an adverse action taken by one person against another person that would not have occurred had the person been of another sex. Discrimination of that nature in certain enumerated circumstances is illegal in many countries.

Currently, discrimination based on sex is defined as adverse action against another person, that would not have occurred had the person been of another sex. This is considered a form of prejudice and is illegal in certain enumerated circumstances in most countries.

Sexual discrimination can arise in different contexts. For instance an employee may be discriminated against by being asked discriminatory questions during a job interview, or because an employer did not hire, promote or wrongfully terminated an employee based on his or her gender, or employers pay unequally based on gender.

In an educational setting there could be claims that a student was excluded from an educational institution, programme, opportunity, loan, student group, or scholarship due to his or her gender. In the housing setting there could be claims that a person was refused negotiations on seeking a house, contracting/leasing a house or getting a loan based on his or her gender. Another setting where there have been claims of gender discrimination is banking; for example, if one is refused credit or is offered unequal loan terms based on one's gender.

Another setting where there is usually gender discrimination is when one is refused to extend his or her credit, refused approval of credit/loan process, and if there is a burden of unequal loan terms based on one's gender.

Socially, sexual differences have been used to justify different roles for men and women, in some cases giving rise to claims of primary and secondary roles.

While there are alleged non-physical differences between men and women, major reviews of the academic literature on gender difference find only a tiny minority of characteristics where there are consistent psychological differences between men and women, and these relate directly to experiences grounded in biological difference.

Unfair discrimination usually follows the gender stereotyping held by a society.

The United Nations had concluded that women often experience a "glass ceiling" and that there are no societies in which women enjoy the same opportunities as men. The term "glass ceiling" is used to describe a perceived barrier to advancement in employment based on discrimination, especially sex discrimination.

In the United States, the Glass Ceiling Commission, a government-funded group, stated: "Over half of all Master's degrees are now awarded to women, yet 95% of senior-level managers, of the top Fortune 1000 industrial and 500 service companies are men. Of them, 97% are white." In its report, it recommended affirmative action, which is the consideration of an employee's gender and race in hiring and promotion decisions, as a means to end this form of discrimination.

Transgender individuals, both male to female and female to male, often experience problems which often lead to dismissals, underachievement, difficulty in finding a job, social isolation, and, occasionally, violent attacks against them.

Language Discrimination

Diversity of language is protected and respected by most nations who value cultural diversity. However, people are sometimes subjected to different treatment because their preferred language is associated with a particular group, class or category. Commonly, the preferred language is just another attribute of separate ethnic groups. Discrimination exists if there is prejudicial treatment against a person or a group of people who speak a particular language or dialect. Language discrimination is suggested to be labeled Linguacism or logocism.

Reverse Discrimination

Some attempts at antidiscrimination have been criticized as reverse discrimination. In particular, minority quotas (e.g. affirmative action) can be said to discriminate against members of a dominant or majority group. In its opposition to race preferences, the American Civil Rights Institute's Ward Connerly stated, "There is nothing positive, affirmative, or equal about 'affirmative action' programs that give preference to some groups based on race." On the other hand, it is argued that critics of antidiscriminatory steps often rely on misconceptions, that policy should take into account the negative effects of discrimination on minorities to reduce existing inequalities.

Disability Discrimination

People with disabilities face discrimination in all levels of society. The attitude that disabled individuals are inferior to non-disabled individuals is called ableism or disablism. Historically, the disabled have been shunned for their problems. These views are reinforced in modern times in media, books, films, comics, art and language.

Chronic pain is a debilitating condition which is often neglected in modern society. According to the American Chiropractic Association, over 50% of all working US citizens complain of back pain each year. An estimated 80% of the population will experience back pain at some point in their life. Many times pain can become chronic and debilitating.

Ergonomic seating and work environments are not only be a reasonable accommodation for those who suffer, they are also a preventative measure to counteract the soaring cost of medical treatment for pain conditions. Ergonomic seating in all public institutions would be a positive step to providing access to public services for all those who need it.

In the United States, the Americans with Disabilities Act provides guidelines for providing wheelchair access for public institutions, but ergonomic devices for those who suffer from pain are something that has yet to be implemented. This is just one of many accessibility issues still faced by disabled individuals.

Disabled people may also face discrimination by employers. They may find problems with securing employment as their disability can be seen as a risk to the company, and once in employment they may find they are overlooked for promotion opportunities. Similarly, if an employee becomes disabled while employed they may also find themselves being managed out the company by HR departments.

Unsympathetic employers can make life very difficult for such employees and can often make their health problems worse. Disability discrimination laws mean that in theory the employee has a method of redress in such instances.

Almost every person with a syndrome is discriminated against. They may not be able to join organizations, and they may even be neglected by schools and other public utilities.

THEORIES

Discrimination

Social theories such as Egalitarianism claim that social equality should prevail. In some societies, including most developed countries, each individual's civil rights include the right to be free from government sponsored social discrimination. Taking into account the capacity to perceive pain and/or suffering that all animals have, 'abolitionist' or 'vegan' egalitarianism maintains that every individual, regardless their species, should have at least the basic right not to be an object. See also speciesism.

Conservative and Anarcho-Capitalist

In contrast, conservative writer and law professor Matthias Storme has claimed that the freedom of discrimination in human societies is a fundamental human right, or more precisely, the basis of all fundamental freedoms and therefore the most fundamental freedom. Author Hans-Hermann Hoppe, in an essay about his book Democracy: The God That Failed, asserts that a natural social order is characterized by increased discrimination. ◆

6
Public International Law

Public international law concerns the structure and conduct of sovereign states and intergovernmental organisations. To a lesser degree, international law also may affect multinational corporations and individuals, an impact increasingly evolving beyond domestic legal interpretation and enforcement. Public international law has increased in use and importance vastly over the twentieth century, due to the increase in global trade, armed conflict, environmental deterioration on a worldwide scale, awareness of human rights violations, rapid and vast increases in international transportation and a boom in global communications.

The field of study combines two main branches: the law of nations (*jus gentium*) and international agreements and conventions (*jus inter gentes*), which have different theoretical foundations and should not be confused.

Public international law should not be confused with "*private international law*", which is concerned with the resolution of conflict of laws. In its most general sense, international law "consists of rules and principles of general application dealing with the conduct of states and of intergovernmental organizations and with their relations *inter se*, as well as with some of their relations with persons, whether natural or juridical."

Public international law establishes the framework and the criteria for identifying states as the principal actors in the international legal system. As the existence of a state presupposes control and jurisdiction over territory, international law deals with the acquisition of territory, state immunity and the legal responsibility of states in their conduct with each other. International law is similarly concerned with the treatment of individuals within state boundaries. There is thus a comprehensive regime dealing with group rights, the treatment of aliens, the rights of refugees, international crimes, nationality problems, and human rights generally. It further includes the important functions of the maintenance of international peace and security, arms control, the pacific settlement of disputes and the regulation of the use of force in international relations. Even when the law is not able to stop the outbreak of war, it has developed principles to govern the conduct of hostilities and the treatment of prisoners. International law is also used to govern issues relating to the global environment, the global commons such as international waters and outer space, global communications, and world trade.

Whilst municipal law is hierarchical or vertical in its structure (meaning that a legislature enacts binding legislation), international law is horizontal in nature. This means that all states are sovereign and theoretically equal. As a result of the notion of sovereignty, the value and authority of international law is dependent upon the voluntary participation of states in its formulation, observance, and enforcement. Although there may be exceptions, it is thought by many international academics that most states enter into legal commitments with other states out of enlightened self-interest rather than adherence to a body of law that is higher than their own. As D. W. Greig notes, "international law cannot exist in isolation from the political factors operating in the sphere of international relations".

Breaches of international law raise difficult questions for lawyers. Since international law has no established compulsory judicial system for the settlement of disputes or a coercive penal system, it is not as straightforward as managing breaches within a domestic legal system. However, there are means by which breaches are brought to the attention of the international community and some means for resolution. For example, there are judicial or quasi-judicial tribunals in international law in certain areas such as trade and human rights.

The formation of the United Nations, for example, created a means for the world community to enforce international law upon members that violate its charter through the Security Council.

Traditionally, sovereign states and the Holy See were the sole subjects of international law. With the proliferation of international organisations over the last century, they have in some cases been recognised as relevant parties as well. Recent interpretations of international human rights law, international humanitarian law, and international trade law (e.g., North American Free Trade Agreement (NAFTA) Chapter 11 actions) have been inclusive of corporations, and even of certain individuals.

History of Public International Law

The earliest known treatises on international law was the *Introduction to the Law of Nations* written at the end of the 8th century by Muhammad al-Shaybani (d. 804), a jurist of the Hanafi school of Islamic law and jurisprudence, and other Islamic jurists soon followed with a number of treatises written on international law (*Siyar* in Arabic). These early Islamic legal treatises covered the application of Islamic ethics, Islamic economic jurisprudence and Islamic military jurisprudence to international law, and were concerned with a number of international law topics, including the law of treaties; the treatment of diplomats, hostages, refugees and prisoners of war; the right of asylum; conduct on the battlefield; protection of women, children and non-combatant civilians; contracts across the lines of battle; the use of poisonous weapons; and devastation of enemy territory. The first European treatises on international law was later written by Francisco de Vitoria in the 16th century; Hugo Grotius, in the early 17th century, developed the subject further. He and other European legal scholars may have been influenced by early Islamic international law.

Beginning with the Peace of Westphalia in 1648, the 17th, 18th and 19th centuries saw the growth of the concept of the sovereign "nation-state", which consisted of a nation controlled by a centralised system of government. The concept of nationalism became increasingly important as people began to see themselves as citizens of a particular nation with a distinct national identity. Until the mid-19th century, relations between nation-states were dictated by treaty, agreements to behave in a certain way towards another state, unenforceable except by force, and not binding except as matters of honor and faithfulness. But treaties alone became increasingly toothless and wars became increasingly destructive, most markedly towards civilians, and civilised peoples decried their horrors, leading to calls for regulation of the acts of states, especially in times of war.

Perhaps the first instrument of modern public international law was the Lieber Code, passed in 1863 by the Congress of the United States, to govern the conduct of US forces during the United States Civil War and considered to be the first written recitation of the rules and articles of war, adhered to by all civilized nations, the precursor of public international law. Part of the Code follows:

"Military necessity, as understood by modern civilised nations, consists in the necessity of those measures which are indispensable for securing the ends of the war, and which are lawful according to the modern law and usages of war. Military necessity admits of all direct destruction of life or limb of armed enemies, and of other persons whose destruction is incidentally unavoidable in the armed contests of the war; it allows of the capturing of every armed enemy, and every enemy of importance to the hostile government, or of peculiar danger to the captor; it allows of all destruction of property, and obstruction of the ways and channels of traffic, travel, or communication, and of all withholding of sustenance or means of life from the enemy; of the appropriation of whatever an enemy's country affords necessary for the subsistence and safety of the Army, and of such deception as does not involve the breaking of good faith either positively pledged, regarding agreements entered into during the war, or supposed by the modern law of war to exist. (...But...) Men who take up arms against one another in public war do not cease on this account to be moral beings, responsible to one another and to God. Military necessity does not admit of cruelty—that is, the infliction of suffering for the sake of suffering or for revenge, nor of maiming or wounding except in fight, nor of torture to extort confessions. It does not admit of the use of poison in any way, nor of the wanton devastation of a district. It admits of deception, but disclaims acts of perfidy; and, in general, military necessity does not include any act of hostility which makes the return to peace unnecessarily difficult."

This first statement of the previously uncodified rules and articles of war led to the first prosecution for war crimes—in the case of United States prisoners of war held in cruel and depraved conditions at Andersonville, Georgia, in which the Confederate commandant of that camp was tried and hanged, the only Confederate soldier to be punished by death in the aftermath of the entire Civil War.

In the years that followed, other states subscribed to limitations of their conduct, and numerous other treaties and bodies were created to regulate the conduct of states towards one another in terms of these treaties, including, but not limited to, the Permanent Court of Arbitration in 1899; the Hague and Geneva Conventions, the first of which was passed in 1907; the International Court of Justice in 1921; the Genocide Convention; and the International Criminal Court, in the late 1990s. Because international law is a relatively new area of law its development and propriety in applicable areas are often subject to dispute.

Conflicts between Public International Law and National Sovereignty

The conflict between international law and national sovereignty is subject to vigorous debate and dispute in academia, diplomacy, and politics. Certainly, there is a growing trend toward judging a state's domestic actions in the light of international law and standards. Numerous people now view the nation-state as the primary unit of international affairs, and believe that only states may choose to voluntarily enter into commitments under international law, and that they have the right to follow their own counsel when it comes to interpretation of their commitments. Certain scholars and political leaders feel that these modern developments endanger nation states by taking power away from state governments and ceding it to international bodies such as the U.N. and the World Bank, argue that international law has evolved to a point where it exists separately from the mere consent of states, and discern a legislative and judicial process to international law that parallels such processes within domestic law. This especially occurs when states violate or deviate from the expected standards of conduct adhered to by all civilised nations.

A number of states support very narrow interpretations of international law, including the People's Republic of China, the military junta currently holding power in Burma, and the Russian Federation. These states maintain that sovereignty—and thus what some view as the basis of sovereignty, the ultima ratio regum, or last argument of kings (force and coercion, by military or other means)—is the only true international law; thus seeing states as having free rein over their own affairs and their affairs in the larger world. Other states oppose this view. One group of opponents of this point of view, including many European nations, maintain that all civilized nations have certain norms of conduct expected of them, including the prohibition of genocide, slavery and the slave trade, wars of aggression, torture, and piracy, and that violation of these universal norms represents a crime, not only against the individual victims, but against humanity as a whole. States and individuals who subscribe to this view opine that, in the case of the individual responsible for violation of international law, he "is become, like the pirate and the slave trader before him, hostis humani generis, an enemy of all mankind", and thus subject to prosecution in a fair trial before any fundamentally just tribunal, through the exercise of universal jurisdiction. Another group believes that states only commit to international law with express consent, whether through treaty or customary law, and have the right to make their own interpretations of its meaning; and that international courts only function with the consent of states.

Though the European democracies tend to support broad, universalistic interpretations of international law, many other democracies have differing views on international law. Several democracies, including Israel, India, the United States, take a flexible, eclectic approach, recognising aspects of public international law such as territorial rights as universal, regarding other aspects as arising from treaty or custom, and viewing certain aspects as not being subjects of public international law at all. Democracies in the developing world, due to their past colonial histories, often insist on non-interference in their internal affairs, particularly regarding human rights standards or their peculiar institutions, but often strongly support international law at the bilateral and multilateral levels, such as in the United Nations, and especially regarding the use of force, disarmament obligations, and the terms of the UN Charter.

Sources of International Law

Public international law has four primary sources: international treaties, custom, general principles of law and judicial decisions and teachings. International treaty law comprises obligations states expressly and voluntarily accept between themselves in treaties. Customary international law is derived from the consistent practice of States accompanied by *opinio juris*, i.e. the conviction of States that the consistent practice is required by a legal obligation. Judgements of international tribunals as well as scholarly works have traditionally been looked to as persuasive sources for custom in addition to direct evidence of state behaviour (and they are also explicitly mentioned as such in Art. 38 of the Statute of the International Court of Justice, as subsidiary means for the determination of rules of law). Attempts to codify customary international law picked up momentum after the Second World War with the formation of the International Law Commission (ILC), under the aegis of the United Nations. Codified customary law is made the binding interpretation of the underlying custom by agreement through treaty. For states not party to such treaties, the work of the ILC may still be accepted as custom applying to those states. General principles of law are those commonly recognised by the major legal systems of the world. Certain norms of international law achieve the binding force of peremptory norms (*jus cogens*) as to include all states with no permissible derogations.

INTERPRETATION

Where there are disputes about the exact meaning and application of national laws, it is the responsibility of the courts to decide what the law means. In international law interpretation is within the domain of the protagonists, but may also be conferred on judicial bodies such as the International Court of Justice, by the terms of the treaties or by consent of the parties. It is generally the responsibility of states to interpret the law for themselves, but the processes of diplomacy and availability of supra-national judicial organs operate routinely to provide assistance to that end. Insofar as treaties are concerned, the Vienna Convention on the Law of Treaties writes on the topic of interpretation that:

> "A treaty shall be interpreted in good faith in accordance with the ordinary meaning to be given to the terms of the treaty in their context and in the light of its object and purpose." (article 31(1))

This is actually a compromise between three different theories of interpretation:

- The textual approach, a restrictive interpretation, which bases itself on the "ordinary meaning" of the text; that approach assigns considerable weight to the actual text.
- The subjective approach, which takes into consideration (i) the idea behind the treaty, (ii) treaties "in their context", and (iii) what the writers intended when they wrote the text.
- A third approach, which bases itself on interpretation "in the light of its object and purpose", i.e. the interpretation that best suits the goal of the treaty, also called "effective interpretation".

These are general rules of interpretation; specific rules might exist in specific areas of international law.

Enforcement

Since international law exists in a legal environment without an overarching "sovereign" (i.e., an external power able and willing to compel compliance with international norms), "enforcement" of international law is very different than in the domestic context. In many cases, enforcement takes on Coasian characteristics, where the norm is self-enforcing. In other cases, defection from the norm can pose a real risk, particularly if the international environment is changing. When this happens, and if enough states (or enough powerful states) continually ignore a particular aspect of international law, the norm may actually change according to concepts of customary international law. For example, prior to World War I, unrestricted submarine warfare was considered a violation of international law and ostensibly the casus belli for the United States' declaration of war against Germany. By World War II, however, the practice was so widespread that during the Nuremberg trials, the charges against German Admiral Karl Dönitz for ordering unrestricted submarine warfare were dropped, notwithstanding that the activity constituted a clear violation of the Second London Naval Treaty of 1936.

Enforcement by States

Apart from a state's natural inclination to uphold certain norms, the force of international law comes from the pressure that states put upon one another to behave consistently and to honor their obligations. As with any system of law, many violations of international law obligations are overlooked. If addressed, it is almost always purely through diplomacy and the consequences upon an offending state's reputation. Though violations may be common in fact, states try to avoid the appearance of having disregarded international obligations. States may also unilaterally adopt sanctions against one another such as the severance of economic or diplomatic ties, or through reciprocal action. In some cases, domestic courts may render judgment against a foreign state (the realm of private international law) for an injury, though this is a complicated area of law where international law intersects with domestic law.

It is implicit in the Westphalian system of nation-states, and explicitly recognised under Article 51 of the Charter of the United Nations, that all states have the inherent right to individual and collective self-defence if an armed attack occurs against them. Article 51 of the UN Charter guarantees the right of states to defend themselves until (and unless) the Security Council takes measures to keep the peace.

Enforcement by International Bodies

Violations of the UN Charter by members of the United Nations may be raised by the aggrieved state in the General Assembly for debate. The General Assembly cannot make binding resolutions, only 'recommendations', but through its adoption of the "Uniting for Peace" resolution (A/RES/377 A), of 3 November 1950, the Assembly declared that it has the power to authorize the use of force, under the terms of the UN Charter, in cases of breaches of the peace or acts of aggression, provided that the Security Council, owing to the negative vote of a permanent member, fails to act to address the situation. The Assembly also declared, by its adoption of resolution 377 A, that it could call for other collective measures—such as economic and diplomatic sanctions—in situations constituting the milder "threat to the Peace".

The Uniting for Peace resolution was initiated by the United States in 1950, shortly after the outbreak of the Korean War, as a means of circumventing possible future Soviet vetoes in the Security Council. The legal significance of the resolution is unclear, given that the General Assembly cannot issue binding resolutions. However, it was never argued by the "Joint Seven-Powers" that put forward the draft resolution, during the corresponding discussions, that it in any way afforded the Assembly new powers. Instead, they argued that the resolution simply declared what the Assembly's powers already were, according to the UN Charter, in the case of a dead-locked Security Council. The Soviet Union was the only permanent member of the Security Council to vote against the Charter interpretations that were made law by the Assembly's adoption of resolution 377 A.

Alleged violations of the Charter can also be raised by states in the Security Council. The Security Council could subsequently pass resolutions under Chapter VI of the UN Charter to recommend the "Pacific Resolution of Disputes." Such resolutions are not binding under international law, though they usually are expressive of the Council's convictions. In rare cases, the Security Council can adopt resolutions under Chapter VII of the UN Charter, related to "threats to Peace, Breaches of the Peace and Acts of Aggression," which are legally binding under international law, and can be followed up with economic sanctions, military action, and similar uses of force through the auspices of the United Nations.

It has been argued that resolutions passed outside of Chapter VII can also be binding; the legal basis for that is the Council's broad powers under Article 24(2), which states that "in discharging these duties (exercise of primary responsibility in international peace and security), it shall act in accordance with the Purposes and Principles of the United Nations". The mandatory nature of such resolutions was upheld by the International Court of Justice (ICJ) in its advisory opinion on Namibia. The binding nature of such resolutions can be deduced from an interpretation of their language and intent.

States can also, upon mutual consent, submit disputes for arbitration by the International Court of Justice, located in The Hague, Netherlands. The judgments given by the Court in these cases are binding, although it possesses no means to enforce its rulings. The Court may give an advisory opinion on any legal question at the request of whatever body may be authorized by or in accordance with the Charter of the United Nations to make such a request. Some of the advisory cases brought before the court have been controversial with respect to the court's competence and jurisdiction.

Often enormously complicated matters, ICJ cases (of which there have been less than 150 since the court was created from the

Permanent Court of International Justice in 1945) can stretch on for years and generally involve thousands of pages of pleadings, evidence, and the world's leading specialist public international lawyers. As of June 2009, there are 15 cases pending at the ICJ. Decisions made through other means of arbitration may be binding or non-binding depending on the nature of the arbitration agreement, whereas decisions resulting from contentious cases argued before the ICJ are always binding on the involved states.

Though states (or increasingly, international organisations) are usually the only ones with standing to address a violation of international law, some treaties, such as the International Covenant on Civil and Political Rights have an optional protocol that allows individuals who have had their rights violated by member states to petition the international Human Rights Committee.

INTERNATIONAL LEGAL THEORY

Natural Law

The intellectual seeds of modern international law germinated in the 16th and 17th centuries, when the influence of the Roman Catholic Church in international affairs gradually weakened. Many early international legal theorists were concerned with axiomatic truths thought to be reposed in natural law. Among the early natural law writers, Francisco de Vitoria, Dominican professor of theology at the University of Salamanca, examined the question of just war and Spanish authority in the Americas. He did so while Spain was at the height of its power, after the violent Spanish conquest of Peru in 1536.

Eclectic School

Central in the development of modern international law was Hugo Grotius a Dutch theologian, humanist and jurist. In his principal work *De jure Belli ac Pacis Libri Tres* ("Three Books on the Law of War and Peace"; 1625), Grotius claimed that nations as well as persons ought to be governed by universal principle based on morality and divine justice. Much of Grotius's content drew from the Bible and from classical history (just war theory of Augustine of Hippo). Drawing also from domestic contract law, he also noted that relations between polities were governed by *jus gentium*, the law of peoples, which had been established by the consent of the community of nations.

The fundamental facets of the Grotian or eclectic school, especially the doctrines of legal equality, territorial sovereignty, and independence of states, became definitive to international law in Europe. These principles were recognised in the Peace of Westphalia and became the foundation for the treaties of Osnabrück and Münster.

Another eclectic thinker, German philosopher Christian von Wolff, contended that the foundation for international community should come as a world superstate (*civitas maxima*), having authority over the component member states. This view was rejected by the Swiss diplomat Emmerich de Vattel, who favoured a rationale of equality of states as articulated by 18th century natural law. Vattel suggested in his major work *Le droit des gens* that the law of nations was composed of custom and law on the one hand, and natural law on the other.

Legal Positivism

The early positive school emphasised the importance of custom and treaties as sources of international law. Among the early positivists was Alberico Gentili, a professor of civil law at Oxford who used historical examples to posit that positive law (*jus voluntarium*) was determined by general consent. Another professor at Oxford, Richard Zouche, published the first manual of international law in 1650.

In the 18th century legal positivism became popular and found its way into international legal philosophy. The principal figure among 18th century positivists was Cornelius van Bynkershoek, a celebrated Dutch jurist who asserted that the bases of international law were customs and treaties commonly consented to by various states. A second positivist, John Jacob Moser was a prolific German scholar who emphasised the importance of state practice in international law. A contemporary German scholar, Georg Friedrich von Martens, published the first systematic manual on positive international law, *Precis du droit des gens moderne de l'Europe*.

The growth of nationalism and Hegelian philosophy in the 19th century pushed natural law farther from the legal realm. Commercial law became nationalised into private international law, distinct from public international law. Positivism narrowed the range of international practice that might qualify as law, favouring rationality to morality and ethics. The Congress of Vienna in 1815 marked formal recognition of the political and international legal system based on the conditions of Europe.

INTERNATIONAL HUMANITARIAN LAW

International Humanitarian Law (IHL), often referred to as the laws of war, the laws and customs of war or the law of armed conflict, is the legal corpus "comprised of the Geneva Conventions and the Hague Conventions, as well as subsequent treaties, case law, and customary international law." It defines the conduct and responsibilities of belligerent nations, neutral nations and individuals engaged in warfare, in relation to each other and to *protected persons*, usually meaning civilians.

The law is mandatory for nations bound by the appropriate treaties. There are also other customary unwritten rules of war, many of which were explored at the Nuremberg War Trials. By extension, they also define both the *permissive* rights of these powers as well as *prohibitions* on their conduct when dealing with irregular forces and non-signatories.

Two Historical Streams: The Law of Geneva and The Law of The Hague

Modern International Humanitarian Law is made up of two historical streams: the law of The Hague referred to in the past as the law of war proper and the law of Geneva or humanitarian law. The two streams take their names from a number of international conferences which drew up treaties relating to war and conflict, in particular the Hague Conventions of 1899 and 1907, and the Geneva Conventions, the first which was drawn up in 1863. Both are branches of *jus in bello*, international law regarding acceptable practices while engaged in war and armed conflict.

The Law of The Hague or the Laws of War proper,"determines the rights and duties of belligerents in the conduct of operations and limits the choice of means in doing harm." In particular, it concerns itself with the definition of combatants, establishes rules relating to the means and methods of warfare, and examines the issue of military objectives.

Systematic attempts to limit the savagery of warfare only began to develop in the 19th century. Such concerns were able to build on the changing view of warfare by states influenced by the Age of Enlightenment. The purpose of warfare was to overcome the enemy state and this was obtainable by disabling the enemy combatants. Thus, "(t)he distinction between combatants and civilians, the requirement that wounded and captured enemy combatants must be treated humanely, and that quarter must be given, some of the pillars of modern humanitarian law, all follow from this principle."

The Law of Geneva

The massacre of civilians in the midst of armed conflict has a long and dark history. Selected examples include: Moses, speaking for the god of the Israelites, ordering the killing of all the Midianite women and male children; the massacres of the Kalingas by Ashoka in India, the massacre of some 100,000 Hindus by the Muslim troops of Timur (Tamerlane) or the Crusader massacres of Jews and Muslims in the Siege of Jerusalem (1099), to name a few examples drawn from a long list in history. Fritz Munch sums up historical military practice before 1800: "The essential points seem to be these: In battle and in towns taken by force, combatants and non-combatants were killed and property was destroyed or looted. In the 17th century, the Dutch jurist Hugo Grotius wrote "Wars, for the attainment of their objects, it cannot be denied, must employ force and terror as their most proper agents."

Humanitarian Norms in History

However, even in the midst of the carnage of history, there were expressions of humanitarian norms to protect the victims of armed conflicts, i.e. the wounded, the sick and the shipwrecked which date back to ancient times.

In the Old Testament, the King of Israel prevents the slaying of the captured following the prophet, Elisha's admonition, to spare enemy prisoners: In answer to a question from the King, he said, "You shall not slay them. Would you slay those whom you have taken captive with your sword and with your bow? Set bread and water before them, that they may eat and drink and go to their master."

In ancient India there are records, for example the Laws of Manu, describing the types of weapons that should not be used. "When he fights with his foes in battle, let him not strike with weapons concealed (in wood), nor with (such as are) barbed, poisoned, or the points of which are blazing with fire. There is also the command not to strike the enemy "who folds his hands in supplication....Nor one who sleeps, nor one who has lost his coat of mail, nor one who is naked, nor one who is disarmed, nor one who looks on without taking part in the fight..."

Islamic law indicates that "noncombatants who did not take part in fighting such as women, children, monks and hermits, the aged, blind, and insane" were not to be molested. The first Caliph, Abu Bakr, proclaimed "Do not mutilate. Do not kill little children or old men or women. Do not cut off the heads of palm trees or burn them. Do not cut down fruit trees. Do not slaughter livestock except for food." Islamic jurists have held that a prisoner should not be killed as he "cannot be held responsible for mere acts of belligerency." Islamic law did not spare all non-combatants. In the case of those who refused to convert to Islam or pay an alternative tax, "were allowed in principle to kill any one of them, combatants or noncombatants, provided they were not killed treacherously and with mutilation."

Codification of Humanitarian Norms

However, it wasn't until second half of the 18th century that more systematic approach was initiated. In the United States, a German immigrant, Francis Lieber, drew up a code of conduct in 1863, the Lieber Code, for the Northern army which included the humane treatment of civilian populations in the areas of conflict. It also forbade the execution of POWs. At the same time, the involvement of a number of individuals such as Florence Nightingale during the Crimean War and Henry Dunant a Genevese businessman who had worked with wounded soldiers at the Battle of Solferino led to more systematic efforts to try and prevent the suffering of war victims. Dunant wrote a book, A Memory of Solferino, which described the horrors he had witnessed. His reports led to the founding of the International Committee of the Red Cross (ICRC) in 1863 and the convening of a conference in Geneva in 1864 which drew up the Geneva Convention for the Amelioration of the Condition of the Wounded in Armies in the Field.

The Law of Geneva, is directly inspired by the principle of humanity. It relates to those who are not participating in the conflict as well as military personnel hors de combat. It provides the legal basis for protection and humanitarian assistance carried out by impartial humanitarian organizations such as the ICRC. This focus can be found in the Geneva Conventions.

Geneva Conventions

The Geneva Conventions are the result of a process that developed in a number of stages between 1864 and 1949 which focused on the protection of civilians and those who can no longer fight in an armed conflict. As a result of World War II, all four conventions were revised based on previous revisions and partly on some of the 1907 Hague Conventions and readopted by the international community in 1949. Later conferences have added provisions prohibiting certain methods of warfare and addressing issues of civil wars.

The Geneva Conventions are:

- First Geneva Convention *"for the Amelioration of the Condition of the Wounded and Sick in Armed Forces in the Field"* (first adopted in 1864, last revision in 1949)
- Second Geneva Convention *"for the Amelioration of the Condition of Wounded, Sick and Shipwrecked Members of Armed Forces at Sea"* (first adopted in 1949, successor of the 1907 Hague Convention X)
- Third Geneva Convention *"relative to the Treatment of Prisoners of War"* (first adopted in 1929, last revision in 1949)
- Fourth Geneva Convention *"relative to the Protection of Civilian Persons in Time of War"* (first adopted in 1949, based on parts of the 1907 Hague Convention IV)

In addition, there are three additional amendment protocols to the Geneva Convention:

- Protocol I (1977): Protocol Additional to the Geneva Conventions of 12 August 1949, and relating to the Protection of Victims of International Armed Conflicts. As of 12 January 2007 it had been ratified by 167 countries.
- Protocol II (1977): Protocol Additional to the Geneva Conventions of 12 August 1949, and relating to the Protection of Victims of Non-International Armed Conflicts. As of 12 January 2007 it had been ratified by 163 countries.
- Protocol III (2005): Protocol Additional to the Geneva Conventions of 12 August 1949, and relating to the Adoption of an Additional Distinctive Emblem. As of June 2007 it had

been ratified by 17 countries and signed but not yet ratified by an additional 68 countries.

While the Geneva Conventions of 1949 can be seen as the result of a process which began in 1864, today, they have "achieved universal participation with 194 parties." This means that they apply to almost any international armed conflict.

Historical Convergence between IHL and the Laws of War

With the adoption of the 1977 Protocols to the Geneva Conventions, the two strains of law began to converge. Already before, articles focusing on humanity could be found in the Law of The Hague (i.e. the protection of certain prisoners of war and civilians in occupied territories) articles which were later incorporated into the Law of Geneva in 1929 and 1949). However the Protocols of 1977 relating to the protection of victims in both international and internal conflict not only incorporated aspects of both the Law of The Hague and the Law of Geneva, but also important human rights aspects.

Basic Rules of IHL

1. Persons hors de combat and those not taking part in hostilities shall be protected and treated humanely.
2. It is forbidden to kill or injure an enemy who surrenders or who is hors de combat.
3. The wounded and sick shall be cared for and protected by the party to the conflict which has them in its power. The emblem of the red cross or the red crescent must be respected as the sign of protection.
4. Captured combatants and civilians must be protected against acts of violence and reprisals. They shall have the right to correspond with their families and to receive relief.
5. No one shall be subjected to torture, corporal punishment or cruel or degrading treatment.

6. Parties to a conflict and members of their armed forces do not have an unlimited choice of methods and means of warfare.

7. Parties to a conflict shall at all times distinguish between the civilian population and combatants. Attacks shall be directed solely against military objectives.

Examples

Well-known examples of such rules include the prohibition on attacking doctors or ambulances displaying a Red Cross. It is also prohibited to fire at a person or vehicle bearing a white flag, since that indicates an intent to surrender or a desire to communicate. In either case, the persons protected by the Red Cross or white flag are expected to maintain neutrality, and may not engage in warlike acts; in fact, engaging in war activities under a white flag or red cross is itself a violation of the laws of war.

These examples of the laws of war address declaration of war, *(the UN charter (1945) Art 2, and some other Arts in the charter, curtails the right of member states to declare war; as does the older and toothless Kellogg-Briand Pact of 1928 for those nations who ratified it but used against Germany in the Nuremberg War Trials)*, acceptance of surrender and the treatment of prisoners of war; the avoidance of atrocities; the prohibition on deliberately attacking civilians; and the prohibition of certain inhumane weapons. It is a violation of the laws of war to engage in combat without meeting certain requirements, among them the wearing of a distinctive uniform or other easily identifiable badge and the carrying of weapons openly. Impersonating soldiers of the other side by wearing the enemy's uniform and fighting in that uniform, is forbidden, as is the taking of hostages.

International Committee of the Red Cross

The ICRC is the only institution explicitly named under international humanitarian law (IHL) as a controlling authority. The legal mandate of the ICRC stems from the four Geneva Conventions of 1949, as well as its own Statutes.

The International Committee of the Red Cross (ICRC) is an impartial, neutral, and independent organization whose exclusively humanitarian mission is to to protect the lives and dignity of victims of war and internal violence and to provide them with assistance.

—Mission of ICRC

VIOLATIONS AND PUNISHMENT

During conflict, punishment for violating the laws of war may consist of a specific, deliberate and limited violation of the laws of war in reprisal.

Soldiers who break specific provisions of the laws of war lose the protections and status afforded as prisoners of war but only after facing a "*competent tribunal*" (GC III Art 5). At that point they become an unlawful combatant but they must still be "*treated with humanity and, in case of trial, shall not be deprived of the rights of fair and regular trial*", because they are still covered by GC IV Art 5.

Spies and "terrorists" are only protected by the laws of war if the *power* which holds them is in a state of armed conflict or war and until they are found to be an *unlawful combatant*. Depending on the circumstances, they may be subject to civilian law or military tribunal for their acts and in practice have been subjected to torture and/or execution. The laws of war neither approve nor condemn such acts, which fall outside their scope. Countries that have signed the *UN Convention Against Torture* have committed themselves not to use torture on anyone for any reason.

After a conflict has ended, persons who have committed any breach of the laws of war, and especially atrocities, may be held individually accountable for war crimes through process of law.

International Human Rights Law

International human rights law is a system of laws, both domestic, regional and international, designed to promote human rights. Human rights law is made up of various international human rights instruments which are binding to its parties (nation-states that have ratified the treaty).

An important concept within human rights law is that of universal jurisdiction. This concept, which is not widely accepted, is that any nation is authorized to prosecute and punish violations of human rights wherever and whenever they may have occurred. Some customary peremptory norms of human rights are also recognised, and these are considered binding on all nations, even those that have not ratified the relevant treaty.

In principle human rights law is enforced on a domestic level and nation states that ratify human rights treaties commit themselves to enact domestic human rights legislations.

In addition to international human rights law, human rights law has been created on a regional level. The three regional human rights instrument that form binding human rights law to party states are: African Charter on Human and Peoples' Rights, the American Convention on Human Rights (the Americas) and the European Convention on Human Rights.

Human rights law is related to, but not the same as International Humanitarian Law and Refugee Law. War crimes, crimes against humanity and genocide have their own treaty law.

Universal Declaration of Human Rights

The Universal Declaration of Human Rights is a declaration that does not form binding international human rights law. Although some legal scholars cite the UDHR as evidence for customary international law and more broadly the UDHR has become an authoritative human rights reference. The UDHR has provided the basis for subsequent international human rights instruments that form binding international human rights law.

The Two Covenants

The Universal Declaration of Human Rights (UDHR) was adopted as binding international treaty into two distinct and different covenants, the International Covenant on Civil and Political Rights(ICCPR) and the International Covenant on Economic, Social and Cultural Rights (ICESCR). The two Covenants form treaty law, that is international human rights law, and ratifying parties (nation states) to the Covenant commit themselves to implement the contained rights in their domestic jurisdictions. Note that some states have signed but not ratified the Covenants. Both covenants came in force in 1976 when a sufficient number of countries had ratified the Covenants.

International Human Rights Treaties

Since the adoption of the two Covenants a number of other treaties (pieces of legislation) have been adopted at the international level.

They are generally known as *human rights instruments*. Some of the most significant include:

- Convention on the Elimination of All Forms of Racial Discrimination (CERD) (adopted 1966, entry into force: 1969)
- Convention on the Elimination of All Forms of Discrimination Against Women (CEDAW) (entry into force: 1981)
- United Nations Convention Against Torture (CAT) (adopted 1984, entry into force: 1984)
- Convention on the Rights of the Child (CRC) (adopted 1989, entry into force: 1989)

International Convention on the Protection of the Rights of All Migrant Workers and Members of their Families (ICRMW) (adopted 1990)

Regional Human Rights Instruments

There are three key regional human rights instruments which have established human rights law on a regional basis. These are:

- the African Charter on Human and Peoples' Rights for Africa (1981, in force since 1986)

- the American Convention on Human Rights for the Americas (1969, in force since 1978)
- the European Convention on Human Rights for Europe (1950, in force since 1953)

Organisation of American States and Council of Europe, like UN, have also adopted (but, unlike UN, later) separate treaties (with weaker implementation mechanisms) containing catalogues of economic, social and cultural rights, as opposed to their aforementioned conventions dealing mostly with civil and political rights.

- European Social Charter for Europe (1961, in force since 1965, complaints mechanism created under 1995 Additional Protocol, in force since 1998)
- Protocol of San Salvador to the ACHR for the Americas (1988, in force since 1999)

Enforcement of Human Rights Law

There is currently no international court to administer international human rights law, however, quasi-judicial bodies exists under some UN treaties (e.g., Human Rights Committee under ICCPR). The International Criminal Court (ICC) has jurisdiction over the crime of genocide, war crimes and crimes against humanity. While the European Court of Human Rights, and the Inter-American Court of Human Rights enforce regional human rights law. Although these same international bodies also hold jurisdiction over cases regarding international humanitarian law, it is crucial to recognize that the two frameworks constitute distinctly different legal regimes.

The United Nations Human Rights Bodies do have some quasi legal enforcement mechanisms. These include the Treaty Bodies attached to the current seven active treaties, and the Human Rights Council complaints procedures, known as the 1235 and 1503 mechanisms

The enforcement of international human rights law is the responsibility of the Nation State, and it is the primary responsibility of the State to make human rights a reality.

In practice, many human rights are very difficult to legally enforce due to the absence of consensus on the application of certain rights, the lack of relevant national legislation or of bodies empowered to take legal action to enforce them.

In over 110 countries national human rights institutions (NHRIs) have been setup to protect, promote or monitor human rights with jurisdiction in a given country. Although not all NHRIs are compliant with the Paris Principles, the number and effect of these institutions is increasing. The Paris Principles were defined at the first International Workshop on National Institutions for the Promotion and Protection of Human Rights in Paris on 7-9 October 1991, and adopted by United Nations Human Rights Commission Resolution 1992/54 of 1992 and the General Assembly Resolution 48/134 of 1993. The Paris Principles list a number of responsibilities for national institutions.

Universal Jurisdiction

Universal jurisdiction is a controversial principle in international law whereby states claim criminal jurisdiction over persons whose alleged crimes were committed outside the boundaries of the prosecuting state, regardless of nationality, country of residence, or any other relation with the prosecuting country. The state backs its claim on the grounds that the crime committed is considered a crime against all, which any state is authorized to punish. The concept of universal jurisdiction is therefore closely linked to the idea that certain international norms are erga omnes, or owed to the entire world community, as well as the concept of jus cogens. In 1993 Belgium passed a *law of universal jurisdiction* to give its courts jurisdiction over crimes against humanity in other countries, and in 1998 Augusto Pinochet was arrested in London following an indictment by Spanish judge Baltasar Garzón under the universal jurisdiction principle. The principle is supported by Amnesty International and other human rights organisations as they believe certain crimes pose a threat to the international community as a whole and the community has a moral duty to act, but others, including Henry Kissinger argue that "widespread agreement that human rights violations and crimes against humanity must be prosecuted has hindered active consideration of the proper role of international courts. Universal jurisdiction risks creating universal tyranny – that of judges". ◆

7

Universal Declaration of Human Rights

The Universal Declaration of Human Rights (UDHR) is a declaration adopted by the United Nations General Assembly (10 December 1948 at the Palais de Chaillot, Paris). The *Guinness Book of Records* describes the UDHR as the "Most Translated Document" in the world. The Declaration arose directly from the experience of the Second World War and represents the first global expression of rights to which all human beings are respectfully entitled to. It consists of 30 articles which have been elaborated in subsequent international treaties, regional human rights instruments, national constitutions and laws. The International Bill of Human Rights consists of the Universal Declaration of Human Rights, the International Covenant on Economic, Social and Cultural Rights, and the International Covenant on Civil and Political Rights and its two Optional Protocols. In 1966 the General Assembly adopted the two detailed Covenants, which complete the International Bill of Human Rights; and in 1976, after the Covenants had been ratified by a sufficient number of individual nations, the Bill took on the force of international law.

Precursors

The morals and values of human rights can be traced through the history of religious beliefs and cultures around the world. European philosophers of the enlightenment period developed theories of natural law that influenced the adoption of documents such as the Bill of Rights of England, the Bill of Rights in the United States, and the Declaration of the Rights of Man and of the Citizen in France.

During World War II, the Allies adopted the Four Freedoms: freedom of speech, freedom of assembly, freedom from fear and freedom from want, as their basic war aims. The United Nations Charter "reaffirmed faith in fundamental human rights, and dignity and worth of the human person" and committed all member states to promote "universal respect for, and observance of, human rights and fundamental freedoms for all without distinction as to race, sex, language or religion".

When the atrocities committed by Nazi Germany and her enemies became apparent after the World War II, the consensus within the world community was that the United Nations Charter did not sufficiently define the rights it referenced. A universal declaration that specified the rights of individuals was necessary to give effect to the Charter's provisions on human rights. Such a declaration was proposed by Cuban diplomats Guy Pérez Cisneros and Ernesto Dihigo.

Drafting

Canadian John Peters Humphrey was called upon by the United Nations Secretary-General to work on the project and became the Declaration's principal drafter. At the time Humphrey was newly appointed as Director of the Division of Human Rights within the United Nations Secretariat. The Commission on Human Rights, a standing body of the United Nations, was constituted to undertake the work of preparing what was initially conceived as an International Bill of Rights. The membership of the Commission was designed to be broadly representative of the global community with representatives of the following countries serving: Australia, Belgium, Byelorussian Soviet Socialist Republic, Chile, China, Cuba, Egypt, France, India, Iran, Lebanon, Panama, Philippines, United Kingdom, United States, Soviet Union, Uruguay and Yugoslavia. Well known members of the Commission included Eleanor Roosevelt of the United States, who was Chairman, Jacques Maritain and René Cassin of France, Charles Malik of Lebanon and P. C. Chang of China, among others. Humphrey provided the initial draft which became the working text of the Commission.

According to *Globalising Family Values*, the Declaration's pro-family phrases were the result of the Christian Democratic movement's influence on Cassin and Malik.

ADOPTION

The Universal Declaration was adopted by the General Assembly on 10 December 1948 by a vote of 48 in favour, 0 against, with 8 abstentions (all Soviet Bloc states [i.e., Byelorussia, Czechoslovakia, Poland, Ukraine, USSR] and Yugoslavia, South Africa and Saudi Arabia).

The following countries voted in favour of the Declaration: Afghanistan, Argentina, Australia, Belgium, Bolivia, Brazil, Burma, Canada, Chile, China, Colombia, Costa Rica, Cuba, Denmark, the Dominican Republic, Ecuador, Egypt, El Salvador, Ethiopia, France, Greece, Guatemala, Haiti, Iceland, India, Iran, Iraq, Lebanon, Liberia, Luxembourg, Mexico, Netherlands, New Zealand, Nicaragua, Norway, Pakistan, Panama, Paraguay, Peru, Philippines, Thailand, Sweden, Syria, Turkey, United Kingdom, United States, Uruguay and Venezuela.

Despite the central role played by Canadian John Humphrey, the Canadian Government at first abstained from voting on the Declaration's draft, but later voted in favour of the final draft in the General Assembly.

Structure

The underlying structure of the Universal Declaration was introduced in its second draft which was prepared by Rene Cassin. Cassin worked from a first draft prepared by John Peters Humphrey. The structure was influenced by the Code Napoleon, including a preamble and introductory general principles. Cassin compared the Declaration to the portico of a Greek temple, with a foundation, steps, four columns and a pediment. Articles 1 and 2 are the foundation blocks, with their principles of dignity, liberty, equality and brotherhood. The seven paragraphs of the preamble, setting out the reasons for the Declaration, are represented by the steps. The main body of the Declaration forms the four columns. The first column (articles 3–11) constitutes rights of the individual, such as the right to life and the prohibition of slavery. The second column (articles 12–17) constitutes the rights of the individual in civil and political society. The third column (articles 18–21) is concerned with spiritual, public and political freedoms such as freedom of religion and freedom of association. The fourth column (articles 22–27) sets out social, economic and cultural rights. In Cassin's model, the last three articles of the Declaration provide the pediment which binds the structure together. These articles are concerned with the duty of the individual to society and the prohibition of use of rights in contravention of the purposes of the United Nations.

Preamble

The Universal Declaration begins with a preamble consisting of seven paragraphs followed by a statement "proclaiming" the Declaration.

Each paragraph of the preamble sets out a reason for the adoption of the Declaration. The first paragraph asserts that the recognition of human dignity of all people is the foundation of justice and peace in the world. The second paragraph observes that disregard and contempt for human rights have resulted in barbarous acts which have outraged the conscience of mankind and that the four freedoms: freedom of speech, belief, freedom from want, and freedom from fear – which is "proclaimed as the highest aspiration" of the people. The third paragraph states that so that people are not compelled to rebellion against tyranny, human rights should be protected by rule of law. The fourth paragraph relates human rights to the development of friendly relations between nations. The fifth paragraph links the Declaration back to the United Nations Charter which reaffirms faith in fundamental human rights and dignity and worth of the human person. The sixth paragraph notes that all members of the United Nations have pledged themselves to achieve, in cooperation with the United Nations, the promotion of universal respect for and observance of human rights and fundamental freedoms. The seventh paragraph observes that "a common understanding" of rights and freedoms is of "the greatest importance" for the full realisation of that pledge.

These paragraphs are followed by the "proclamation" of the Declaration as a "common standard of achievement" for "all peoples and all nations", so that "all individuals" and "all organs of society" should by teaching and education, promote respect for these rights and freedoms and by progressive measures, national and international, secure their universal and effective recognition and observance.

The Preamble is:

Whereas recognition of the inherent dignity and of the equal and inalienable rights of all members of the human family is the foundation of freedom, justice and peace in the world,

Whereas disregard and contempt for human rights have resulted in barbarous acts which have outraged the conscience of mankind, and the advent of a world in which human beings shall enjoy freedom of speech and belief and freedom from fear and want has been proclaimed as the highest aspiration of the common people,

Whereas it is essential, if man is not to be compelled to have recourse, as a last resort, to rebellion against tyranny and oppression, that human rights should be protected by the rule of law,

Whereas it is essential to promote the development of friendly relations between nations,

Whereas the peoples of the United Nations have in the Charter reaffirmed their faith in fundamental human rights, in the dignity and worth of the human person and in the equal rights of men and women and have determined to promote social progress and better standards of life in larger freedom,

Whereas Member States have pledged themselves to achieve, in co-operation with the United Nations, the promotion of universal respect for and observance of human rights and fundamental freedoms,

Whereas a common understanding of these rights and freedoms is of the greatest importance for the full realization of this pledge,

Now, Therefore THE GENERAL ASSEMBLY proclaims THIS UNIVERSAL DECLARATION OF HUMAN RIGHTS as a common standard of achievement for all peoples and all nations, to the end that every individual and every organ of society, keeping this Declaration constantly in mind, shall strive by teaching and education to promote respect for these rights and freedoms and by progressive measures, national and international, to secure their universal and effective recognition and observance, both among the peoples of Member States themselves and among the peoples of territories under their jurisdiction.

Human Rights Set Out in the Declaration

The following reproduces the articles of the Declaration which set out the specific human rights that are recognised in the Declaration.

Article 1

All human beings are born free and equal in dignity and rights. They are endowed with reason and conscience and should act towards one another in a spirit of brotherhood.

Article 2

Everyone is entitled to all the rights and freedoms set forth in this Declaration, without distinction of any kind, such as race, colour, sex, language, religion, political or other opinion, national or social origin, property, birth or other status. Furthermore, no distinction shall be made on the basis of the political, jurisdictional or international status of the country or territory to which a person belongs, whether it be independent, trust, non-self-governing or under any other limitation of sovereignty.

Article 3

Everyone has the right to life, liberty and security of person.

Article 4

No one shall be held in slavery or servitude; slavery and the slave trade shall be prohibited in all their forms.

Article 5

No one shall be subjected to torture or to cruel, inhuman or degrading treatment or punishment.

Article 6

Everyone has the right to recognition everywhere as a person before the law.

Article 7

All are equal before the law and are entitled without any discrimination to equal protection of the law. All are entitled to equal protection against any discrimination in violation of this Declaration and against any incitement to such discrimination.

Article 8

Everyone has the right to an effective remedy by the competent national tribunals for acts violating the fundamental rights granted him by the constitution or by law.

Article 9

No one shall be subjected to arbitrary arrest, detention or exile.

Article 10

Everyone is entitled in full equality to a fair and public hearing by an independent and impartial tribunal, in the determination of his rights and obligations and of any criminal charge against him.

Article 11

1. Everyone charged with a penal offence has the right to be presumed innocent until proved guilty according to law in a public trial at which he has had all the guarantees necessary for his defence.

2. No one shall be held guilty of any penal offence on account of any act or omission which did not constitute a penal offence, under national or international law, at the time when it was committed. Nor shall a heavier penalty be imposed than the one that was applicable at the time the penal offence was committed.

Article 12

No one shall be subjected to arbitrary interference with his privacy, family, home or correspondence, nor to attacks upon his honour and reputation. Everyone has the right to the protection of the law against such interference or attacks.

Article 13

1. Everyone has the right to freedom of movement and residence within the borders of each state.
2. Everyone has the right to leave any country, including their own, and to return to their country.

Article 14

1. Everyone has the right to seek and to enjoy in other countries asylum from persecution.
2. This right may not be invoked in the case of prosecutions genuinely arising from non-political crimes or from acts contrary to the purposes and principles of the United Nations.

Article 15

1. Everyone has the right to a nationality.
2. No one shall be arbitrarily deprived of his nationality nor denied the right to change his nationality.

Article 16

1. Men and women of full age, without any limitation due to race, nationality or religion, have the right to marry and to found a family. They are entitled to equal rights as to marriage, during marriage and at its dissolution.
2. Marriage shall be entered into only with the free and full consent of the intending spouses.
3. The family is the natural and fundamental group unit of society and is entitled to protection by society and the State.

Article 17

1. Everyone has the right to own property alone as well as in association with others.

2. No one shall be arbitrarily deprived of his property.

Article 18

Everyone has the right to freedom of thought, conscience and religion; this right includes freedom to change his religion or belief, and freedom, either alone or in community with others and in public or private, to manifest his religion or belief in teaching, practice, worship and observance.

Article 19

Everyone has the right to freedom of opinion and expression; this right includes freedom to hold opinions without interference and to seek, receive and impart information and ideas through any media and regardless of frontiers.

Article 20

1. Everyone has the right to freedom of peaceful assembly and association.

2. No one may be compelled to belong to an association.

Article 21

1. Everyone has the right to take part in the government of their country, directly or through freely chosen representatives.

2. Everyone has the right of equal access to public service in their country.

3. The will of the people shall be the basis of the authority of government; this will shall be expressed in periodic and genuine elections which shall be by universal and equal suffrage and shall be held by secret vote or by equivalent free voting procedures.

Article 22

Everyone, as a member of society, has the right to social security and is entitled to realization, through national effort and international co-operation and in accordance with the organisation and resources of each State, of the economic, social and cultural rights indispensable for his dignity and the free development of his personality.

Article 23

1. Everyone has the right to work, to free choice of employment, to just and favourable conditions of work and to protection against unemployment.
2. Everyone, without any discrimination, has the right to equal pay for equal work.
3. Everyone who works has the right to just and favourable remuneration ensuring for himself and his family an existence worthy of human dignity, and supplemented, if necessary, by other means of social protection.
4. Everyone has the right to form and to join trade unions for the protection of his interests.

Article 24

Everyone has the right to rest and leisure, including reasonable limitation of working hours and periodic holidays with pay.

Article 25

1. Everyone has the right to a standard of living adequate for the health and well-being of himself and of his family, including food, clothing, housing and medical care and necessary social services, and the right to security in the event of unemployment, sickness, disability, widowhood, old age or other lack of livelihood in circumstances beyond his control.
2. Motherhood and childhood are entitled to special care and assistance. All children, whether born in or out of wedlock, shall enjoy the same social protection.

Article 26

1. Everyone has the right to education. Education shall be free, at least in the elementary and fundamental stages. Elementary education shall be compulsory. Technical and professional education shall be made generally available and higher education shall be equally accessible to all on the basis of merit.

2. Education shall be directed to the full development of the human personality and to the strengthening of respect for human rights and fundamental freedoms. It shall promote understanding, tolerance and friendship among all nations, racial or religious groups, and shall further the activities of the United Nations for the maintenance of peace.

3. Parents have a prior right to choose the kind of education that shall be given to their children.

Article 27

1. Everyone has the right freely to participate in the cultural life of the community, to enjoy the arts and to share in scientific advancement and its benefits.

2. Everyone has the right to the protection of the moral and material interests resulting from any scientific, literary or artistic production of which he is the author.

Article 28

Everyone is entitled to a social and international order in which the rights and freedoms set forth in this Declaration can be fully realised.

Article 29

1. Everyone has duties to the community in which alone the free and full development of his personality is possible.

2. In the exercise of his rights and freedoms, everyone shall be subject only to such limitations as are determined by law

solely for the purpose of securing due recognition and respect for the rights and freedoms of others and of meeting the just requirements of morality, public order and the general welfare in a democratic society.

3. These rights and freedoms may in no case be exercised contrary to the purposes and principles of the United Nations.

Article 30

Nothing in this Declaration may be interpreted as implying for any State, group or person any right to engage in any activity or to perform any act aimed at the destruction of any of the rights and freedoms set forth herein.

Commemoration: International Human Rights Day

The adoption of the Universal Declaration is a significant international commemoration marked each year on 10 December and is known as Human Rights Day or International Human Rights Day. The commemoration is observed by individuals, community and religious groups, human rights organisations, parliaments, governments and the United Nations. Decadal commemorations are often accompanied by campaigns to promote awareness of the Declaration and human rights. 2008 marked the 60th anniversary of the Declaration and was accompanied by year long activities around the theme "Dignity and justice for all of us".

SIGNIFICANCE AND LEGAL EFFECT

In the preamble, governments commit themselves and their peoples to measures to secure the universal and effective recognition and observance of the human rights set out in the Declaration. Eleanor Roosevelt supported the adoption the UDHR as a declaration, rather than as a treaty, because she believed that it would have the same kind of influence on global society as the United States Declaration of Independence had within the United States. In this she proved to be correct. Even though not formally legally binding, the Declaration has been adopted in or influenced most national constitutions since 1948. It also serves as the foundation for a growing number of international treaties and national laws and international, regional, national and sub-national institutions protecting and promoting human rights.

Legal Effect

While not a treaty itself, the Declaration was explicitly adopted for the purpose of defining the meaning of the words "fundamental freedoms" and "human rights" appearing in the United Nations Charter, which is binding on all member states. For this reason, the Universal Declaration is a fundamental constitutive document of the United Nations. Many international lawyers, in addition, believe that the Declaration forms part of customary international law and is a powerful tool in applying diplomatic and moral pressure to governments that violate any of its articles. The 1968 United Nations International Conference on Human Rights advised that it "constitutes an obligation for the members of the international community" to all persons. The declaration has served as the foundation for two binding UN human rights covenants, the International Covenant on Civil and Political Rights and the International Covenant on Economic, Social and Cultural Rights and the principles of the Declaration are elaborated in international treaties such as the International Convention on the Elimination of All Forms of Racial Discrimination, the International Convention on the Elimination of Discrimination Against Women, the United Nations Convention on the Rights of the Child, the United Nations Convention Against Torture and many more. The Declaration continues to be widely cited by governments, academics, advocates and constitutional courts and individual human beings who appeal to its principles for the protection of their recognised human rights.

Reaction

Praise

The Universal Declaration has received praise from a number of notable people. Charles Malik, Lebanese philosopher and diplomat, called it "an international document of the first order of importance," while Eleanor Roosevelt, first chairwoman of the Commission on Human Rights (CHR) that drafted the Declaration, stated that it "may well become the international Magna Carta of all men everywhere." 10 December 1948. In a speech on 5 October 1995, Pope John Paul II called the UDHR "one of the highest expressions of the human conscience of our time." And in a statement on 10 December 2003 on behalf of the European Union, Marcello Spatafora said that "it placed human rights at the centre of the framework of principles and obligations shaping relations within the international community."

Censorship

The Cuban government has been accused of ordering copies of the Universal Declaration of Human Rights to be burned or otherwise destroyed.

Criticism

Some Islamic countries have criticised the Universal Declaration of Human Rights for its perceived failure to take into the account the cultural and religious context of Islamic countries. In 1982, the Iranian representative to the United Nations, Said Rajaie-Khorassani, articulated the position of his country regarding the Universal Declaration of Human Rights, by saying that the UDHR was "a secular understanding of the Judeo-Christian tradition", which could not be implemented by Muslims without trespassing the Islamic law. On 30 June 2000, Muslim nations that are members of the Organisation of the Islamic Conference officially resolved to support the Cairo Declaration on Human Rights in Islam, an alternative document that says people have "freedom and right to a dignified life in accordance with the Islamic Shari'ah". It is important to acknowledge that there are many voices within Islam and Shari'a law can and is interpreted variously by different Islamic jurists. The voiced opposition against the UDHR needs to be taken within that context. Religion, culture and politics are intertwined, the position of women and the lack of due legal process in many Islamic societies can not be entirely attributed to the application of Shari'a.

Property Rights Criticism

Libertarians and some conservatives believe the positive rights that must be provided by others through forceful extraction (for example taxation) negate other peoples' inalienable rights.

Education

Some proponents of alternative education, particularly unschooling, take issue with the right to compulsory education stated in Article 26. In the philosophies of John Holt and others, compulsory education itself violates the right of a person to follow their own interests:

> No human right, except the right to life itself, is more fundamental than this. A person's freedom of learning is part of his freedom of thought, even more basic than his freedom of speech. If we take from someone his right to decide what he will be curious about, we destroy his freedom of thought. We say, in effect, you must think not about what interests you and concerns you, but about what interests and concerns us.
>
> – John Holt, *Escape from Childhood*

The Right to Refuse to Kill

Groups such as Amnesty International and War Resisters International have advocated for "The Right to Refuse to Kill" to be added to the UDHR. War Resisters International has stated that the right to conscientious objection to military service is primarily derived from, but not yet explicit in, Article 18 of the UDHR: the right to freedom of thought, conscience and religion.

Steps have been taken within the UN to make this right more explicit (see Conscientious Objector); but those steps have been limited to secondary, more "marginal" UN documents. That is why Amnesty International would like to have this right brought "out of the margins" and explicitly into the primary document, namely the UDHR itself.

To the rights enshrined in the Universal Declaration of Human Rights one more might, with relevance, be added. It is "The Right to Refuse to Kill."

– Assistant Secretary General of the United Nations, and Nobel Peace Laureate, Sean MacBride, *1974 Nobel Lecture*

Bangkok Declaration

In the Bangkok Declaration adopted by Ministers of Asian states meeting in 1993 in the lead up to the World Conference on Human Rights, Asian governments reaffirmed their commitment to the principles of the United Nations Charter and the Universal Declaration of Human Rights. They stated their view of the interdependence and indivisibility of human rights and stressed the need for universality, objectivity and non-selectivity of human rights.

Article 29 Section 3

The Declaration's assertion that, "These rights and freedoms may in no case be exercised contrary to the purposes and principles of the United Nations." is criticised by some as a "fail-safe" clause; supposedly allowing any previous right to be suspended at whim based on changes in UN policy.

International Covenant on Civil and Political Rights

The International Covenant on Civil and Political Rights (ICCPR) is a United Nations treaty based on the Universal Declaration of Human Rights, created on 16 December 1966 and entered into force on 23 March 1976.

The International Covenant on Civil and Political Rights is monitored by the Human Rights Committee (a separate body to the Human Rights Council which replaced the Commission on Human Rights under the UN Charter in 2006) with permanent standing, to consider periodic reports submitted by member States on their compliance with the treaty. Members of the Human Rights Committee are elected by member states, but do not represent any State. The

Covenant contains two Optional Protocols. The first optional protocol creates an individual complaints mechanism whereby individuals in member States can submit complaints, known as communications, to be reviewed by the Human Rights Committee. Its rulings under the first optional protocol have created the most complex jurisprudence in the UN international human rights law system.

The second optional protocol abolishes the death penalty; however, countries were permitted to make a reservation allowing for use of death penalty for the most serious crimes of a military nature, committed during wartime.

Genesis

The ICESCR and the ICCPR have their roots in the same process that led to the Universal Declaration of Human Rights. As the UDHR was not expected to impose binding obligations, the United Nations Commission on Human Rights began drafting a pair of binding Covenants on human rights intended to impose concrete obligations on their parties. Due to disagreements between member states on the relative importance of negative Civil and Political versus positive Economic, Social and Cultural rights, two separate Covenants were created. These were presented to the UN General Assembly in 1954, and adopted in 1976.

Convention Provisions

Five categories:

1. Protection on individual's physical integrity (against things such as execution, torture, and arbitrary arrest).
2. Procedural fairness in law (rule of law, rights upon arrest, trial, basic conditions must be met when imprisoned, rights to a lawyer, impartial process in trial).
3. Protection based on gender, religious, racial or other forms of discrimination.
4. Individual freedom of belief, speech, association, freedom of press, right to hold assembly.

5. Right to political participation (organise a political party, vote, voice contempt for current political authority).

Two optional protocols:

1. Mechanism by which individuals can launch complaints against member states.

2. Abolition of the death penalty.

NATIONAL IMPLEMENTATION AND EFFECTS

The International Covenant on Civil and Political Rights has been signed by 174 states, 8 of which have yet to ratify the treaty. A country-by-country list of declarations and reservations made upon ratification, accession or succession can be seen.

New Zealand

While New Zealand has not incorporated the ICCPR into law, it took measures to give effect to many of the rights contained within it by passing the New Zealand Bill of Rights Act in 1990.

United States

The United States Senate ratified the ICCPR in 1992, with 5 reservations, 5 understandings, and 4 declarations. Some have noted that with so many reservations, its implementation has little domestic effect. Included in the Senate's ratification was the declaration that "the provisions of Article 1 through 27 of the Covenant are not self-executing", and in a Senate Executive Report stated that the declaration was meant to "clarify that the Covenant will not create a private cause of action in U.S. Courts."

Effect on Domestic Law

Where a treaty or covenant is not self-executing, and where Congress has not acted to implement the agreement with legislation, no private right of action is created by ratification. *Sei Fujii v. State* 38 Cal.2d 718, 242 P.2d 617 (1952); also see *Buell v. Mitchell* 274 F.3d 337 (6th Cir., 2001) (discussing ICCPR's relationship to death penalty cases, citing to other ICCPR cases). Thus while the ICCPR is *ostensibly* binding upon the United States as a matter of international law, it does not form part of the domestic law of the nation.

International Law

Prominent critics in the human rights community, such as Prof. Louis Henkin (non-self-execution declaration incompatible with the Supremacy Clause) and Prof. Jordan Paust ("Rarely has a treaty been so abused.") have denounced the United States' ratification subject to the non-self-execution declaration as a blatant fraud upon the international community, especially in light of its subsequent failure to conform domestic law to the minimum human rights standards as established in the Covenant over the last fifteen years. In 1994, the United Nations' Human Rights Committee expressed similar concerns:

Of particular concern are widely formulated reservations which essentially render ineffective all Covenant rights which would require any change in national law to ensure compliance with Covenant obligations. No real international rights or obligations have thus been accepted. And when there is an absence of provisions to ensure that Covenant rights may be sued on in domestic courts, and, further, a failure to allow individual complaints to be brought to the Committee under the first Optional Protocol, all the essential elements of the Covenant guarantees have been removed.

Indeed, the United States has not accepted a single international obligation required under the Covenant. It has not changed its domestic law to conform with the strictures of the Covenant. See *Hain v. Gibson,* 287 F.3d 1224 (10th Cir. 2002) (noting that Congress has not done so). Its subjects are not permitted to sue to enforce their basic human rights under the Covenant, as noted above. It has not ratified the Optional Protocol. As such, the Covenant has been rendered ineffective, with the bone of contention being United States officials' insistence upon preserving a vast web of sovereign, judicial, prosecutorial, and executive branch immunities that often deprives its subjects of the "effective remedy" under law the Covenant is intended to guarantee. In 2006, the Human Rights Committee expressed concern over what it interprets as material non-compliance, exhorting the United States to take immediate corrective action:

> The Committee notes with concern the restrictive interpretation made by the State party of its obligations under the Covenant, as a result in particular of ... (b) its failure to take fully into consideration its obligation under the Covenant not only to respect, but also to ensure the rights prescribed by the Covenant; and (c) its restrictive approach to some substantive provisions of the Covenant, which is not in conformity with the interpretation made by the Committee before and after the State party's ratification of the Covenant.
>
> The State party should review its approach and interpret the Covenant in good faith, in accordance with the ordinary meaning to be given to its terms in their context, including subsequent practice, and in the light of its object and purpose. The State party should in particular ... (b) take positive steps, when necessary, to ensure the full implementation of all rights prescribed by the Covenant; and (c) consider in good faith the interpretation of the Covenant provided by the Committee pursuant to its mandate.

As a reservation that is "incompatible with the object and purpose" of a treaty is void as a matter of international law, Vienna Convention on the Law of Treaties, art. 19, 1155 U.N.T.S. 331 (entered into force Jan. 27, 1980) (specifying conditions under which signatory States can offer "reservations"), there is some issue as to whether the non-self-execution declaration is even legal under domestic law. At this point, the United States certainly appears to be a signatory in name only.

States not Member of the Covenant

The majority of states in the world are parties to the ICCPR. As of August 2009 the following 29 states have either not yet signed the convention, or have signed but have not yet ratified the convention.

Signed but not ratified:

1. China
2. Comoros
3. Cuba
4. Guinea-Bissau
5. Laos
6. Nauru
7. Pakistan
8. São Tomé and Príncipe

Neither signed nor ratified:

1. Antigua and Barbuda
2. Bahamas
3. Bhutan
4. Brunei
5. Burma (Myanmar)
6. Fiji
7. Kiribati
8. Malaysia
9. Marshall Islands
10. Micronesia
11. Oman
12. Palau
13. Qatar
14. Saint Kitts and Nevis
15. Saint Lucia
16. Saudi Arabia
17. Singapore
18. Solomon Islands
19. Tonga
20. United Arab Emirates
21. Vanuatu
22. Vatican City (through the Holy See)

8

European Convention on Human Rights

The Convention for the Protection of Human Rights and Fundamental Freedoms (also called the "European Convention on Human Rights" and "ECHR"), was adopted under the auspices of the Council of Europe in 1950 to protect human rights and fundamental freedoms in Europe. All Council of Europe member states are party to the Convention and new members are expected to ratify the convention at the earliest opportunity.

The Convention established the European Court of Human Rights. Any person who feels his or her rights have been violated under the Convention by a state party can take a case to the Court. The decisions of the Court are not automatically legally binding, but the Court does have the power to award damages. The establishment of a Court to protect individuals from human rights violations is an innovative feature for an international convention on human rights, as it gives the individual an active role on the international arena (traditionally, only states are considered actors in international law). The European Convention is still the only international human rights agreement providing such a high degree of individual protection. State parties can also take cases against other state parties to the Court, although this power is rarely used.

The Convention has several protocols. For example, Protocol 13 prohibits the death penalty. The protocols accepted vary from State Party to State Party, though it is understood that state parties should be party to as many protocols as possible.

The Convention was drafted by the Council of Europe after World War II. Sir David Maxwell-Fyfe was the Chair of the Council's legal and administrative division from 1949 to 1952, and oversaw the drafting of Convention. It was designed to incorporate a traditional civil liberties approach to securing "effective political democracy", from the strongest traditions in the United Kingdom, France and other member states of Europe. The Convention was opened for signature on 4 November 1950 in Rome. It was ratified and entered into force on 3 September 1953. It is overseen by the European Court of Human Rights in Strasbourg, and the Council of Europe. Until recently, the Convention was also overseen by a European Commission on Human Rights.

Drafting

The Convention is drafted in broad terms, in a similar (albeit more modern) manner to the English Bill of Rights, the American Bill of Rights, the French Declaration of the Rights of Man or the first part of the German Basic law. Statements of principle are, from a legal point of view, not determinative and require extensive "interpretation" by courts to bring out meaning in particular factual situations.

Convention Articles

As amended by Protocol 11, the Convention consists of three parts. The main rights and freedoms are contained in Section I, which consists of Articles 2 to 18. Section II (Articles 19 to 51) sets up the Court and its rules of operation. Section III contains various concluding provisions.

Before the entry into force of Protocol 11, Section II (Article 19) set-up the Commission and the Court, Sections III (Articles 20 to 37) and IV (Articles 38 to 59) included the high-level machinery for the operation of, respectively, the Commission and the Court, and Section V contained various concluding provisions.

Many of the Articles in Section I are structured in two paragraphs: the first sets out a basic right or freedom (such as Article 2(1) – the right to life) but the second contains various exclusions, exceptions or limitations on the basic right (such as Article 2(2) – which excepts certain uses of force leading to death).

Article 1 - Respecting Rights

Article 1 simply binds the signatory parties to secure the rights under the other Articles of the Convention "within their jurisdiction". In exceptional cases, "jurisdiction" may not be confined to a Contracting State's own national territory; the obligation to secure Convention rights then also extends to foreign territory, such as occupied land in which the State exercises effective control.

Article 2 - Life

Article 2 protects the right of every person to their life. The first paragraph of the article contains an exception for the lawful executions, while the second paragraph provides that death resulting from defending one self or others, arresting a suspect or fugitive, or suppressing riots or insurrections, will not contravene the Article when the use of force involved is "no more than absolutely necessary".

This right does also not derogate under Article 15 of the convention during peacetime. The exemption for the case of lawful executions is further restricted by Protocols 6 and 13, for those parties who are also parties to those protocols.

The European Court of Human Rights did not rule upon the right to life until 1995, when in *McCann v. United Kingdom* it ruled that the exception contained in the second paragraph do not constitute situations when it is permitted to kill, but situations where it is permitted to use force which might result in the deprivation of life.

The Court has ruled that states have three main duties under Article 2:

1. a duty to refrain from unlawful killing,
2. a duty to investigate suspicious deaths and,
3. in certain circumstances, a positive duty to prevent foreseeable loss of life.

Article 3 - Torture

Article 3 prohibits torture, and "inhuman or degrading treatment or punishment". There are no exceptions or limitations on this right. This provision usually applies, apart from torture, to cases of severe police violence and poor conditions in detention.

The Court have emphasised the fundamental nature of Article 3 in holding that the prohibition is made in "absolute terms ... irrespective of a victim's conduct." The Court has also held that states cannot deport or extradite individuals who might be subjected to torture, inhuman or degrading treatment or punishment, in the recipient state.

Initially the Court took a restrictive view on what consisted of torture, preferring to find that states had inflicted inhuman and degrading treatment. Thus the court held that practices such as sleep deprivation, subjecting individual to intense noise and requiring them to stand against a wall with their limbs outstretched for extended periods of time, did not constitute torture. In fact, the Court only found a state guilty of torture in 1996 in the case of a detainee who was suspended by his arms whilst his hands were tied behind his back. Since then the Court has appeared to be more open to finding states guilty of torture and has even ruled that since the Convention is a "living instrument", treatment which it had previously characterised as inhuman or degrading treatment might in future be regarded as torture.

Article 4 - Servitude

Article 4 prohibits slavery, servitude and forced labour but exempts labour:

1. done as a normal part of imprisonment,
2. in the form of compulsory military service or work done as an alternative by conscientious objectors,
3. required to be done during a state of emergency, and
4. considered to be a part of a person's normal "civic obligations."

Article 5 - Liberty and Security

Article 5 provides that everyone has the right to liberty and security of person. Liberty and security of the person are taken as a "compound" concept - security of the person has not been subject to separate interpretation by the Court.

Article 5 provides the right to liberty, subject only to lawful arrest or detention under certain other circumstances, such as arrest on suspicion of a crime or imprisonment in fulfilment of a sentence. The article also provides the right to be informed in a language one understands of the reasons for the arrest and any charge against them, the right of prompt access to judicial proceedings to determine the legality of one's arrest or detention and to trial within a reasonable time or release pending trial, and the right to compensation in the case of arrest or detention in violation of this Article.

Steel v. United Kingdom (1998) 28 EHRR 603.

Article 6 - Fair Trial

Article 6 provides a detailed right to a fair trial, including the right to a public hearing before an independent and impartial tribunal within reasonable time, the presumption of innocence, and other minimum rights for those charged with a criminal offence (adequate time and facilities to prepare their defence, access to legal representation, right to examine witnesses against them or have them examined, right to the free assistance of an interpreter).

The majority of Convention violations that the Court finds today are excessive delays, in violation of the "reasonable time" requirement, in civil and criminal proceedings before national courts, mostly in Italy and France. Under the "independent tribunal" requirement, the Court has ruled that military judges in Turkish state security courts are incompatible with Article 6.

Another significant set of violations concerns the "confrontation clause" of Article 6 (i.e. the right to examine witnesses or have them examined). In this respect, problems of compliance with Article 6 may arise when national laws allow the use in evidence of the testimonies of absent, anonymous and vulnerable witnesses.

Article 7 - Retrospectivity

Prohibits the retrospective criminalisation of acts and omissions. No person may be punished for an act that was not a criminal offence at the time of its commission. The Article states that a criminal offence is one under either national or international law, which would permit a party to prosecute someone for a crime which was not illegal under their domestic law at the time, so long as it was prohibited by international law. The Article also prohibits a heavier penalty being imposed than was applicable at the time when the criminal act was committed.

Article 7 incorporates the legal principle *nullum crimen, nulla poena sine lege* into the convention.

Article 8 - Privacy

Article 8 provides a right to respect for one's "private and family life, his home and his correspondence", subject to certain restrictions that are "in accordance with law" and "necessary in a democratic society". This Article clearly provides a right to be free of unlawful searches, but the Court has given the protection for "private and family life" that this Article provides a broad interpretation, taking for instance that prohibition of private consensual homosexual acts violates this Article. This may be compared to the jurisprudence of the United States Supreme Court, which has also adopted a somewhat broad interpretation of the right to privacy. Furthermore, Article 8 sometimes comprises positive obligations: whereas classical human rights are formulated as prohibiting a State from interfering with rights, and thus *not* to do something (e.g. not to separate a family under family life protection), the effective enjoyment of such rights may also include an obligation for the State to become active, and to *do* something (e.g. to enforce access for a divorced father to his child).

Article 9 - Conscience and Religion

Article 9 provides a right to freedom of thought, conscience and religion. This includes the freedom to change a religion or belief, and to manifest a religion or belief in worship, teaching, practice and observance, subject to certain restrictions that are "in accordance with law" and "necessary in a democratic society"

Article 10 - Expression

Article 10 provides the right to freedom of expression, subject to certain restrictions that are "in accordance with law" and "necessary in a democratic society". This right includes the freedom to hold opinions, and to receive and impart information and ideas.

- *Lingens v Austria* (1986) 8 EHRR 407
- *The Observer and The Guardian v United Kingdom* (1991) 14 EHRR 153, the "Spycatcher" case.
- *Bowman v United Kingdom* (1998) 26 EHRR 1
- *Communist Party v Turkey* (1998) 26 EHRR 1211
- *Appleby v United Kingdom* (2003) 37 EHRR 38

Article 11 - Association

Article 11 protects the right to freedom of assembly and association, including the right to form trade unions, subject to certain restrictions that are "in accordance with law" and "necessary in a democratic society".

- *Vogt v Germany*
- *Yazar, Karatas, Aksoy and Hep v Turkey* (2003) 36 EHRR 59

Article 12 - Marriage

Article 12 provides a right for men and women of marriageable age to marry and establish a family.

Despite a number of invitations, the Court has so far refused to apply the protections of this Article to same-sex marriage. The

Court has defended this on the grounds that the Article was intended to apply only to different-sex marriage, and that a wide margin of appreciation must be granted to parties in this area.

Prohibiting a transsexual person from marrying somebody whose sex is different from that person's affirmed gender is a breach of Article 12. *(Goodwin v. United Kingdom; I. v. United Kingdom.)* This 2002 holding represented a reversal of the Court's previous opinion *(Rees v. United Kingdom).* It did not, however, alter the understanding that Article 12 protects only different-sex couples. The United Kingdom Gender Recognition Act now requires married couples, one of whom is a transsexual person, to annul their marriage before the trans partner can be granted a Gender Recognition Certificate. Although this provision is apparently in breach of the article the Court has thus far found the UK Government to be within its margin of appreciation *Parry v UK (2006).*

Article 13 - Effective Remedy

Article 13 provides for the right for an effective remedy before national authorities for violations of rights under the Convention. The inability to obtain a remedy before a national court for an infringement of a Convention right is thus a free-standing and separately actionable infringement of the Convention.

Article 14 - Discrimination

Article 14 contains a prohibition of discrimination. This prohibition is broad in some ways, and narrow in others. On the one hand, the article protects against discrimination based on any of a wide range of grounds. The Article provides a list of such grounds, including sex, race, colour, language, religion and several other criteria, and most significantly providing that this list is non-exhaustive. On the other hand, the article's scope is limited only to discrimination with respect to rights under the Convention. Thus, an applicant must prove discrimination in the enjoyment of a specific right that is guaranteed elsewhere in the Convention (e.g. discrimination based on sex – Article 14 – in the enjcyment of the right to freedom of expression – Article 10). Protocol 12 extends this prohibition to cover discrimination in any legal right, even when that legal right is not protected under the Convention, so long as it is provided for in national law.

Article 15 - Derogations

Article 15 allows contracting states to derogate from the rights guaranteed by the Convention in time of "war or other public emergency threatening the life of the nation". Derogation from the rights in the Convention, however, is subject to a number of qualifying criteria, these are that: the state of affairs relied on is temporary and exceptional; the circumstances are grave enough to threaten the organised life of the entire community; the emergency is actual or imminent in that the emergency is about to occur; the threat is to the life of the nation which seeks to derogate; and the measures for which the derogation is required are "strictly required by the exigencies of the situation".

In November 2001 the United Kingdom government held that there was such a dire state of emergency in the country that it was necessary to implement Part 4 of the Anti-terrorism, Crime and Security Act 2001 and detain a number of terrorist suspects indefinitely without charge in Belmarsh Prison pending deportation. This lasted until April 2005, after the Law Lords ruled on 16 December 2004 that the claim was not consistent with the Convention. Lord Hoffmann went further to say:

> The real threat to the life of the nation, in the sense of a people living in accordance with its traditional laws and political values, comes not from terrorism but from laws such as these. That is the true measure of what terrorism may achieve. It is for Parliament to decide whether to give the terrorists such a victory.

Other instances where this derogation has been used have been in Ireland between July and December 1957, Greece in 1969, Ireland in 1978, Northern Ireland from 1988, and Turkey in 1996.

Article 16 - Aliens

Article 16 allows states to restrict the political activity of foreigners.The Court has ruled that European Union member states cannot consider the nationals of other member states to be aliens.

Article 17 - Abuse of Rights

Article 17 provides that no one may use the rights guaranteed by the Convention to seek the abolition or limitation of rights guaranteed in the Convention. This addresses instances where states seek to restrict a human right in the name of another human right, or where individuals rely on a human right to undermine other human rights (for example where an individual issues a death threat).

Article 18 - Permitted Restrictions

Article 18 provides that any limitations on the rights provided for in the Convention may be used only for the purpose for which they are provided. For example, Article 5, which guarantees the right to personal freedom, may be explicitly limited in order to bring a suspect before a judge. To use pre-trial detention as a means of intimidation of a person under a false pretext is therefore a limitation of right (to freedom) which does not serve an explicitly provided purpose (to be brought before a judge), and is therefore contrary to Article 18.

CONVENTION PROTOCOLS

As of February 2006, fourteen protocols to the Convention have been opened for signature. These can be divided into two main groups: those changing the machinery of the convention, and those adding additional rights to those protected by the convention. The former require unanimous ratification before coming into force, while the latter are optional protocols which only come into force between ratifying member states (normally after a small threshold of states has been reached).

For the first Protocol, Monaco and Switzerland have signed but never ratified. Andorra has neither signed nor ratified.

Protocol 1, Article 1 - Property

Article 1 provides for the rights to the peaceful enjoyment of one's possessions.

Protocol 1, Article 2 - Education

Article 2 provides for the right not to be denied an education and the right for parents to have their children educated in accordance with their religious and other views. It does not however guarantee any particular level of education of any particular quality (*Belgian linguistic case*).

Protocol 1, Article 3 - Elections

Article 3 provides for the right to regular, free and fair elections.

- *Matthews v. United Kingdom* (1999) 28 EHRR 361

Protocol 4 - Civil Imprisonment, Free Movement, Expulsion

Article 1 prohibits the imprisonment of people for breach of a contract. Article 2 provides for a right to freely move within a country once lawfully there and for a right to leave any country. Article 3 prohibits the expulsion of nationals and provides for the right of an individual to enter a country of his or her nationality. Article 4 prohibits the collective expulsion of foreigners.

Spain, Turkey and the United Kingdom have signed but never ratified Protocol 4. Andorra, Greece and Switzerland have neither signed nor ratified this protocol.

Protocol 6 - Restriction of Death Penalty

Requires parties to restrict the application of the death penalty to times of war or "imminent threat of war".

Every Council of Europe member state has signed and ratified Protocol 6, except Russia who has signed but not ratified.

Protocol 7 - Crime and Family

- Article 1 provides for a right to fair procedures for lawfully resident foreigners facing expulsion.

- Article 2 provides for the right to appeal in criminal matters.
- Article 3 provides for compensation for the victims of miscarriages of justice.
- Article 4 prohibits the re-trial of anyone who has already been finally acquitted or convicted of a particular offence (Double jeopardy).
- Article 5 provides for equality between spouses.

Despite having signed the protocol more than twenty years ago, Belgium, Germany, the Netherlands, Spain and Turkey have never ratified it. The United Kingdom has neither signed nor ratified the protocol.

Protocol 12 - Discrimination

Applies the current expansive and indefinite grounds of prohibited discrimination in Article 14 to the exercise of any legal right and to the actions (including the obligations) of public authorities.

The Protocol entered into force on 1 April 2005 and has (As of July 2009) been ratified by 17 member states. Several member states — namely Bulgaria, Denmark, France, Lithuania, Malta, Monaco, Poland, Sweden, Switzerland and the United Kingdom — have not signed the protocol.

The United Kingdom Government has declined to sign Protocol 12 on the basis that they believe the wording of protocol is too wide and would result in a flood of new cases testing the extent of the new provision. They believe that the phrase "rights set forth by law" might include international conventions to which the UK is not a party, and would result in incorporation of these instruments by stealth. It has been suggested that the protocol is therefore in a kind of catch-22, since the UK will decline to either sign or ratify the protocol until the European Court of Human Rights has addressed the meaning of the provision, while the court is hindered in doing so by the lack of applications to the court concerning the protocol caused by the decisions of Europe's most populous states — including the UK — not to ratify the protocol. The UK Government, nevertheless, "agrees in principle that the ECHR should contain a provision against discrimination that is free-standing and not parasitic on the other Convention rights".

Protocol 13 - Complete Abolition of Death Penalty

Provides for the total abolition of the death penalty.

Procedural and Institutional Protocols

The Convention's provisions affecting institutional and procedural matters has been altered several times by mean of protocols. These amendments have, with of the exception of Protocol 2, amended the text of the convention. Protocol 2 did not amend the text of the convention as such, but stipulated that it was to be treated as an integral part of the text. All of these protocols have required the unanimous ratification of all the member states of the Council of Europe to enter into force.

Protocol 11

Protocols 2, 3, 5, 8, 9 and 10 have now been superseded by Protocol 11 which entered into force on 1 November 1998. It established a fundamental change in the machinery of the convention. It abolished the Commission, allowing individuals to apply directly to the Court, which was given compulsory jurisdiction and altered the latter's structure. Previously states could ratify the Convention without accepting the jurisdiction of the Court of Human Rights. The protocol also abolished the judicial functions of the Committee of Ministers.

Protocol 14

Protocol 14 follows on from Protocol 11 in further improving the efficiency of operation of the Court. It seeks to "filter" out cases that have less chance of succeeding along with those that are broadly similar to cases brought previously against the same member state. Furthermore a case will not be considered admissible where an applicant has not suffered a "significant disadvantage". This latter ground can only be used when an examination of the application on the merits is not considered necessary and where the subject-matter of the application had already been considered by a national court.

A new mechanism is introduced with Protocol 14 to assist enforcement of judgements by the Committee of Ministers. The Committee can ask the Court for an interpretation of a judgement and can even bring a member state before the Court for non-compliance of a previous judgement against that state.

Protocol 14 also allows the European Union to accede to the Convention, an issue which is also dependent on the ratification of the Lisbon Treaty, in light of the fact that the European Community currently lacks the competence to accede to human rights treaties.

The protocol has been signed by every Council of Europe member state. Currently only Russia has not yet ratified the protocol. It will only come into force only when it has been ratified by all Council of Europe member states.

In 2009, a provisional Protocol No. 14b was opened for signature. It allows single judges to reject manifestly inadmissible applications against protocol's member states and extends the competence of three-judge committees to declare applications against protocol's member states admissible and decide on their merits where there already is a well-established case law of the Court.

Citation

The ECHR may be cited in academic works in a number of ways. The European Treaty Series citation is "*Convention for the Protection of Human Rights and Fundamental Freedoms*, ETS 5, Article 1, para 2" for the second paragraph of the first article. Citation of the treaty is never by page number. ◆

9

American Convention on Human Rights

The American Convention on Human Rights (also known as the Pact of San José) is an international human rights instrument. It was adopted by the nations of the Americas meeting in San José, Costa Rica, in 1969. It came into force after the eleventh instrument of ratification (that of Grenada) was deposited on 18 July 1978.

The bodies responsible for overseeing compliance with the Convention are the Inter-American Commission on Human Rights and the Inter-American Court of Human Rights, both of which are organs of the Organisation of American States (OAS).

Content and Purpose

According to its preamble, the purpose of the Convention is "to consolidate in this hemisphere, within the framework of democratic institutions, a system of personal liberty and social justice based on respect for the essential rights of man."

Chapter I establishes the general obligation of the states parties to uphold the rights set-forth in the Convention to all persons under their jurisdiction, and to adapt their domestic laws to bring them into line with the Convention. The 23 articles of Chapter II give a list of individual civil and political rights due to all persons, including the right to life "in general, from the moment of conception", to humane treatment, to a fair trial, to privacy, to freedom of conscience, freedom of assembly, freedom of movement, etc. The single article in Chapter III deals with economic, social, and cultural rights. The somewhat cursory treatment given to this issue here was expanded some ten years later with the Protocol of San Salvador.

Describes those circumstances in which certain rights can be temporarily suspended, such as during states of emergency, and the formalities to be followed for such suspension to be valid. With a nod to the balance between rights and duties enshrined in the earlier American Declaration of the Rights and Duties of Man, points out that individuals have responsibilities as well as rights.

Contain provisions for the creation and operation of the two bodies responsible for overseeing compliance with the Convention: the Inter-American Commission, based in Washington, D.C., United States, and the Inter-American Court, headquartered in San José, Costa Rica. Deals with mechanisms for ratifying the Convention, amending it or placing reservations in it, or denouncing it. Various transitory provisions are set-forth.

Additional Protocols

In the ensuing years, the states parties to the American Convention have supplemented its provisions with two additional protocols.

The first, the Additional Protocol to the American Convention on Human Rights in the area of Economic, Social, and Cultural Rights (more commonly known as the "Protocol of San Salvador"), was opened for signature in the city of San Salvador, El Salvador, on 17 November 1988. It represented an attempt to take the inter-American human rights system to a higher level by enshrining its protection of so-called second-generation rights in the economic, social, and cultural spheres.

The protocol's provisions cover such areas as the right to work, the right to health, the right to food, and the right to education. It came into effect on 16 November 1999 and has been ratified by 14 nations.

The second, the Protocol to the American Convention on Human Rights to Abolish the Death Penalty, was adopted at Asunción, Paraguay, on 8 June 1990. While Article 4 of the American Convention had already placed severe restrictions on the states' ability to impose the death penalty – only applicable for the most serious crimes; no reinstatement once abolished; not to be used for political offenses or common crimes; not to be used against those aged under 18 or over 70, or against pregnant women – signing this protocol formalises a state's solemn commitment to refrain from using capital punishment in any peacetime circumstance. To date it has been ratified by 11 nations (see below).

Ratifications

Country	*Ratification date*	*1st additional protocol*	*2nd additional protocol*
Argentina	14 August 1984	30 June 2003	18 June 2008
Barbados	5 December 1981		
Bolivia	20 June 1979	12 July 2006	
Brazil	9 July 1992	8 August 1996	31 July 1996
Chile	8 August 1990		4 August 2008
Colombia	28 May 1973	10 October 1997	
Costa Rica	2 March 1970	9 September 1999	30 March 1998
Dominica	3 June 1993		
Dominican Republic	21 January 1978		
Ecuador	8 December 1997	2 February 1993	5 February 1998
El Salvador	20 June 1978	4 May 1995	
Grenada	14 July 1978		
Guatemala	27 April 1978	30 May 2000	
Haiti	14 September 1977		
Honduras	5 September 1977		

Country	*Ratification date*	*1st additional protocol*	*2nd additional protocol*
Jamaica	19 July 1978		
Mexico	2 March 1981	8 March 1996	28 June 2007
Nicaragua	25 September 1979		24 March 1999
Panama	8 May 1978	28 October 1992	27 June 1991
Paraguay	18 August 1989	28 May 1997	31 October 2000
Peru	12 July 1978	17 May 1995	
Suriname	12 December 1987	28 February 1990	
Uruguay	26 March 1985	21 December 1995	8 February 1994
Venezuela	23 June 1977		24 August 1992

Trinidad and Tobago suspended its ratification on 26 May 1998 (effective 26 May 1999) over the death penalty issue.

The treaty is open to all OAS member states, although to date it has not been ratified by Canada or several of the English-speaking Caribbean nations; the United States signed it in 1977 but has not proceeded with ratification.

Canada did at one point seriously consider ratification, but has decided against it, despite being in principle in favour of such a treaty. The ACHR, having been largely drafted by the predominantly Roman Catholic nations of Latin America, contains anti-abortion provisions, specifically, Article 4.1:

> *"Every person has the right to have his life respected. This right shall be protected by law and, in general, from the moment of conception. No one shall be arbitrarily deprived of his life."*

This conflicts with the current legality of abortions in Canada. Although Canada could ratify the convention with a reservation with respect to abortion (as did Mexico), that would contradict Canada's stated opposition to the making of reservations to human rights treaties. Another solution would be for the other states to remove the anti-abortion provisions, but that is unlikely to occur due to strong Catholic feeling in those countries.

Freedom of Association

Freedom of association is the individual right to come together with other individuals and collectively express, promote, pursue and defend common interests. The right to freedom of association has been included in a number of national constitutions and human rights instruments, including the US constitution and the European Convention on Human Rights.

Freedom of association in the sense of workers' right to organise and collectively bargain is also recognised in the Universal Declaration of Human Rights and International Labour Organisation Conventions.

The right to freedom of association is sometimes used interchangeably with the freedom of assembly. More specifically the freedom of assembly is understood in a political context, although depending on the source *(constitution, human rights instrument etc.)* the right to freedom of association may be understood to include the right to freedom of assembly.

Concept

Democracy and Civil Society

Jeremey McBride argues that respect for the freedom of association by all public authorities and the exercising of this freedom by all sections of society are essential both to establish a "genuine democracy" and to ensure that, once achieved, it remains "healthy and flourishing". In this regard he sees the formation of political parties as a significant manifestation of the freedom of association.

The freedom of association is however not only exercised in the political sense, but also for a vast array of interests – such as culture, recreation, sport and social and humanitarian assistance. Jeremey McBride agues that the formation of non-governmental organisations (NGOs), which he equates with civil society, is the "fruit of associational activity".

Libertarian

Freedom of association is a term popular in libertarian literature. It is used to describe the concept of absolute freedom to live in a community or be part of an organisation whose values or culture are closely related to one's preferences; or, on a more basic level, to associate with any individual one chooses.

The libertarian concept of freedom of association is often rebuked from a moral/ethical context. Under laws in such a system, business owners could refuse service to anyone for whatever reason. Opponents argue that such practices are regressive and would lead to greater prejudice within society. Right-libertarians sympathetic to freedom of association, such as Richard Epstein, respond that in a case of refusing service (which thus is a case of the freedom of contract) unjustified discrimination incurs a cost and therefore a competitive disadvantage. Left-libertarians argue that such refusal would place those businesses at an economic disadvantage to those who provide services to all, making them less profitable and eventually leading them to close down.

Libertarians also argue that freedom of association, in a political context, is merely the extension of the right to determine with whom to associate in one's personal life. For example, somebody who valued good manners or etiquette may not relish associating with someone who was not decent or was uncouth. Or, a homophobe probably would not enjoy associating with gay people. In both instances, a person is voluntarily deciding with whom to associate, based on his/her own volition. Libertarians believe that freedom of association, in the political sphere, is not such a fanciful or unrealistic notion, since individual human beings already choose with whom they would like to associate based on a variety of reasons.

CONSTITUTIONS

South African Constitution – Bill of Rights

The South African Constitution's Bill of Rights enshrines the right to freedom of association in Section 18, which states "Everyone has the right to freedom of association." Furthermore Section 17 states "Everyone has the right, peacefully and unarmed, to assemble, to demonstrate, to picket and to present petitions", effectively enshrining the right of freedom of assembly. Workers' right to freedom of association in terms of the right to form trade unions and collective bargaining is recognised separately, in Section 23.

US Constitution

While the United States Constitution's First Amendment identifies the rights to assemble and to petition the government, the text of the First Amendment does not make specific mention of a right to association. Nevertheless, the United States Supreme Court held in NAACP *v.* Alabama that the freedom of association is an essential part of the Freedom of Speech because, in many cases, people can engage in effective speech only when they join with others. The Supreme Court has found the Constitution to protect the freedom of association in two cases (NAACP *v.* Alabama, 1958 and Roberts *v.* United States Jaycees, 1984).

1. *Intimate Associations.* A fundamental element of personal liberty is the right to choose to enter into and maintain certain intimate human relationships. These intimate human relationships are known as "intimate associations." The paradigmatic "intimate association" is the family.
2. *Expressive Associations.* Expressive associations are groups that engage in activities protected by the First Amendment—speech, assembly, petitioning government for a redress of grievances, and the free exercise of religion.

Limitation

However, the implicit First Amendment right of association in the U.S. Constitution has been limited by court rulings. For example, it is illegal in the United States to consider race in the making and enforcement of private contracts other than marriage or taking affirmative action. This limit on freedom of association results from Section 1981 of Title 42 of the United States Code, as balanced against the First Amendment in the 1976 decision of *Runyon v. McCrary*.

The holding of *Runyon* is that the defendant private schools were free to *express* and teach their views, such as white separatism, but could not discriminate on the basis of race in the *provision* of services to the general public. So, if the plaintiff African-American children wished to attend such private schools, *and* were clearly qualified in all respects (but race) and were able to pay the fees, *and* were willing to attend *despite* the fact that the school's professed principles were inconsistent with admitting them, then the schools were required by Section 1981 to admit them. This doctrine rests on the interpretation of a private contract as a "badge" of slavery when either party considers race in choosing the other.

Workers' Freedom of Association

The organisation of labour was commonly resisted during the 19th century, with even relatively liberal countries such as the United Kingdom banning it for various periods (in the UK's case, between 1820 and 1824).

In the international labour movement, the freedom of association is a right identified under international labour standards as the right of workers to organise and collectively bargain. Freedom of association, in this sense, is recognised as a fundamental human right by a number of documents including the Universal Declaration of Human Rights and International Labour Organisation Convention C87 and Convention C98 — two of the eight fundamental, core international labour standards. 'Freedom of Association' can also refer to legal bans on private contracts negotiated between a private employer and their employees requiring workers at a particular workplace to join a union as a term and condition of employment. Supporters of this sort of private freedom of association claim that the right to join a union incorporates a right not to join a union. In the United States, the term 'right to work' is more common for this type of law. ◆

10
Self-Determination

Self-determination is defined as free choice of one's own acts without external compulsion; and especially as the freedom of the people of a given territory to determine their own political status or independence from their current state. In other words, it is the right of the people of a certain nation to decide how they want to be governed without the influence of any other country. The latter is a complex concept with conflicting definitions and legal criteria for determining which groups may legitimately claim the right to self-determination. This often coincides with various nationalist movements.

History of Pre-20th Century

Just as colonisation and colonialism have been practiced throughout human history, political self-determination has been cherished by people through history, the ancient Mesopotamian and later Greek city-states being early examples.

The revolt of the British colonists in North America has been defined as the first assertion of the right of national and democratic self-determination because of the explicit invocation of natural law, the natural rights of man and consent of, and sovereignty by, the people, ideas inspired particularly by John Locke's writings. Thomas Jefferson furthered promoted the notion that the will of the people was supreme, especially through authorship of the Declaration of Independence which inspired Europeans throughout the 19th century. The French Revolution also was motivated by and legitimatised ideas of self-determination.

During the early 1800s most of the nations of South America achieved independence from Spain. The American public, organised groups and even Congressional resolutions, often supported such movements, especially the Greek War of Independence (1821-29) and the demands of Hungarian revolutionaries in 1848. However, such support never became official government policy. After the American Civil War the United States government opposed self-determination for the West Indian islands of Saint Thomas and Saint John in 1868, the Hawaiian Islands in 1868. By the conclusion of the Spanish-American War in 1899 the United States supported its annexation without the consent of the peoples the former Spanish colonies of Guam, Puerto Rico and the Philippines; it retained "quasi-suzerainty" over Cuba.

World War I and II

Woodrow Wilson revived the American commitment to self-determination, at least for European states, during World War I. When the Bolsheviks came to power in Russia in November 1917, they called for Russia's immediate withdrawal as a member of the Allies of World War I. They also supported the right of all nations, including colonies, to self-determination. (As early as 1914 Lenin wrote: " would be wrong to interpret the right to self-determination as meaning anything but the right to existence as a separate state.") The 1918 Constitution of the Soviet Union acknowledged the right of secession for its constituent republics.

This presented a challenge to Wilson's more limited demands. In January 1918 Wilson issued his Fourteen Points of January 1918 which, among other things, called for adjustment of colonial claims, as long as the interests of colonial powers had equal weight with the claims of subject peoples. The Treaty of Brest-Litovsk in March 1918 led to Russia's exit from the war and the independence of Finland, Estonia, Latvia, Ukraine, Lithuania and Poland. The end of the war led to the dissolution of the defeated Austro-Hungarian Empire and the creation by the Allies of Czechoslovakia and the union of the State of Slovenes, Croats and Serbs and the Kingdom of Serbia as new states. However, this imposition of states where some nationalities (especially Poles, Czechs, and Serbs and Romanians) were given power over nationalities who disliked and distrusted them eventually helped lead to World War II. The defeated Ottoman empire was dissolved into the Republic of Turkey and several smaller nations, plus the new Middle East Allied "protectorates" of Syria, Palestine, Iraq and Yemen. The League of Nations was proposed as much as a means of consolidating these new states, as a path to peace.

During the 1920s and 1930s there were some successful movements for self-determination in the beginnings of the process of decolonisation. In the Statute of Westminster Great Britain granted independence to Canada, New Zealand, Newfoundland, the Irish Free State, the Commonwealth of Australia, and the Union of South Africa after the British parliament declared itself as incapable of passing laws over them without their consent. Egypt, Afghanistan and Iraq also achieved independence from Britain and Lebanon from France. Other efforts were unsuccessful, like the Indian independence movement. And Italy, Japan and Germany all initiated new efforts to bring certain territories under their control, leading to World War II.

The UN Charter

In 1941 Allies of World War II signed the Atlantic Charter and accepted the principle of self-determination. In January 1942 twenty-six nations signed the Declaration by United Nations, which accepted those principles. The ratification of the United Nations Charter in 1945 at the end of World War II placed the right of self-determination into the framework of international law and diplomacy.

- Chapter 1, Article 1, part 2 states that purpose of the UN Charter is: "To develop friendly relations among nations based on respect for the principle of equal rights and self-determination of peoples, and to take other appropriate measures to strengthen universal peace."
- Article 1 in both the International Covenant on Civil and Political Rights (ICCPR) and the International Covenant on

Economic, Social and Cultural Rights (ICESCR). Both read: "All peoples have the right of self-determination. By virtue of that right they freely determine their political status and freely pursue their economic, social and cultural development."

- The United Nations Universal Declaration of Human Rights article 15 states that everyone has the right to a nationality and that no one should be arbitrarily deprived of a nationality or denied the right to change nationality.

However, the charter and other resolutions did not insist on full independence as the best way of obtaining self-government, nor did they include an enforcement mechanism. Moreover, nations were recognised by the legal doctrine of uti possidetis juris, meaning that old administrative boundaries would become international boundaries upon independence, even if they had little relevance to linguistic, ethnic, and cultural boundaries. Nevertheless, justified by the language of self-determination, between 1946 and 1960, the peoples of thirty-seven new nations freed themselves from colonial status in Asia, Africa, and the Middle East. The territoriality issue inevitably would lead to more conflicts and independence movements within many nations and challenges to the assumption that territorial integrity is as important as self-determination.

The Soviet Union's successful post-war efforts to turn Eastern Germany and the countries of Eastern Europe into Soviet satellite states contrasted with decolonisation. The additional success of communists in creating the People's Republic of China led to the Cold War with western nations. These nations became willing to support authoritarian governments as long as they remained anti-communist and began to suspect all self-determinations movements of being communist-inspired or controlled. Thus the United States entered into a 10 year war in Vietnam, taking over from French colonialists, and supported Portugal in its attempts to hold on to Angola. The Soviet Union also violated principles of self-determination by suppressing the Hungarian revolution of 1956 and the Prague Spring Czechoslovak reforms of 1968. It invaded Afghanistan to support an increasingly unpopular communist government assailed by local tribal groups.

The Cold War began to wind down after Mikhail Gorbachev assumed power in March 1985. With the cooperation of U.S. president Ronald Reagan, Gorbachev wound down the size of the Soviet Armed Forces and reduced nuclear arms in Europe, while liberalising the economy. In 1989 in rapid succession, communist regimes collapsed in Poland, Hungary, Czechoslovakia, East Germany, and Romania. In December 1991, Gorbachev resigned as president and the Soviet Union dissolved relatively peacefully into fifteen sovereign republics, all of which rejected communism and most of which adopted democratic reforms and free-market economies. Yugoslavia began a much more violent break up in 1990.

Current Issues

Since the early 1990s, the legitimatisation of the principle of national self-determination has led to an increase in the number of conflicts within states, as sub-groups seek greater self-determination and even full secession, and as their conflicts for leadership within groups and with other groups and with the dominant state become violent. The international reaction to these new movements has been uneven and often dictated more by politics than principle. The year 2000 United Nations Millennium Declaration failed to deal with these new demands, mentioning only "the right to self-determination of peoples which remain under colonial domination and foreign occupation."

In an issue of Macquarie University Law Journal Associate professor Aleksandar Pavkovic and Senior Lecturer Peter Radan outlined current legal and political issues in self-determination. These include:

Defining "Peoples"

There is not yet a recognised legal definition of "peoples" in international law. Vita Gudeleviciute of Vytautas Magnus University Law School, reviewing international law and UN resolutions, finds in cases of non-self-governing peoples (colonised and/or indigenous) and foreign military occupation "a people" is the entire population of the occupied territorial unit, no matter their other differences. In cases where people lack representation by a state's government, the unrepresented become a separate people. Present international law does not recognise ethnic and other minorities as separate peoples. Other definitions offered are "peoples" being self-evident (from ethnicity, language, history, etc.), or defined by "ties of mutual affection or sentiment," i.e. "loyalty," or by mutual obligations among peoples. Or the definition may be simply that a people is a group of individuals who unanimously choose a separate state. If the "people" are unanimous in their desire for self-determination, it strengthens their claim. For example, the populations of federal units of the Yugoslav federation were considered a people in the breakup of Yugoslavia, even though some of those units had very diverse populations. Libertarians who argue for self-determination distinguish between the voluntary nation (the land, the culture, the terrain, the people) and the state, the coercive apparatus, which they have a right to choose or self-determine.

Self-determination *versus* Territorial Integrity

National self-determination challenges the principle of territorial integrity (or sovereignty) of states because it is the will of the people that makes a state legitimate. This implies a people should be free to choose their own state and its territorial boundaries. However, there are far more self-identified nations than there are existing states and there is no legal process to redraw state boundaries according to the will of these peoples.

Pavkovic and Radan describe three theories of international relations relevant to self-determination.

- The realist theory of international relations insists that territorial sovereignty is more important than national self-determination. This policy was pursued by the major powers during the Cold War.
- Liberal internationalism has become an alternative since that time. It promotes the abolition of war among states as well

as increased individual liberty within states, and holds the expansion of global markets and cross-border cooperation diminishes the significance of territorial integrity, allowing for somewhat greater recognition of greater self-determination of peoples.

- Cosmopolitan liberalism calls for political power to shift to a world government which would make secession and change of boundaries a relatively easy administrative matter. However, also would mean the de facto end of self-determination of national groups.

Allen Buchanan, author of seven books on self-determination and secession, supports territorial integrity as a moral and legal aspect of constitutional democracy. However, he also advances a "Remedial Rights Only Theory" where a group has "a general right to secede if and only if it has suffered certain injustices, for which secession is the appropriate remedy of last resort." He also would recognise secession if the state grants, or the constitution includes, a right to secede.

Vita Gudeleviciute holds that in cases of non-self-governing peoples and foreign military occupation the principle of self-determination trumps that of territorial integrity. In cases where people lack representation by a state's government, they also may be considered a separate people, but under current law cannot claim the right to self-determination. On the other hand, he finds that secession within a single state is a domestic matter not covered by international law. Thus there are no on what groups may constitute a seceding people.

Methods of Increasing Minority Rights

In order to accommodate demands for minority rights and avoid secession and the creation of a separate new state, many states decentralise or devolve greater decision-making power to new or existing subunits or even autonomous areas. More limited measures might include restricting demands to the maintenance of national cultures or granting non-territorial autonomy in the form of national associations which would assume control over cultural matters. This would be available only to groups that abandoned secessionist demands and the territorial state would retain political and judicial control, but only if would remain with the territorially organised state.

Self-determination *versus* Majority Rule/Equal Rights

Pavkoviæ explores how national self-determination, in the form of creation of a new state through secession, could override the principles of majority rule and of equal rights, which are primary liberal principles. This includes the question of how an unwanted state can be imposed upon a minority. He explores five contemporary theories of secession. In "anarcho-capitalist" theory only landowners have the right to secede. In communitarian theory, only those groups that desire direct or greater political participation have the right, including groups deprived of rights, per Allen Buchanan. In two nationalist theories, only national cultural groups have a right to secede. Australian professor Harry Beran's democratic theory endorses the equality of the right of secession to all types of groups. Unilateral secession against majority rule is justified if the group allows secession of any other group within its territory.

CONSTITUTIONAL LAW

Most sovereign states do not recognise the right to self-determination through secession in their constitutions. Many expressly forbid it. However, there are several existing models of self-determination through greater autonomy and through secession.

In liberal constitutional democracies the principle of majority rule has dictated whether a minority can secede. In the United States Abraham Lincoln acknowledged that secession might be possible through amending the United States Constitution. The Supreme Court in Texas *v* White, held secession could occur "through revolution, or through consent of the States." The British Parliament in 1933 held that Western Australia only could secede from Australia upon vote of a majority of the country as a whole; the previous two-thirds majority vote for secession via referendum in Western Australia was insufficient.

The Chinese Communist Party followed the Soviet Union in including the right of secession in its 1931 constitution in order to entice ethnic nationalities and Tibet into joining. However, once in control of the territories the party eliminated the right to secession from the constitution. The 1947 Constitution of the Union of Burma contained an express state right to secede from the union under a number of procedural conditions. It was eliminated in the 1974 constitution of the Socialist Republic of the Union of Burma (officially the "Union of Myanmar"). Burma still allows "local autonomy under central leadership."

As of 1996 the constitutions of Austria, Ethiopia, France, Singapore, Saint Kitts and Nevis Republics have express or implied rights to secession. Switzerland allows for the secession from current and the creation of new cantons. In the case of proposed Quebec separation from Canada the Supreme Court of Canada in 1998 ruled that only both a clear majority of the province and a constitutional amendment confirmed by all participants in the Canadian federation could allow secession.

The 2003 draft of the European Union Constitution allowed for the voluntary withdrawal of member states from the union. There was much discussion about such self-determination by minorities before the final document underwent the unsuccessful ratification process in 2005.

Drawing New Borders

Once groups exercise self-determination through secession, the issue of the proposed borders may prove more controversial than the fact of secession. The bloody Yugoslav wars in the 1990s were related mostly to borders issues because the international community applied a version of uti possidetis juris in transforming existing internal borders of the various Yugoslav republics into international borders, despite the conflicts of ethnic groups within those boundaries. The northern two-thirds of Quebec already has made it clear it will resist by force being incorporated into a Quebec nation.

The border between Northern Ireland and the Irish Free State was based on the borders of existing counties and did not include all of historic Ulster. A Boundary Commission was established to consider re-drawing it. Its proposals, which amounted to a small net transfer to Northern Ireland, were leaked to the press and then not acted upon. In December 1925, the governments of the Irish Free State, Northern Ireland, and the United Kingdom agreed to accept the existing border. Most Irish Nationalists and Irish Republicans claim all of Northern Ireland and are not particularly interested in new borders.

Current Movements

For past movements see list of historical autonomist and secessionist movements and lists of decolonised nations. Also see list of autonomous areas by country and list of territorial autonomies and list of active autonomist and secessionist movements.

Australia

Recently (2003 onwards), self-determination has become the topic of some debate in Australia in relation to Aborigines (indigenous Australians). In the 1970s, the Aboriginal community approached the Federal Government and requested the right to administer their own communities. This encompassed basic local government functions, ranging from land dealings and management of community centres to road maintenance and garbage collection, as well as setting education programmes and standards in their local schools.

Balochistan Province

Since 1948, Baloch nationalists in Pakistan, Iran, and Afghanistan have been seeking independence as a separate state for the Baloch people from elements outside the country. The movement has culminated in several armed uprisings in both Pakistan and Iran, that have been crushed, especially during the 1970s. The movement is strongest in Balochistan (Pakistan), where it is led by the Balochistan Liberation Army and the Baloch Students Organisation.

Basque Country

The Basque Country (Basque: *Euskal Herria*, Spanish: *País Vasco*, French: *Pays Basque*) as a cultural region (not to be confused with the homonym Autonomous Community of the Basque country) is a European region in the western Pyrenees that spans the border between France and Spain, on the Atlantic coast. It comprises the autonomous communities of the Basque Country and Navarre in Spain and then the Northern Basque Country in France. Since the 19th century, Basque nationalism has demanded the right of some kind of self-determination. This desire for independence is particularly stressed among leftist Basque nationalists. The right of self-determination was asserted by the Basque Parliament in 1990, 2002 and 2006. Since self-determination is not recognised in the Spanish Constitution of 1978, some Basques abstained and some even voted against it in the referendum of December 6 of that year. However, it was approved by a clear majority at the Spanish level, and simple majority at Navarrese and Basque levels. The derived autonomous regimes for the BAC was approved in later referendum but the autonomy of Navarre (*amejoramiento del fuero*: "improvement of the charter") was never subject to referendum but just approved by the Navarrese Cortes (parliament). There are not many sources on the issue for the French Basque country.

Euskadi Ta Askatasuna (ETA) Euskadi Ta Askatasuna or ETA (English: *Basque Homeland and Freedom*; pronounced [È[Ðta]), is an armed Basque nationalist and separatist organisation. Founded in 1959, it evolved from a group advocating traditional cultural ways to a paramilitary group with the goal of Basque independence. Its ideology is Marxist-Leninist.

Biafra

Biafra Republic was first declared in 1967 by Lt. Col Chukwuemeka Odumegwu Ojukwu but the state could only survive for 30 months during which Nigerian government fought the break-away republic to annex it. Over 3 million Igbos lost their lives in the ensuing war.

In 1999, a new group of activists formed an organisation Movement for the Actualisation of the Sovereign Republic of Biafra (MASSOB). Various other groups have been formed with similar agenda.

Catalan Countries

Països Catalans (in catalan, often literally translated into English as *Catalan Countries*) refers to the territories where Catalan language was historically spoken. These territories in the past were in the, talking in contemporary terms, Confederation of the Crown of Aragon (which included the Kingdom of Aragon, the Kingdom of Valencia, the Kingdom of Majorca, Sicily, Malta and Sardinia, and for a brief period, Provence, the Kingdom of Naples, the Duchy of Neopatria, and the Duchy of Athens.).

Nowadays there are a lot of movements which supports the independence of Catalan Countries from Spain and France. Some of the politic parties of Catalonia, Valencian community, and Balear islands that follow this idea are Republican Left of Catalonia and Republican Left of the Valencian Country, Estat Català, Partit Republicà Català, Popular Unity Candidates, Valencian Nationalist Bloc, Bloc per Mallorca,...etc. Furthermore, there are some other Catalan groups and movements that want the independence of Catalan Countries, such as: Sobirania i Progrés, Deu Mil per l'autodeterminació, Catalunya Estat Lliure , Sobirania Valenciana ,...etc. All these political parties and movements follow a non-violence way to express their ideas.

Chechnya

Under Dzhokkar Dudayev, Chechnya declared independence as the Chechen Republic of Ichkeria, using self-determination, Russia's history of bad treatment of Chechens, and a history of independence before belonging to Russia as main motives. Russia has now reconquered Chechnya, but the separatist government functions still in exile, though it has been split into two entities: the Achmed Zakayev-run pro-Western Chechen Republic (based in Poland, the UK and the US), and the Islamist-backed Caucasus Emirate.

Germany

Under conditions of peace and in democratic state the focus of German public addresses weaker topics, as especially the *Rights of informational self-determination*. This is a new topic in the context of surveillance of public areas and surveillance at work.

Israel and Palestine

The right to self-determination as outlined in public international law is often referenced by both sides in the ongoing Israel-Palestinian conflict.

Kosovo

Kosovo is a largely ethnic-Albanian nation (Albanians 88%, Serbs 6%, Bosniaks 3%, Roma 2%, Turks 1%. which seeks independence on territories long held by ethnic Serbs, including as part of Yugoslavia. Conflict between the two culminated in the 1996-1999 Kosovo War between the Kosovo Liberation Army (KLA) and the then Federal Republic of Yugoslavia led by Slobodan Miloševiæ. This culminated in the 1999 United States/NATO attacks on Serbia, withdrawal of Serbian troops and entry of the NATO Kosovo Force. International negotiations to determine the final status of Kosovo were unsuccessful. On 17 February 2008, 109 members (10 members including all Kosovo Serbs were absent) of the Kosovo Assembly voted unanimously for a unilateral declaration of independence. Serbia rejected the decision. Kosovo is independent, supervised by the international community following the conclusion of the political process to determine Kosovo's final status envisaged in UN Security Council Resolution 1244. As of April 2009, the independence of Kosovo has been recognised by 58 countries.

Kurdistan

Kurdistan is the land of the Kurdish people of the middle east. The territory is currently part of 4 states Turkey, Iraq, Syria and Iran. There are Kurdish self determination movements in each of the 4 states. Iraqi Kurdistan has to date achieved the largest degree of self-determination through the formation of the Kurdistan Regional Government, an entity recognised by the Iraqi Federal Constitution.

Although the right of the creation of a Kurdish state was recognised following World War I in the Treaty of Sèvres, the treaty was then annulled by the Treaty of Lausanne. To date two separate Kurdish republics and one Kurdish Kingdom have declared sovereignty. The Republic of Ararat (Northern Kurdistan/Eastern Turkey), the Republic of Mehabad (Eastern Kurdistan/Iranian Kurdistan) and the Kingdom of Kurdistan (Southern Kurdistan/Northern Iraq), each of these fledgling states was crushed by military intervention. The Patriotic Union of Kurdistan which currently holds the Iraqi presidency and the Kurdistan Democratic Party which governs the Kurdistan Regional Government both explicitly commit themselves to the development of Kurdish self-determination.

Jammu and Kashmir

There is a democratic movement for independence from both Indian and Pakistani rule led by the Hurriyat Conference, realising the pre-1948 state of Jammu and Kashmir which want the application of the UN Resolutions calling for plebiscite in Kashmir. Hurriyat Conference in Jammu and Kashmir are currently trying to seek full independence for the whole region from India, Pakistan and China on the claim of its right to self-determination. Indian armed forces and the Pakistani ISI stand accused of aggression and violation of human rights of ordinary citizens of Kashmir and neglecting the development of Northern Areas respectively.

New Zealand

Secession movements have surfaced several times in the South Island of New Zealand. The Premier of New Zealand, Sir Julius Vogel, was amongst the first people to make this call,, which was voted on by the Parliament of New Zealand as early as 1865. The desire for South Island independence was one of the main factors in moving the capital of New Zealand from Auckland to Wellington that year.

The South Island Party with a pro-South agenda, fielded candidates in the 1999 General Election and a new South Island Party was formed before the 2008 General Election. Today, the question of South Island Independence remains a matter of public debate rather than a political issue.

Taiwan

Taiwan is the focus of a self-determination dispute in the East Asia region. The government of the People's Republic of China claims the entirety of Taiwan as its territory. However, Taiwanese independence advocates argue that there is no legal claim to Taiwan, as no legally binding treaty ever transferred sovereignty to China following World War II, an assertion that both the People's Republic of China and the Republic of China disagree with. At the same time, the *de facto* government of Taiwan, the Republic of China still has not formally withdrawn its claims to the mainland and several other areas. In practice, however, this claim essentially died off through the 1990s and is no longer pressed by Taiwan's elected government.

Turkish Cypriots

Since Turkey's invaision and continued occupation of Cyprus in 1974, following ethnic clashes and turmoil on the island, an administration recognised by Turkey only was declared in 1983 – the Turkish Republic of Northern Cyprus. It is questionable whether it is the Turkish Cypriot community who claimed the right of self-determination in ending their partnership with the Republic of Cyprus given that they are greatly out-numbered by the Turkish settlers who were brought to the area by Turkey.

United States

The colonisation of the North American continent and its Native American population has been the source of legal battles since the early 1800s. Surviving Native American were resettled to separate tracts of land (reservations) which have been given a certain degree of autonomy within the United States federal government.

The Chicano Movement (or Chicano nation) seeks to recreate Aztlán, the legendary homeland of the Aztecs comprising the Southwestern United States which is home to the majority of Mexican Americans.

There is an active Hawaiian sovereignty movement which aims at rectifying the overthrow of the Hawaiian monarchy in the late 19th century which resulted in the incorporation of Hawai'i into the United States.

Since 1972, the U.N. Decolonisation Committee has called for Puerto Rico's decolonisation and for the U.S. to recognise the island's right to self-determination and independence. In 2007 the Decolonisation Subcommittee called for the United Nations General Assembly to review the political status of Puerto Rico, a power reserved by the 1953 Resolution. This follows the 1967 passage of a plebiscite Act that provided for a vote on the status of Puerto Rico with three status options: continued commonwealth, statehood, and independence. In the first plebscite the commonwealth option won with 60.4% of the votes but U.S. congressional committees failed to enact legislation to address the status issue. In subsequent plebiscites in 1993 and 1998 the status quo was upheld.

Many current U.S. state, regional and city secession groups use the language of self-determination. A 2008 Zogby International poll revealed that 22% of Americans believe that "any state or region has the right to peaceably secede and become an independent republic."

Sri Lanka

The Sri Lankan Tamils people seek self-determination due to claimed discrimination by the majority Sinhala government's so called institutionalised discrimination in language, education, jobs, and civil liberties. The early non violent protests developed into a violent confrontation with the state and eventual civil war.

Right to Work

The right to work is the concept that people have a human right to work, and may not be prevented from doing so. The right to work is enshrined in the Universal Declaration of Human Rights and recognised in international human rights law through its inclusion in the International Covenant on Economic, Social and Cultural Rights, where the right to work emphasises economic, social and cultural development.

Human Right

Article 23.1 of the Universal Declaration of Human Rights states:

> "Everyone has the right to work, to free choice of employment, to just and favourable conditions of work and to protection against unemployment."

The International Covenant on Economic, Social and Cultural Rights elaborates the right to work in the context of individual freedoms and economic, social and cultural development. The Covenant also elaborates the role of the state in realising this human right. Article 6 states:

> "(1) The State Parties to the present Covenant recognise the right to work, which includes the right of everyone to the opportunity to gain his living by work which he freely chooses or accepts, and will take appropriate steps to safeguard this right. (2) The steps to be taken by a State party to the present Covenant to achieve the full realisation of this right shall include technical and vocational guidance and training programmes, policies and techniques to achieve steady economic, social and cultural development and full and productive employment under conditions safeguarding fundamental political and economic freedoms to the individual."

The African Charter on Human and Peoples' Rights also recognises the right, emphasising conditions and pay, i.e. labour rights. Article 15, states:

> "Every individual shall have the right to work under equitable and satisfactory conditions, and shall receive equal pay for equal work."

Soviet Union

The 1977 Soviet Constitution also emphasises conditions of work, or labor rights, and revered to economic, social and cultural development. Article 40 stated:

> "Citizens of the USSR have the right to rest and leisure. This right is ensured by the establishment of a working week not exceeding 41 hours, for workers and other employees, a shorter working day in a number of trades and industries, and shorter hours for night work; by the provision of paid annual holidays, weekly days of rest, extension of the network of cultural, educational, and health-building institutions, and the development on a mass scale of sport, physical culture, and camping and tourism; by the provision of neighbourhood recreational facilities, and of other opportunities for rational use of free time. The length of collective farmers' working and leisure time is established by their collective farms."

Criticism

Paul Lafargue, in The Right to Be Lazy, wrote: "And to think that the sons of the heroes of the Terror have allowed themselves to be degraded by the religion of work, to the point of accepting, since 1848, as a revolutionary conquest, the law limiting factory labour to twelve hours. They proclaim as a revolutionary principle the Right to Work. Shame to the French proletariat! Only slaves would have been capable of such baseness." ◆

11
Economic Freedom

Economic freedom is a term used in economic research and policy debates. As with freedom generally, there are various definitions, but no universally accepted concept of economic freedom. One major approach to economic freedom comes from the libertarian tradition emphasising free markets and private property, while another extends the welfare economics study of individual choice, with greater economic freedom coming from a "larger" (in some technical sense) set of possible choices. Another more philosophical perspective emphasises its context in distributive justice and basic freedoms of all individuals.

Today the term is most commonly associated with a classical liberal (or free market) viewpoint, and defined as the freedom to produce, trade and consume any goods and services acquired without the use of force, fraud or theft. This is embodied in the rule of law, property rights and freedom of contract, and characterised by external and internal openness of the markets, the protection of property rights and freedom of economic initiative.

Indices of economic freedom attempt to measure (free market) economic freedom, and empirical studies based on these rankings have found them to be correlated with higher living standards, economic growth, income equality, less corruption and less political violence. These economic freedom indices are sometimes used to rank countries by economic freedom, and are usually topped by Hong Kong and Singapore. Between 1985 and 2005, only a small number of surveyed countries did not increase their *Economic Freedom of the World* score. Some empirical analysis suggests that the index is not closely correlated with economic growth, but regression analysis of the disaggregated components suggests that some specific freedoms contribute to economic growth while others hamper it.

Other conceptions of economic freedom include freedom from want and the freedom to engage in collective bargaining.

CLASSICAL LIBERAL VIEWPOINT

Classical liberals argue that the rule of law both requires, and is required for economic freedom. Friedrich Hayek argued that the certainty of law contributed to the prosperity of the West more that any other single factor. Other important principles of the rule of law are the generality and equality of the law, which require that all legal rules apply equally to everybody. These principles can be seen as safeguards against severe restrictions on liberty, because they require that all laws equally apply to those with political and coercive power as well as those who are governed. Principles of the generality and equality of the law exclude special privileges and arbitrary application of law, that is laws favouring one group at the expense of other citizens. According to Friedrich Hayek, equality before the law is incompatible with any activity of the government aiming to achieve the material equality of different people. He asserts that a state's attempt to place people in the same (or similar) material position leads to an unequal treatment of individuals and to a compulsory redistribution of income. Both of those actions are contributing to a decline in economic freedom.

PRIVATE PROPERTY RIGHTS

According to the classical liberal view, a secure system of private property rights is an essential part of economic freedom. Such systems include two main rights: the right to control and benefit from property and the right to transfer property by voluntary means. These rights offer people the possibility of autonomy and self-determination according to theirs personal values and goals. Economist Milton Friedman sees property rights as "the most basic of human rights and an essential foundation for other human rights." With property rights protected, people are free to choose the use of their property, earn on it, and transfer it to anyone else, as long as they do it on a voluntary basis and do not resort to force, fraud or theft. In such conditions most people can achieve much greater personal freedom and development than under a regime of government coercion. A secure system of property rights also reduces uncertainty and encourages investments, creating favorable conditions for an economy to be successful. Empirical evidence suggests that countries with strong property rights systems have economic growth rates almost twice as high as those of countries with weak property rights systems, and that a market system with significant private property rights is an essential condition for democracy. According to Hernando de Soto, much of the poverty in the Third World countries is caused by the lack of Western systems of laws and well-defined and universally recognised property rights. De Soto argues that because of the legal barriers poor people in those countries cannot utilise their assets to produce more wealth. Pierre Proudhon, a socialist and anarchist thinker, argued that property is both theft and freedom.

Freedom of Contract

Freedom of contract is the right to choose one's contracting parties and to trade with them on any terms and conditions one sees fit. Contracts permit individuals to create their own enforceable legal rules, adapted to their unique situations. Parties decide whether contracts are profitable or fair, but once a contract is made they are obliged to fulfil its terms, even if they are going to sustain losses by doing so. Through making binding promises people are free to pursue their own interests. The main economic function of contracts is to provide transferability of property rights. Transferability largely depends on the enforceability of contracts, which is enabled by the judicial system. In Western societies the state does not enforce all types of contracts, and in some cases it intervenes by prohibiting certain arrangements, even if they are made between willing parties. However, not all contracts need to be enforced by the state. For example, in the United States there is a large number of third-party arbitration tribunals which resolve disputes under private commercial law. Negatively understood, freedom of contract is freedom from government interference and from imposed value judgments of fairness. The notion of "freedom of contract" was given one of its most famous legal expressions in 1875 by Sir George Jessel MR:

> *If there is one thing more than another public policy requires it is that men of full age and competent understanding shall have the utmost liberty of contracting, and that their contracts when entered into freely and voluntarily shall be held sacred and shall be enforced by courts of justice. Therefore, you have this paramount public policy to consider – that you are not lightly to interfere with this freedom of contract.*

Economic and Political Freedom

Some classical liberals argue that political and civil liberties have simultaneously expanded with market-based economies, and present empirical evidence to support the claim that economic and political freedoms are linked.

In *Capitalism and Freedom* (1962), Friedman developed the argument that economic freedom, while itself an extremely important component of total freedom, is also a necessary condition for political freedom. He commented that centralised control of economic activities was always accompanied with political repression. In his view, voluntary character of all transactions in a free market economy and wide diversity that it permits are fundamental threats to repressive political leaders and greatly diminish power to coerce. Through elimination of centralised control of economic activities, economic power is separated from political power, and the one can serve as counterbalance to the other. Friedman feels that competitive capitalism is especially important to minority groups, since impersonal market forces protect people from discrimination in their economic activities for reasons unrelated to their productivity.

In *The Road to Serfdom*, Hayek argued that "Economic control is not merely control of a sector of human life which can be separated from the rest; it is the control of the means for all our ends." Hayek criticised socialist policies as the slippery slope that can lead to totalitarianism. Gordon Tullock has argued that "the Hayek-Friedman argument" predicted totalitarian governments in much of Europe in the late 20th century. He uses Sweden, in which the government at that time controlled 63 percent of GNP, as an example to support his argument that the basic problem with *The Road to Serfdom* is "that it offered predictions which turned out to be false. The steady advance of government in places such as Sweden has not led to any loss of non-economic freedoms." While criticising Hayek, Tullock still praises the classical liberal notion of economic freedom, saying, "Arguments for political freedom are strong, as are the arguments for economic freedom. We needn't make one set of arguments depend on the other." However, according to Robert Skidelsky, Hayek "safeguarded himself from such retrospective refutation." Skidelsky argues that Hayek's argument was contingent, and that, "By the 1970s there was some evidence of the slippery slope...and then there was Thatcher. Hayek's warning played a critical part in her determination to 'roll back the state.'"

Austrian School economist Ludwig von Mises argued that economic and political freedom were mutually dependent: "The idea that political freedom can be preserved in the absence of economic freedom, and vice versa, is an illusion. Political freedom is the corollary of economic freedom. It is no accident that the age of capitalism became also the age of government by the people."

Walter E. Williams argues that economic freedom is not necessarily associated with political freedom, noting the example of Singapore, which is highly ranked on measures of economic freedom and little political freedom.

Indices of Economic Freedom

The annual surveys *Economic Freedom of the World* (EFW) and *Index of Economic Freedom* (IEF) are two indices which attempt to measure the degree of economic freedom in the world's nations. The EFW index, originally developed by Gwartney, Lawson and Block at the Fraser Institute was likely the most used in empirical studies as of 2000. The other major major index, which was developed by the Heritage Institute and the Wall Street Journal appears superior for data work, although as it only goes back to 1995, it is less useful for historical comparisons.

According to the creators of the indices, these rankings correlate strongly with higher average income per person, higher income of the poorest 10%, higher life expectancy, higher literacy, lower infant mortality, higher access to water sources and less corruption. The people living in the top one-fifth of countries enjoy an average income of $23,450 and a growth rate in the 1990s of 2.56 percent per year; in contrast, the bottom one-fifth in the rankings had an average income of just $2,556 and a -0.85 percent growth rate in the 1990s. The poorest 10 percent of the population have an average income of just $728 in the lowest ranked countries compared with over $7,000 in the highest ranked countries. The life expectancy of people living in the highest ranked nations is 20 years longer than for people in the lowest ranked countries.

Higher economic freedom, as measured by both the Heritage and the Fraser indices, correlates strongly with higher self-reported happiness.

Erik Gartzke of the Fraser Institute estimates that countries with a high EFW are significantly less likely to be involved in wars, while his measure of democracy had little or no impact.

The *Economic Freedom of the World* score for the entire world has grown considerably in recent decades. The average score has increased from 5.17 in 1985 to 6.4 in 2005. Of the nations in 1985, 95 nations increased their score, seven saw a decline, and six were unchanged. Using the 2008 Index of Economic Freedom methodology world economic freedom has increased 2.6 points since 1995.

Members of the World Bank Group also use *Index of Economic Freedom* as the indicator of investment climate, because it covers more aspects relevant to the private sector in wide number of countries.

Worldwide index of economic freedom 2009 - top and bottom 15 rankings

published by The Wall Street Journal and the Heritage Foundation

Rank	*Country*	*Freedom %*	*Rank*	*Country*	*Freedom %*
1	Hong Kong	90	143	Guinea-Bissau	45.4
2	Singapore	87.1	144	Congo, Republic of	45.4
3	Australia	82.6	145	Belarus	45
4	Ireland	82.2	146	Iran	44.6
5	New Zealand	82	147	Turkmenistan	44.2
6	United States	80.7	148	São Tomé and Príncipe	43.8
7	Canada	80.5	149	Libya	43.5
8	Denmark	79.6	150	Comoros	43.3
9	Switzerland	79.4	151	Congo, Demo.Republic	42.8
10	United Kingdom	79	152	Venezuela	39.9
11	Chile	78.3	153	Eritrea	38.5
12	Netherlands	77	154	Burma	37.7
13	Estonia	76.4	155	Cuba	27.9
14	Iceland	75.9	156	Zimbabwe	27.2
15	Luxembourg	75.2	157	Korea, North	2

The nature of economic freedom is often in dispute. Some economists, socialists and anarchists contend that the existing indicators of economic freedom are too narrowly defined, and should take into account a broader conception of economic freedoms. Critics of the indices (e.g. Thom Hartmann) also oppose the inclusion business-related measures like corporate charters and intellectual property protection. John Miller in Dollars & Sense has stated that the indices are "a poor barometer of either freedom more broadly construed or of prosperity." He argues that the high correlation between living standards and economic freedom as measured by IEF is the result of choices made in the construction of the index that guarantee this result. For example, the treatment of a large informal sector (common in poor countries) as an indicator of restrictive government policy, and the use of the change in the ratio of government spending to national income, rather than the level of this ratio. Hartman argues that these choices cause the social democratic European countries to rank higher than countries where the government share of the economy is small but growing.

Economists Dani Rodrik and Jeffrey Sachs have separately noted that there appears to be little correlation between measured economic freedom and economic growth when the least free countries are disregarded, as indicated by the strong growth of the Chinese economy in recent years. Morris Altman found that there is a relatively large correlation between economic freedom and both per capita income and per capita growth. He argues that this is especially true when it comes to sub-indices relating to property rights and sound money, while he calls into question the importance of sub-indices relating to labor regulation and big government once certain threshold values are passed. John Miller further observes that Hong Kong and Singapore, both only "partially free" according to Freedom House, are leading countries on both economic freedom indices and casts doubt on the claim that measured economic freedom is associated with political freedom . However, according to the Freedom House, "there is a high and statistically significant correlation between the level of political freedom as measured by Freedom House and economic freedom as measured by the Wall Street Journal/Heritage Foundation survey."

Alternative Views of Economic Freedom

Franklin D. Roosevelt included freedom from want in his Four freedoms speech. Roosevelt stated that freedom from want "translated into world terms, means economic understandings which will secure to every nation a healthy peacetime life for its inhabitants-everywhere in the world". In terms of US policy, Roosevelt's New Deal included economic freedoms such as freedom of trade union organisation, as well as a wide range of policies of government intervention and redistributive taxation aimed at promoting freedom from want. Internationally, Roosevelt favored the policies associated with the

Bretton Woods Agreement which fixed exchange rates and established international economic institutions such as the World Bank and International Monetary Fund.

Herbert Hoover saw economic freedom as a fifth freedom, which secures survival of Roosevelt's Four freedoms. He described economic freedom as freedom "for men to choose their own calling, to accumulate property in protection of their children and old age, freedom of enterprise that does not injure others."

Positive and Negative Freedom

The differences between alternative views of economic freedom have been expressed in terms of Isaiah Berlin's distinction between positive freedom and negative freedom. Classical liberals favour a focus on negative freedom as did Berlin himself. By contrast Amartya Sen argues for an understanding of freedom in terms of capabilities to pursue a range of goals. One measure which attempts to assess freedom in the positive sense is Goodin, Rice, Parpo, and Eriksson's measure of discretionary time, which is an estimate of how much time people have at their disposal during which they are free to choose the activities in which they participate, after taking into account the time they need to spend acquiring the necessities of life.

Freedom of Association and Union Organisation

The Philadelphia Declaration "Constitution of the International Labour Organisation". of the International Labour Organisation states that "all human beings, irrespective of race, creed or sex, have the right to pursue both their material well-being and their spiritual development in conditions of freedom and dignity, of economic security and equal opportunity". The ILO further states that "The right of workers and employers to form and join organisations of their own choosing is an integral part of a free and open society."

Political Freedom

Political freedom can be described as the absence of interference with the sovereignty of an individual by the use of coercion or aggression, a definition which is also known as negative liberty. Political freedom can also be described as having the power and resources to act to fulfil one's own potential, as in the definition of positive liberty. Presumably within both definitions, the members of a free society have full dominion over their public and private lives but positive liberty addresses the notion of human agency, whereas, the definition attributed to negative liberty addresses only an individual's actions and not his/her social circumstances.

The opposite of a free society would be a totalitarian state, which highly restricts political freedom in order to regulate almost every aspect of behavior. In this sense 'freedom' refers solely to the relation of humans to other humans, and the only infringement on it is coercion by humans, as suggested within the definition of negative liberty.

Types

The concept of political freedom is very closely allied with the concepts of civil liberties and individual rights, which in most democratic societies is the profession characterised by various freedoms which are afforded the legal protection of the state. Some of these freedoms may include (in alphabetical order):

- Freedom of assembly
- Freedom of association
- Freedom of education
- Freedom of movement
- Freedom of religion
- Freedom of speech
- Freedom of the press
- Freedom of thought
- Freedom from unreasonable searches and seizures, which is related to freedom of privacy
- Freedom to bear arms

- Intellectual freedom
- Sexual freedom
- Suffrage

Views

Various groups along the political spectrum naturally differ on what they believe constitutes "true" political freedom.

Left wing political philosophy generally couples the notion of freedom with that of positive liberty, or the enabling of an individual to realize his or her own potential. Freedom, in this sense, may include freedom from poverty, starvation, treatable disease, and oppression, as well as freedom from force and coercion, from whomever they may issue.

However, Friedrich Hayek, a well-known classical liberal, criticised this as a misconception of freedom, instead emphasising the aspects of negative liberty.

the use of 'liberty' to describe the physical 'ability to do what I want', the power to satisfy our wishes, or the extent of the choice of alternatives open to us...has been deliberately fostered as part of the socialist argument... Once this identification of freedom with power is admitted, there is no limit to the sophisms by which the attractions of the word 'liberty' can be used to support measures which destroy individual liberty, no end to the tricks by which people can be exhorted in the name of liberty to give up their liberty. It has been with the help of this equivocation that the notion of collective power over circumstances has been substituted for that of individual liberty and that in totalitarian states liberty has been suppressed in the name of liberty.

Hayek also famously noted that "liberty" and "freedom" have probably been the most abused words in recent history.

Milton Friedman, another classical liberal, strongly incorporated the absence from coercion into his description of political freedom.

The essence of political freedom is the absence of coercion of one man by his fellow men. The fundamental danger to political freedom is the concentration of power. The existence of a large measure of power in the hands of a relatively few individuals enables them to use it to coerce their fellow men. Preservation of freedom requires either the elimination of power where that is possible or its dispersal where it cannot be eliminated.

Many social anarchists see negative and positive liberty as complementary concepts of freedom. They describe the negative liberty-centric view endorsed by capitalists as "selfish freedom". According to Anarchism FAQ:

The right-libertarian does not address or even acknowledge that the (absolute) right of private property may lead to extensive control by property owners over those who use, but do not own, property (such as workers and tenants). Thus a free-market capitalist system leads to a very selective and class-based protection of "rights" and "freedoms." For example, under capitalism, the "freedom" of employers inevitably conflicts with the "freedom" of employees. When stockholders or their managers exercise their "freedom of enterprise" to decide how their company will operate, they violate their employee's right to decide how their labouring capacities will be utilised. In other words, under capitalism, the "property rights" of employers will conflict with and restrict the "human right" of employees to manage themselves. Capitalism allows the right of self-management only to the few, not to all. Or, alternatively, capitalism does not recognise certain human rights as universal which anarchism does.

Some people treat freedom as if it were almost synonymous with democracy, while other people see conflicts or even opposition between the two concepts. For example, some people argue that Iraq was free under Paul Bremer on the grounds that it was a rational, humanist, non-subjugating government, long before elections were held. Others have argued that Iraq was free under Saddam Hussein because Iraq was not a colony, while a third one's claim is that neither dictatorial nor colonial rule in Iraq are examples of political freedom.

Environmentalists often argue that political freedoms should include some constraint on use of ecosystems. They maintain there is no such thing, for instance, as "freedom to pollute" or "freedom to deforest" given that such activities create negative externalities. The popularity of SUVs, golf, and urban sprawl has been used as evidence that some ideas of freedom and ecological conservation can clash. This leads at times to serious confrontations and clashes of values reflected in advertising campaigns, e.g. that of PETA regarding fur.

There have been numerous philosophical debates over the nature of freedom, the claimed differences between various types of freedom, and the extent to which freedom is desirable. Determinists argue that all human actions are pre-determined and thus freedom is an illusion. Isaiah Berlin saw a distinction between negative liberty and positive liberty.

In jurisprudence, freedom is the right to determine one's own actions autonomously; generally it is granted in those fields in which the subject has no obligations to fulfil or laws to obey, according to the interpretation that the hypothetical natural unlimited freedom is limited by the law for some matters.

Joseph Garcia (not the politician) states his belief that freedom in politics is generally used as a governing tool: "For what we call freedom is given only to those who obey, it is then when you stand for what you believe and fight back against oppression you lose those freedoms, and when what is taken away should be your inalienable rights what choice does one have but to obey?"

FREEDOM OF ASSEMBLY

Freedom of assembly, sometimes used interchangeably with the freedom of association, is the individual right to come together with other individuals and collectively express, promote, pursue and defend common interests. The right to freedom of association is recognized as a human right, a political freedom and a civil liberty.

Freedom of assembly and freedom of association may be used to distinguish between the freedom to assemble in public places and the freedom of joining an association. Freedom of assembly is often used in the context of the right to protest, while freedom of association is used in the context of labor rights and the right to collective bargaining, for example by joining a trade union. Freedom of assembly as guaranteed in the Canadian Constitution and the Constitution of the United States are interpreted to mean both the freedom to assemble and the freedom to join an association.

Human Rights Instruments

The freedom of assembly is enshrined in the following human rights instruments:

- Universal Declaration of Human Rights - Article 20
- International Covenant on Civil and Political Rights - Article 21
- European Convention of Human Rights - Article 11
- American Convention on Human Rights - Article 15. ◆

12
Freedom of Movement

Freedom of movement, mobility rights or the right to travel is a human rights concept which is respected in the constitutions of numerous states. It asserts that a citizen of a state, in which that citizen is present, generally has the right to leave that state, travel wherever the citizen is welcome, and, with proper documentation, return to that state at any time; and also (of equal or greater importance) to travel to, reside in, and/or work in, any part of the state the citizen wishes without interference from the state. Some immigrants' rights advocates assert that human beings have a fundamental human right to mobility not only across states but across nations. Ray Ybarra, an immigrants rights activist and filmmaker, coined the concept of human mobility to apply to international freedom of movement. According to Ybarra, human mobility is a fundamental human right.

Common Limitations

Nevertheless, restrictions on international freedom of movement (immigration or emigration) are commonplace. Within countries, freedom of movement is often more limited for minors, and penal law can modify this right as it applies to persons charged with or convicted of crimes (for instance, parole, probation, registration). In some countries, freedom of movement has historically been limited for women, and for members of disfavoured racial and social groups. Circumstances, both legal and practical, may operate to limit this freedom. For example, a nation that is generally permissive with respect to travel may restrict that right during time of war. In some instances, the laws of a nation may assert a guarantee of this right, but lawless conditions may make unfettered movement impossible. In other instances, a nation whose written laws codify such rights may fail to actually provide them. Other common political-legal restrictions on freedom of movement are:

- national and regional official minimum wage tariff barriers to labour market entry (free movement or migration of workers);
- official identity cards (internal passports, citizenship licenses) that must be carried and produced on demand;
- obligations on persons to register change of address or partner with the state authorities;
- protectionist local-regional barriers to housebuilding and therefore settlement in particular districts; and
- road toll barriers to the free movement of persons by motor cars.

Freedom of Movement between Private Parties

Freedom of movement is not construed as a right to permit an individual to enter private property of another. Such an unauthorised entry constitutes a trespass, often punishable as a tort or a crime, for which the private landowner can summon public officials to remove a trespasser from the landowner's property. In some jurisdictions, questions have arisen as to the extent to which a private owner of land can exclude certain persons from land used for public purposes, such as a shopping mall or a park. There is also a rule of law that a landowner whose property is completely boxed in by that of other private landowners shall have the right to cross private land if that is necessary to reach a public thoroughfare. The concept is also used as the basis for enacting laws to prevent alternate use of streets, roads and right-of-ways from blocking or restricting freedom of movement such as block parties and playing basketball.

There is a converse duty for a private person not to impede the free movement of another. Where a person prevents another from freely leaving an area, either by physically imprisoning them or by threats, that person may be subject to a lawsuit for false imprisonment, and to criminal charges for kidnapping.

Exit restrictions in certain countries

Some countries, such as the defunct Soviet Union, required that their citizens, and sometimes foreign travellers, obtain an exit visa in order to be allowed to leave the country. Currently, foreign students in Russia are issued only an entry visa on being accepted to University there, and must obtain an exit visa to return home.

Citizens of the People's Republic of China who are residents of the mainland are required to apply for special permits in order to enter the Special Administrative Regions of Hong Kong and Macau (and SAR residents require a Home Return Permit to visit the mainland).

Saudi Arabia requires all resident foreigners, but not citizens, to obtain an exit visa before leaving the kingdom.

Sometimes restrictions are placed on leaving that are specific to the intended destination. In the United States travel to Cuba is restricted with the ostensible goal of putting pressure on Cuba by denying it income from American travellers.

History

When Augustus established the Roman Empire in 27 BC, he assumed monarchical powers over the new Roman province of Egypt and was able to prohibit Senators from travelling there without his permission. However, Augustus would also allow more liberty to travel at times. During a famine in 6 AD, he attempted to relieve strain on the food supply by granting senators the liberty to leave Rome and to travel to wherever they wished.

In England in 1215, the right to travel was enshrined in Article 42 of the Magna Carta:

It shall be lawful to any person, for the future, to go out of our kingdom, and to return, safely and securely, by land or by water, saving his allegiance to us, unless it be in time of war, for some short space, for the common good of the kingdom: excepting prisoners and outlaws, according to the laws of the land, and of the people of the nation at war against us, and Merchants who shall be treated as it is said above.

After World War II, the United Nations was established. The new international organisation recognised the importance of freedom of movement through documents such as the Universal Declaration of Human Rights (1948) and the International Covenant on Civil and Political Rights (1966). Article 13 of the Universal Declaration of Human Rights, adopted by the U.N. General Assembly, reads,

> (1) Everyone has the right to freedom of movement and residence within the borders of each State.
>
> (2) Everyone has the right to leave any country, including his own, and to return to his country.

Article 12 of the International Covenant on Civil and Political Rights incorporates this right into treaty law:

> (1) Everyone lawfully within the territory of a State shall, within that territory, have the right to liberty of movement and freedom to choose his residence.
>
> (2) Everyone shall be free to leave any country, including his own.
>
> (3) The above-mentioned rights shall not be subject to any restrictions except those which are provided by law, are necessary to protect national security, public order (ordre public), public health or morals or the rights and freedoms of others, and are consistent with the other rights recognized in the present Covenant.
>
> (4) No one shall be arbitrarily deprived of the right to enter his own country.

The ICCPR entered into force for the initial ratifying states on 23 March 1976, and for additional states following their ratification.

In 1999, the U.N. Human Rights Committee, which is charged with interpreting the treaty, issued its guidelines for Article 12 of the ICCPR in its "General Comment No. 27: Freedom of Movement".

INSTITUTIONAL LAWS BY REGION

Africa

Freedom of movement laws and restrictions vary from country to country on the African continent, however several international agreements beyond those proscribed by the United Nations govern freedom of movement within the African continent. The African Charter on Human and People's Rights, Article 12, guarantees that every individual will have the right to freedom of movement within the borders of their own state so long as they abide by the states laws.The Charter also recognises the right to leave and return to one's country at will, barring concerns of national security, public health, or a threat to the general population. The charter also prevents the mass expulsion of entire groups of people. However, these laws are not necessarily followed or enforced, as evidenced recently by the genocide and mass expulsion in Sudan. There have been attempts to have intellectuals recognized as having special freedom of movement rights, to protect their intellectual ideals as they cross national boundaries.

The Constitution of South Africa also contains express freedoms of movement, in Section 21 of Chapter 2. Freedom of movement is guaranteed to "everyone" in regard to leaving the country but is limited to citizens when entering it or staying in it. Citizens also have a right to a passport.

India

Freedom to move freely throughout the territory of India though reasonable restrictions can be imposed on this right in the interest of the general public, for example, restrictions may be imposed on movement and traveling, so as to control epidemics.

Freedom to reside and settle in any part of the territory of India which is also subject to reasonable restrictions by the State in the interest of the general public or for the protection of the scheduled tribes because certain safeguards as are envisaged here seem to be justified to protect indigenous and tribal peoples from exploitation and coercion.

Burma/Myanmar

The military regime in Burma has been criticised for allegations of restrictions to freedom of movement. These include restrictions on movement by political dissidents, women, and migrant workers. Burmese passports contain a microchip embedded in them which carries identifying information about the passport holder. UN special envoy Razali Ismail, part owner of Iris corporation which won the contract to install the new system, dismissed any security concerns, and said, "Must you think of things in such sinister terms? Anyway, it's only for those people who want to travel outside. In most cases, those will be government people."

Canada

The Constitution of Canada contains mobility rights expressly in section 6 of the Canadian Charter of Rights and Freedoms. The rights specified include the right of citizens to leave and enter the country and the right of both citizens and permanent residents to move within its boundaries. However, the subsections protect poorer regions' affirmative action programmes that favour residents who have lived in the region for longer. Section 6 mobility rights are among the select rights that cannot be limited by the Charter's notwithstanding clause.

Canada's Social Union Framework Agreement, an agreement between governments made in 1999, affirms that "All governments believe that the freedom of movement of Canadians to pursue opportunities anywhere in Canada is an essential element of Canadian citizenship." In the Agreement, it is pledged that "Governments will ensure that no new barriers to mobility are created in new social policy initiatives."

European Union

Within the European Union, residents are guaranteed the right to freely move within the EU's internal borders by the EC Treaty and the European Parliament and Council Directive 2004/38/EC of 29 April 2004. Union residents are given the right to enter any member state for up to three months with a valid passport or identity card. If the citizen does not have a travel document, the member state must afford them every facility in obtaining the documents. Under no circumstances can an entry or exit visa be required. There are some security limitations and public policy restrictions on extended stays by EU residents. For instance, a member state may require that persons register their presence in the country "within a reasonable and non-discriminatory period of time". In general, however, the burden of notification and justification lies with the state. EU citizens also earn a right to permanent residence in member states they have maintained an uninterrupted five year period of legal residence. This residency cannot be subject to any conditions, and is lost only by two successive years absence from the host nation. Family members of EU residents, in general, also acquire the same freedom of travel rights as the resident they accompany, though they may be subject to a short-stay visa requirement. Furthermore, no EU citizen may be declared permanently *persona non grata* within the European Union, or permanently excluded from entry by any member state.

Hong Kong

Under Basic Law of Hong Kong article 31, "Hong Kong residents shall have freedom of movement within the Hong Kong Special Administrative Region and freedom of emigration to other countries and regions. They shall have freedom to travel and to enter or leave the Region. Unless restrained by law, holders of valid travel documents shall be free to leave the Region without special authorisation."

Ireland

In Ireland, the Thirteenth Amendment of the Constitution of Ireland was adopted in November 1992 by a plebiscite of the Irish people in order to ensure the freedom of movement in the specific circumstance of a women travelling abroad to receive an abortion – a practice that is banned in Ireland itself.

Republic of Poland

The freedom of movement in Republic of Poland of Polish nationals holding dual citizenship is or might be unlawfully restricted by Polish government. US Department of State is warning Polish nationals holding dual citizenship, that Polish government despite that Poland joined the Schengen System are obliged to use Polish travel documents (a Polish passport or, as an alternative within the Schengen zone, a Polish National ID card (Dowód Osobisty), or they will NOT be allowed to leave Poland. The latest such incident is recorded as of January 15, 2008. Poland requires Polish citizens (including American citizens who are or can be claimed as Polish citizens), or those who can be suspected to be Polish citizens, to enter and depart Poland using a Polish passport.

Poland does not recognize (although it does not prohibit) dual nationality.

A person holding Polish and U.S. citizenship is deemed by Poland to be a Polish citizen and subject to Polish law. The US Embassy in Poland will not be in a position assist Polish citizens in case of not being allowed to leave Poland.

- Poland - US Department of State: Country Specific Information.
- Dual Citizenship

Syria

The Syrian Constitution states "Every citizen has the right to liberty of movement within the territory of the State unless prohibited therefrom under the terms of a court order or public health and safety regulations.". The United Nations has reported that "in Syria, no laws or measures restrict the liberty of movement or choice of residence of citizens.". Legislative Decree No. 29 of 1970 regulates the right of foreigners to enter, reside in and leave the territory of Syria, and is the controlling document regarding the issuance of passports, visas, and diplomatic travel status. The document specifically states "The latter provision is intended merely to ensure that our country is not the final destination of stateless persons."

However, Syria has been criticised by groups, including Amnesty International for restrictions to freedom of movement. In August 2005, Amnesty International released an "appeal case", citing several freedom of movement restrictions including exit restriction without explanation, refusal to issue passports to political dissidents, detention, restriction from entering certain structures, denial of travel documents, and denial of nationality. The United Nations Human Rights Committee issues regular reports on human rights in Syria, including freedom of movement.

Tibet

Article 5 of the International Convention on the Elimination of all forms of Racial Discrimination explicitly guarantees "...the right to freedom of movement and residence within the border of the State". Under the Chinese household registration citizen, Tibetan residents must receive permission to change their household between a rural and urban area. Tibetans are also forced to agree to Chinese communist party ideals in order to receive a permit to exit the country. It has been reported that Chinese residents in Tibet are not subject to these restrictions, especially if they have access to a Chinese household permit.

United Kingdom

Britons have long enjoyed a comparatively high level of freedom of movement. Apart from Magna Carta, the protection of rights and liberties in this field has tended to come from the common law rather than formal constitutional codes and conventions. Freedom of movement is a basic component of liberty in general and one of the major basic legal constraints on infringements of liberty is the common law ban on all forms of slavery/serfdom.

However, various actions by the UK governing authorities have directly or indirectly curbed personal freedom of movement and residence of citizens in their own country of late.

It has been proposed that a range of specific state restrictions on freedom of movement should be prohibited under a new or comprehensively amended Human Rights Act. The new basic legal prohibitions could include: road tolls and other curbs on freedom of travel and private vehicle ownership and use; personal identity cards (internal passports, citizenship licenses) which have to be produced on demand and/or in order for individuals to access public services and facilities; and legal requirements for citizens to register changes of address or partner with the state authorities.

United States

The Privileges and Immunities Clause of the United States Constitution states, "The Citizens of each State shall be entitled to all Privileges and Immunities of Citizens in the several States." As far back as the circuit court ruling in *Corfield v. Coryell,* 6 Fed. Cas. 546 (1823), the Supreme Court recognised freedom of movement as a fundamental Constitutional right. In *Paul v. Virginia,* 75 U.S. 168 (1869), the Court defined freedom of movement as "right of free ingress into other States, and egress from them."75 U.S. 168 (1868) However, the Supreme Court did not invest the federal government with the authority to protect freedom of movement. Under the "privileges and immunities" clause, this authority was given to the states, a position the Court held consistently through the years in cases such as *Ward v. Maryland,* 79 U.S. 418 (1871), the *Slaughter-House Cases,* 83 U.S. 36 (1873) and *United States v. Harris,* 106 U.S. 629 (1883).

In *United States v. Wheeler,* 254 U.S. 281 (1920), the Supreme Court reiterated its position that the Constitution did not grant the federal government the power to protect freedom of movement. However, *Wheeler* had a significant impact in other ways. For many years, the roots of the Constitution's "privileges and immunities" clause had only vaguely been determined. In 1823, the circuit court in *Corfield* had provided a list of the rights (some fundamental, some not) which the clause could cover. The *Wheeler* court dramatically changed this. It was the first to locate the right to travel in the privileges and immunities clause, providing the right with a specific guarantee of constitutional protection. By reasoning that the clause derived from Article IV of the Articles of Confederation, the decision suggested a narrower set of rights than those enumerated in *Corfield,* but also more clearly defined those rights as absolutely fundamental.

But the Supreme Court began rejecting *Wheeler's* reasoning within a few short years. Finally, in *United States v. Guest,* 383 U.S. 745 (1966), the Supreme Court overruled Chief Justice White's conclusion that the federal government could protect the right to travel only against state infringement.

In *Kent v. Dulles,* 357 U.S. 116 (1958) (overruled by *Regan v. Wald,* 468 U.S. 222, reh'g denied, 469 U.S. 912 (1984)), the United States Secretary of State had refused to issue a passport to an American citizen based on the suspicion that the plaintiff was going abroad to promote communism. Although the Court did not reach the question of constitutionality in this case, Justice William O. Douglas held that the federal government may not restrict the right to travel without due process:

> The right to travel is a part of the 'liberty' of which the citizen cannot be deprived without due process of law under the Fifth Amendment. If that "liberty" is to be regulated, it must be pursuant to the law-making functions of the Congress. . . . . Freedom of movement across frontiers in either direction, and inside frontiers as well, was a part of our heritage. Travel abroad, like travel within the country, . . . may be as close to the heart of the individual as the choice of what he eats, or wears, or reads. Freedom of movement is basic in our scheme of values.

Six years later, the Court struck down a federal ban restricting travel by communists (*Aptheker v. Secretary of State,* 378 U.S. 500 (1964)). But the court struggled to find a way to protect legitimate government interests (such as national security) in light of these decisions. Just a year after *Aptheker,* the Supreme Court fashioned the rational relationship test for constitutionality in *Zemel v. Rusk,* 381 U.S. 1 (1965), as a way of reconciling the rights of the individual with the interests of the state.

The U.S. Supreme Court also dealt with the right to travel in the case of *Saenz v. Roe*, 526 U.S. 489 (1999). In that case, Justice John Paul Stevens, writing for the majority, held that the United States Constitution protected three separate aspects of the right to travel among the states: the right to enter one state and leave another, the right to be treated as a welcome visitor rather than a hostile stranger (protected by the "privileges and immunities" clause in Article IV, § 2), and (for those who become permanent residents of a state) the right to be treated equally to native born citizens (this is protected by the 14th Amendment's Citizenship Clause).

The Court's establishment of a strong constitutional right to freedom of movement has also had far-reaching and unintended effects. For example, the Supreme Court overturned state prohibitions on welfare payments to individuals who had not resided within the jurisdiction for at least one year as an impermissible burden on the right to travel (*Shapiro v. Thompson,* 394 U.S. 618 (1969)). The Court has also struck down one-year residency requirements for voting in state elections (*Dunn v. Blumstein,* 405 U.S. 330 (1972)), one-year waiting periods before receiving state-provided medical care (*Memorial Hospital v. Maricopa County,* 415 U.S. 250 (1974)), civil service preferences for state veterans (*Attorney Gen. of New York v. Soto-Lopez,* 476 U.S. 898 (1986)), and higher fishing and hunting license fees for out-of-state residents (*Baldwin v. Fish & Game Comm'n of Montana,* 436 U.S. 371 (1978)).

A strong right to freedom of movement may yet have even farther-reaching implications. The Supreme Court has acknowledged that freedom of movement is closely related to freedom of association and to freedom of expression. Strong constitutional protection for the right to travel may have significant implications for state attempts to limit abortion rights, ban or refuse to recognise same-sex marriage, and enact anti-crime or consumer protection laws. It may even undermine current Court-fashioned concepts of federalism.

For much of American history, the right to travel included the right to travel by the vehicle of one's choice, and courts occasionally struck down regional regulations that required licenses or government permission to travel on public roadways. With the advent of the automobile, however, courts began upholding laws and regulations requiring licenses to operate vehicles on roadways. Constitutional scholar Roger Roots has referred to the forgotten right to travel without license as "the orphaned right."

The issue of freedom of movement has received new attention in the United States as of 2004, particularly concerning the methods and practices of the Transportation Security Administration. On August 5, 1974, the Air Transportation Security and Anti-Hijacking Acts of 1974 (P.L. 93-366) were signed. Among many important provisions, this landmark aviation security law directed that regulations be prescribed requiring weapons-detecting screening of all passengers and carry-on property. The law is located in Title 49, United States Code (U.S.C.), sections 44901 (Screening passengers and property)and 44902 (Refusal to transport passengers and property). For many decades, an airline ticket's fine print has contained an agreement by the purchaser to submit to a search for unlawful dangerous weapons, explosives or other destructive substances. The Transportation Security Administration (TSA) is responsible for such screening prior to departures from commercial airports within the United States since the signing of the Aviation and Transportation Security Act (P.L. 107-71) on November 19, 2001. Freedom of movement is not denied unless a passenger refuses to submit to a search required by law. There are, however, a number of other safety and homeland security related issues covered in 49 U.S.C. Chapter 449 and Title 49 Code of Federal Regulations in the 1540 series that could impede movement, such as a passenger's name appearing on a "no fly" or "selectee" list. The TSA website is a good source of information on these and other issues.

Another issue of contention deals with freedom of movement across U.S. national borders. The United States has long been lax in permitting persons to cross from Canada into the United States. Concerns about drug trafficking and illegal immigrants seeking employment have led to much stricter controls on those crossing the border from Mexico.

A related issue deals with Free Speech Zones designated during political protests. Although such zones were in use by the 1960s and 1970 due to the Vietnam-era protests, they were not widely reported in the media. However, the controversy over their use has resurfaced strongly due to the 2001-2008 Bush presidency. In essence, Free Speech Zones prevent a person from having complete mobility due to the fact that they are exercising their right to speak freely. Citizens are restricted from traveling (as opposed to being arrested) due to their political communication, despite the fact that the Constitution permits free speech anywhere on U.S. territory. ◆

13
Freedom of Religion

Freedom of religion is a principle that supports the freedom of an individual or community, in public or private, to manifest religion or belief in teaching, practice, worship, and observance; the concept is generally recognised also to include the freedom to change religion or not to follow any religion. Freedom of religion is considered by many people and nations to be a fundamental human right. Thomas Jefferson once said "among the inestimable of our blessings, also, is that ...of liberty to worship our Creator in the way we think most agreeable to His will; ..."

In a country with a state religion, freedom of religion is generally considered to mean that the government permits religious practices of other sects besides the state religion, and does not persecute believers in other faiths.

Many respected scholars consider India as the best example of freedom of religion. The freedom to practise, preach and propagate any religion is a fundamental right outlined in the constitution. India has long been a blend of several religions. It gave the world Hinduism, Buddhism, Jainism and Sikhism. Judaism has been practised here for 2,500 years without any anti-semitism. Christianity arrived here through Saint Thomas in the 1st Century CE as did Islam through Arab traders in the 8th century CE. 80% of India's population practises Hinduism yet India has a Sikh Prime Minister, Dr Manmohan Singh, an Italian-Indian Catholic, Sonia Gandhi as the leader of the largest party and till recently had a Muslim President, Dr Abdul Kalam.

Today there are concerns about the persecution of religious minorities in the Muslim world and in some communist states such as China and North Korea, as well as other forms of intolerance in other countries —for example, the banning of worn religious articles such as the Muslim veil, in certain European countries. Article 18 of the U.N. International Covenant on Civil and Political Rights shows that it is a form of (spiritual) injustice when persons are denied the liberty to exercise their religious freedom. Freedom of religion as a legal concept is related to, but not identical with, religious toleration, separation of church and state, or secular state (*laïcité*).

Where individuals and not governments are concerned, religious toleration is generally taken to refer to an attitude of acceptance towards other people's religions. Such toleration does not require that one view other religions as equally true; rather, the assumption is that each citizen will grant that others have the right to hold and practice their own beliefs. Against this backdrop, proselytism can be a contentious issue, as it could be regarded as an offense against the validity of others' religious beliefs, including irreligious belief.

History of Freedom of Religion

Historically *freedom of religion* has been used to refer to the tolerance of different theological systems of belief, while *freedom of worship* was defined as freedom of individual action. Each of these have existed to varying degrees. While many countries have accepted some form of religious freedom, this has also often been limited in practice through punitive taxation, repressive social legislation, and political disenfranchisement. Compare examples of individual freedom in Italy or the Muslim tradition of dhimmis, literally "protected individuals" professing an officially tolerated non-Muslim religion.

Antiquity

Freedom of religious worship was established in the Maurya Empire of ancient India by Ashoka the Great in the 3rd century BC, which was encapsulated in the Edicts of Ashoka.

In Antiquity a syncretic point-of-view often allowed communities of traders to operate under their own customs. When street mobs of separate quarters clashed in a Hellenistic or Roman city, the issue was generally perceived to be an infringement of community rights. The Greek-Jewish clashes at Cyrene provided one example of cosmopolitan cities as scenes of tumult.

Some of the historical exceptions have been in regions where one of the revealed religions has been in a position of power: Judaism, Zoroastrianism, Christianity and Islam. Others have been where the established order has felt threatened, as shown in the trial of Socrates or where the ruler has been deified, as in Rome, and refusal to offer token sacrifice was similar to refusing to take an oath of allegiance. This was the core for resentment and the persecution of early Christian communities.

Religious freedom for Muslims, Jews and Pagans was declared in the Constitution of Medina by Muhammad in the 7th Century AD. The Islamic Caliphate later guaranteed religious freedom under the conditions that non-Muslim communities accept *dhimmi* (protected) status and their adult males pay the *jizya* tax as a substitute for the *zakat* paid by Muslim citizens.

Europe

The Norman Kingdom of Sicily under Roger II was characterised by its multi-ethnic nature and religious tolerance. Normans, Jews, Muslim Arabs, Byzantine Greeks, Longobards and "native" Sicilians lived in harmony. Rather than exterminate the Muslims of Sicily, Roger II's grandson Emperor Frederick II of Hohenstaufen (1215–1250) allowed them to settle on the mainland and build mosques. Not least, he enlisted them in his – Christian – army and even into his personal bodyguards.

The first full religious freedom law what had "act rank" created by Edict of Turda in Transylvania , and accepted by Hungarian, székely and Saxon part of the diet.

After the fall of the city of Granada Spain in 1492 the Muslim population was promised religious freedom by the Treaty of Granada, but that promise was short-lived. In 1501 Granada's Muslims were given an ultimatum to either convert to Christianity or to emigrate.

The majority converted, but only superficially, continuing to dress and speak as they had before and to secretly practice Islam. The Moriscos (converts to Christianity) were ultimately expelled from Spain between 1609 (Castile) and 1614 (rest of Spain), by Philip III.

The Roman Catholic Church kept a tight rein on religious expression throughout the Middle Ages. Jews were alternately tolerated and persecuted, the most notable examples of the latter being the expulsion of all Jews from Spain in 1492. Some of those who remained and converted were tried as heretics in the Inquisition for allegedly practicing Judaism in secret. Despite the persecution of Jews, they were the most tolerated non-Catholic faith in Europe.

However, the latter was in part a reaction to the growing movement that became the Reformation. As early as 1380, John Wycliffe in England denied transubstantiation and began his translation of the Bible into English. He was condemned in a Papal Bull in 1410, and all his books were burned.

In 1414 Jan Hus, a Bohemian preacher of reformation, was given a safe conduct by the Holy Roman Emperor to attend the Council of Constance. Not entirely trusting in his safety, he made his will before he left. His forebodings proved accurate, and he was burned at the stake on July 6, 1415. The Council also decreed that Wycliffe's remains be disinterred and cast out. This decree was not carried out until 1429.

Martin Luther published his famous 95 Theses in Wittenberg on October 31, 1517. His aim was to stop the sale of indulgences and reform the Church from within, but this was not the result. In 1521 he was given the chance to recant at the Diet of Worms before Charles V, Holy Roman Emperor, then only 19. After he refused to recant he was declared heretic. Partly for his own protection, he was sequestered on the Wartburg in the possessions of Frederick III, Elector of Saxony, where he translated the New Testament into German. He was excommunicated by Papal Bull in 1521.

The Protestant movement, however, continued to gain ground in his absence and spread to Switzerland. Huldrych Zwingli preached reform in Zürich from 1520 to 1523. He opposed the sale of indulgences, celibacy, pilgrimages, pictures, statues, relics, altars, and organs. This culminated in outright war between the Swiss cantons that accepted Protestantism and the Catholics. The Catholics were victorious, and Zwingli was killed in battle in 1531. The Catholic cantons were magnanimous in victory.

In the meantime, in Germany Philip Melanchthon drafted the Augsburg Confession as a common confession for the Lutherans and the free territories. It was presented to Charles V in 1530.

The defiance of Papal authority proved contagious, and in 1533, when Henry VIII of England was excommunicated for his divorce and remarriage to Anne Boleyn, he promptly established a state church with bishops appointed by the crown. This was not without internal opposition, and Thomas More, who had been his prime minister, was executed in 1535 for opposition to Henry.

In 1535 the Swiss canton of Geneva became Protestant. In 1536 the Bernese imposed the reformation on the canton of Vaud by conquest. They sacked the cathedral in Lausanne and destroyed all its art and statuary. John Calvin, who had been active in Geneva was expelled in 1538 in a power struggle, but he was invited back in 1540.

The same kind of seesaw back and forth between Protestantism and Catholicism was evident in England when Mary I of England returned that country briefly to the Catholic fold in 1553 and persecuted Protestants. However, her half-sister, Elizabeth I of England was to restore the Church of England in 1558, this time permanently, though in the process persecute Catholics. The King James Bible commissioned by King James I of England and published in 1611 proved a landmark for Protestant worship, with official Catholic forms of worship being banned.

In the Union of Utrecht, January 20,1579 personal freedom of religion was declared in the struggle between the Northern Netherlands and Spain. The Union of Utrecht was an important step in the establishment of the Dutch Republic (from 1581 to 1795). The establishment of a Jewish community in the Netherlands and New Amsterdam (present day New York)during the Dutch republic is an example of the freedom of religion. When New Amsterdam surrendered to the English in 1664, the freedom of religion was garantied in the Articles of Capitulation.

Intolerance of dissident forms of Protestantism also continued, as evidenced by the exodus of the Pilgrims who sought refuge, first in the Netherlands, and ultimately in America, founding the Plymouth Colony in Massachusetts in 1620. William Penn, the founder of Philadelphia was involved in a case which had a profound effect upon future American law and those of England. In a classic case of jury nullification the jury refused to convict William Penn of preaching a Quaker sermon, which was illegal. Even though the jury was imprisoned for their acquittal, they stood by their decision and helped establish the freedom of religion.

In the Holy Roman Empire, Charles V agreed to tolerate Lutheranism in 1555 at the Peace of Augsburg. Each state was to take the religion of its prince, but within those states, there was not necessarily religious tolerance. Citizens of other faiths could relocate to a more hospitable environment.

In 1558 the Transylvanian Diet of Turda declared free practice of both the Catholic and Lutheran religions, but prohibited Calvinism. Ten years later, in 1568, the Diet extended the freedom to all religions, declaring that "It is not allowed to anybody to intimidate anybody with captivity or expelling for his religion". The Edict of Turda is considered by mostly Hungarian historians as the first legal guarantee of religious freedom in the Christian Europe.

In France, although peace was made between Protestants and Catholics at the Treaty of Saint Germain in 1570, persecution continued, most notably in the Massacre of Saint Bartholomew's Day on August 24, 1572, in which many Protestants throughout France were killed. It was not until the converted Protestant prince Henry IV of France came to the throne that religious tolerance was formalized in the Edict of Nantes in 1598. It would remain in force for over 80 years until its revocation in 1685 by Louis XIV of France. Intolerance remained the norm until the French Revolution, when state religion was abolished and all Church property confiscated.

Bohemia (present-day Czech Republic) enjoyed religious freedom between 1436 and 1620, and became one of the most liberal countries of the Christian world during that period of time. The so-called Basel Compacts of 1436 declared the freedom of religion and peace between Catholics and Utraquists. In 1609 Emperor Rudolf II granted Bohemia greater religious liberty with his Letter of Majesty. The privileged position of the Catholic Church in the Czech kingdom was firmly established after the Battle of White Mountain in 1620. Gradually freedom of religion in Bohemian lands came to an end and Protestants fled or were expelled from the country. A devout Catholic, Emperor Ferdinand II forcibly converted Austrian and Bohemian Protestants.

Poland

Poland has a long tradition of religious freedom. This is first evident in the refusal of Poland to force Christianinty upon the Old Prussian people, but rather persuading them peacefully (these were later almost completely wiped out by the German Teutonic Order). The right to worship freely was a basic right given to all inhabitants of the Commonwealth throughout the 15th and early 16th century, however, complete freedom of religion was officially recognised in Poland in 1573 during the Warsaw Confederation. Poland remained with the religious freedom laws during an era when religious persecution was an everyday occurrence in the rest of Europe.

The General Charter of Jewish Liberties known as the Statute of Kalisz was issued by the Duke of Greater Poland Boleslaus the Pious on September 8, 1264 in Kalisz. The statute served as the basis for the legal position of Jews in Poland and led to creation of the Yiddish-speaking autonomous Jewish nation until 1795. The statute granted exclusive jurisdiction of Jewish courts over Jewish matters and established a separate tribunal for matters involving Christians and Jews. Additionally, it guaranteed personal liberties and safety for Jews including freedom of religion, travel, and trade. The statute was ratified by subsequent Polish Kings: Casimir III of Poland in 1334, Casimir IV of Poland in 1453 and Sigismund I of Poland in 1539. The Commonwealth set a precedent by allowing Jews to become ennobled.

United States

Some of the early colonies, which were founded as a result of religious persecution, were not tolerant of dissident forms of worship. For example, Roger Williams found it necessary to found a new colony in Rhode Island to escape persecution in the theocratically dominated colony of Massachusetts.

It was not until the 18th century that Enlightenment concepts of freedom of individual worship gained ground both in Europe and America.

The modern legal concept of religious freedom as the union of *freedom of belief* and *freedom of worship* with the absence of any state-sponsored religion, originated in the United States of America.

This issue was addressed by Thomas Paine in his pamphlet, *Common Sense* (1776):

> *"As to religion, I hold it to be the indispensable duty of all government, to protect all conscientious professors thereof, and I know of no other business which government hath to do therewith...*

The Virginia Statute for Religious Freedom, written in 1779 by Thomas Jefferson, proclaimed:

> *"o man shall be compelled to frequent or support any religious worship, place, or ministry whatsoever, nor shall be enforced, restrained, molested, or burthened in his body or goods, nor shall otherwise suffer, on account of his religious opinions or belief; but that all men shall be free to profess, and by argument to maintain, their opinions in matters of religion, and that the same shall in no wise diminish, enlarge, or affect their civil capacities."*

Asia

India

Freedom of religion in contemporary India is a fundamental right guaranteed by the country's constitution. Every citizen of India has a right to practice and promote their religions peacefully. However, there is tension between Muslim (and Christian) minorities and the Hindu majority. It has been alleged that the tension is mainly due to the fact that Muslims and Christians actively involve in proselytism, which is disliked by the Hindus.

Freedom of religion in the Indian subcontinent is exemplified by the reign of King Piyadasi (304 B.C to 232 B.C) (Ashoka). One of King Ashoka's main concerns was to reform governmental institutes and exercise moral principles in his attempt to create a just and humane society. Later he promoted the principles of Buddhism, and the creation of a just, understanding and fair society was held as an important principle for many ancient rulers of this time in the East.

The importance of freedom of worship in India was encapsulated in an inscription of Ashoka:

> King Piyadasi (Ashok) dear to the Gods, honours all sects, the ascetics (hermits) or those who dwell at home, he honours them with charity and in other ways. But the King, dear to the Gods, attributes less importance to this charity and these honours than to the vow of seeing the reign of virtues, which constitutes the essential part of them. For all these virtues there is a common source, modesty of speech. That is to say, One must not exalt one's creed discrediting all others, nor must one degrade these others Without legitimate reasons. One must, on the contrary, render to other creeds the honour befitting them.

Religious freedom and the right to worship freely was a practice that had been appreciated and promoted by most ancient India dynasties. As a result, people fleeing religious persecution in other parts of the world including Christians, Jews and Zoroastrians fled to India as a place of refuge where they could enjoy religious freedom. This had been the underlying attitude of most rulers of India until 1200 AD.

The initial entry of Islam into South Asia came in the first century after the death of the Prophet Muhammad. When around 1210 AD the Islamic Sultanates invaded India from the north-west, gradually the principle of freedom of religion deteriorated in this part of the world. They were subsequently replaced by another Islamic invader in the form of Babur. The Mughal empire was founded by the Mongol leader Babur in 1526, when he defeated Ibrahim Lodi, the last of the Delhi Sultans at the First Battle of Panipat. The word "Mughal" is the Indo-Iranian version of Mongol.

On the main Asian continent, the Mongols were very tolerant of religions. People could worship as they wished freely and openly.

CONTEMPORARY DEBATES

The contemporary idea of religious freedom as a human right remains a contested topic. The major areas of debate are listed below.

Christianity

The Roman Catholic Church affirmed religious freedom for all in the Second Vatican Council Declaration *Dignitatis Humanae*. This was itself inspired by the work of the Jesuit theologian John Courtney Murray. Some Orthodox Christians, especially those living in democratic countries, support religious freedom for all, as evidenced by the position of the Ecumenical Patriarchate. Many Protestant Christian churches, including some Baptists, Churches of Christ, Seventh-day Adventist Church and main line churches have a commitment to religious freedoms. The Church of Jesus Christ of Latter-Day Saints (Latter-Day Saints) also affirm religious freedom.

However others, such as African scholar Makau Mutua, have argued that Christian insistence on the propagation of their faith to native cultures as an element of religious freedom has resulted in a corresponding denial of religious freedom to native traditions and led to their destruction. As he states in the book produced by the Oslo

Coalition on Freedom of Religion or Belief — "Imperial religions have necessarily violated individual conscience and the communal expressions of Africans and their communities by subverting African religions."

In fact, the belief of some Christians that non-Christians need to be converted to Christianity in order to be "saved" may be regarded as an affront to the religious freedom of those who follow other faiths or identify as atheists. Because of this prevalent belief among Christians, Christianity has been said to be inherently counter to religious freedom, and many Christians have denounced this proselytizing aspect of their faith.

Islam

Some Islamic theologians quote the Quran ("There is no compulsion in religion," Sura 2:257, and "Say: O you who reject faith, I do not worship what you worship, nor do you worship what I worship...To you be your religion, and to me be mine," Sura 109:1-6, i.e. Sura Al-Kafirun) to show scriptural support for religious freedom. However, other verses and the Hadith mandate severe treatment for unbelievers, which is reflected in the high levels of intolerance shown in many past and contemporary Islamic societies, and some Muslim scholars have disagreed with such ill-treatment.

In Sura 2:190-194, refers to the bloody war against Pagans, Christians and Jews during the Battle of Badr in Medina, of which it was indicating that Muslims are only allowed to fight against those who intend to harm them (right of self-defence) and that if their enemies surrender, they must also stop because God does not like those who transgress limits.

> In Bukhari: V9 N316, Jabir ibn 'Abdullah narrated that a Bedouin accepted Islam and then when he got a fever he demanded that Muhammad to cancel his pledge (allow him to renounce Islam). Muhammad refused to do so. The Bedouin man repeated his demand once, but Muhammad once again refused. Then, he (the Bedouin) left Medina. Muhammad said, "Madinah is like a

pair of bellows (furnace): it expels its impurities and brightens and clear its good." In this narration, there was no evidence demonstrating that Muhammad ordered the execution of the Bedouin for wanting to renounce Islam.

In addition, in Sura 5:3, which is believed to be God's final revelation to Muhammad, states that Muslims are to fear God and not those who reject Islam, and 53:39 every one is accountable only to one's own actions. Therefore, it postulates that in Islam, in the matters of practising a religion, it does not relate to a worldly punishment, but rather these actions are accountable to God in the afterlife. Thus, this supports the argument against the execution of apostates in Islam.

However, on the other hand, some Muslims support the practice of executing apostates who leave Islam, as in Bukhari:V4 B52 N260; "The Prophet said, 'If a Muslim discards his religion, kill him."

In Iran, the constitution recognizes four religions whose status is formally protected: Zoroastrianism, Judaism, Christianity, and Islam. The constitution, however, also set the groundwork for the institutionalized persecution of Bahá'ís, who have been subjected to arrests, beatings, executions, confiscation and destruction of property, and the denial of civil rights and liberties, and the denial of access to higher education. In Egypt, a December 16, 2006 judgment of the Supreme Administrative Council created a clear demarcation between recognized religions — Islam, Christianity and Judaism — and all other religious beliefs; no other religious affiliation is officially admissible. The ruling leaves members of other religious communities, including Bahá'ís, without the ability to obtain the necessary government documents to have rights in their country, essentially denying them of all rights of citizenship. They cannot obtain ID cards, birth certificates, death certificates, marriage or divorce certificates, and passports; they also cannot be employed, educated, treated in public hospitals or vote, among other things. See Egyptian identification card controversy.

Changing Religion

Among the most contentious areas of religious freedom is the right of an individual to change or abandon his or her own religion (apostasy), and the right to evangelise individuals seeking to convince others to make such a change.

Other debates have centered around restricting certain kinds of missionary activity by religions. Many Islamic states, and others such as China, severely restrict missionary activities of other religions. Greece, among European countries, has generally looked unfavourably on missionary activities of denominations others than the majority church and proselytising is constitutionally prohibited.

A different kind of critique of the freedom to propagate religion has come from non-Abrahamic traditions such as the African and Indian. African scholar Makau Mutua criticises religious evangelism on the ground of cultural annihilation by what he calls "proselytising universalist faiths."

The (human) rights regime incorrectly assumes a level playing field by requiring that African religions compete in the marketplace of ideas. The rights corpus not only forcibly imposes on African religions the obligation to compete—a task for which as nonproselytising, noncompetitive creeds they are not historically fashioned—but also protects the evangelizing religions in their march towards universalisation ... it seems inconceivable that the human rights regime would have intended to protect the right of certain religions to destroy others.

Some Indian scholars have similarly argued that the right to propagate religion is not culturally or religiously neutral.

In Sri Lanka there have been debates regarding a bill on religious freedom that seeks to protect indigenous religious traditions from certain kinds of missionary activities. Debates have also occurred in various states of India regarding similar laws, particularly those that restrict conversions using force, fraud or allurement.

In 2008 Christian Solidarity Worldwide, a Christian human rights non-governmental organisation which specialises in religious freedom, launched an in-depth report on the human rights abuses faced by individuals who leave Islam for another religion. The report is the product of a year long research project in six different countries. It calls on Muslim nations, the international community, the UN and the international media to resolutely address the serious violations of human rights suffered by apostates.

Secular Law

Religious practice may also conflict with secular law creating debates on religious freedom. For instance, even though polygamy is permitted in Islam it is prohibited in secular law in many Western countries. Does prohibiting polygamy then curtail the religious freedom of Muslims? The USA and India have taken two different views of this. In India polygamy is permitted, but only for Muslims, under Muslim Personal Law. In the USA polygamy is prohibited for all. This was a major source of conflict between the early Mormon Church and the United States until the Church amended its position on polygamy.

Similar issues have also arisen in the context of the religious use of psychedelic substances by Native American tribes in the United States as well as other Native practices.

International Law

In international law the freedom of religion and belief is protected by the International Covenant on Civil and Political Rights (ICCPR). This protection extends to specifically non-religious beliefs, such as Humanism. However, minority or disfavored religions still receive the spiritual injustice of persecution in many parts of the world.

Children's Rights

The law in Germany provides the term of "religious majority" (*Religionsmündigkeit*) with a minimum age for minors to follow their own religious beliefs even if their parents don't share those or don't approve. Children 14 and older have the unrestricted right to enter or exit any religious community. Children 12 and older cannot be compelled to change to a different belief. Children 10 and older have to be heard before their parents change their religious upbringing to a different belief. There are similar laws in Austria and in Switzerland.

US Foreign Relations

The United States formally considers religious freedom in its foreign relations. The International Religious Freedom Act of 1998 established the United States Commission on International Religious Freedom which investigates the records of over 200 other nations with respect to religious freedom, and makes recommendations to submit nations with egregious records to ongoing scrutiny and possible economic sanctions. Many human rights organisations have urged the United States to be still more vigorous in imposing sanctions on countries that do not permit or tolerate religious freedom.

Some critics charge that the United States policy on religious freedom is largely directed towards the rights of Christians, particularly the ability for Christian missionaries to evangelise, in other countries.

◆

14
Human Rights in India

The situation of human rights in India is a complex one, as a result of the country's large size and tremendous diversity, its status as a developing country and a sovereign, secular, democratic republic, and its history as a former colonial territory. The Constitution of India provides for Fundamental rights, which include freedom of religion. Clauses also provide for Freedom of Speech, as well as separation of executive and judiciary and freedom of movement within the country and abroad.

It is often held, particularly by Indian human rights groups and activists, that members of the Dalit or Untouchable caste have suffered and continue to suffer substantial discrimination. Although human rights problems do exist in India, the country is generally not regarded as a human rights concern, unlike other countries in South Asia. Based on these considerations, the report Freedom in the World 2006 by Freedom House gave India a political rights rating of 2, and a civil liberties rating of 3, earning it the designation of *free*

Chronology of Human Rights in India

- 1829 - The practice of sati was formally abolished by Governor General William Bentick after years of campaigning by Hindu reform movements such as the Brahmo Samaj of Ram Mohan Roy against this orthodox Hindu funeral custom of self-immolation of widows after the death of their husbands.
- 1929 - *Child Marriage Restraint Act*, prohibiting marriage of minors is passed.
- 1947 - India achieves political independence from the British Raj.

- 1950 - The Constitution of India establishes a sovereign democratic republic with universal adult franchise. Part 3 of the Constitution contains a Bill of Fundamental Rights enforceable by the Supreme Court and the High Courts. It also provides for reservations for previously disadvantaged sections in education, employment and political representation.

- 1952 - *Criminal Tribes Act 1871* repealed by government, former "criminal tribes" categorised as "denotified" and Habitual Offenders Act (1952) enacted.

- 1955 - Reform of family law concerning Hindus gives more rights to Hindu women.

- 1958 - *Armed Forces (Special Powers) Act, 1958.*

- 1973 - Supreme Court of India rules in *Kesavananda Bharati* that the basic structure of the Constitution (including many fundamental rights) is unalterable by a constitutional amendment.

- 1975-77 - State of Emergency in India – extensive rights violations take place.

- 1978 - SC rules in *Menaka Gandhi v. Union of India* that the right to life under Article 21 of the Constitution cannot be suspended even in an emergency.

- 1978-*Jammu and Kashmir Public Safety Act, 1978.*

- 1984 - Operation Blue Star and the subsequent 1984 Anti-Sikh riots.

- 1985-6 - The Shah Bano case, where the Supreme Court recognised the Muslim woman's right to maintenance upon divorce, sparks protests from Muslim clergy. To nullify the decision of the Supreme Court, the Rajiv Gandhi government enacted *The Muslim Women (Protection of Rights on Divorce) Act 1986.*

- 1989 - *Scheduled Caste and Scheduled Tribe (Prevention of Atrocities) Act, 1989* is passed.
- 1989-present - Kashmiri insurgency sees ethnic cleansing of Kashmiri Pandits, desecrating Hindu temples, killing of Hindus and Sikhs, and abductions of foreign tourists and government functionaries.
- 1992 - A constitutional amendment establishes Local Self-Government (Panchayati Raj) as a third tier of governance at the village level, with one-third of the seats reserved for women. Reservations were provided for scheduled castes and tribes as well.
- 1992 - Babri Masjid demolished by Hindu mobs, resulting in riots across the country.
- 1993 - National Human Rights Commission is established under the *Protection of Human Rights Act*.
- 2001 - Supreme Court passes extensive orders to implement the right to food.
- 2002 - Violence in Gujarat, chiefly targeting its Muslim minority, claims many lives.
- 2005 - A powerful *Right to Information Act* is passed to give citizen's access to information held by public authorities.
- 2005 - *National Rural Employment Guarantee Act (NREGA)* guarantees universal right to employment.
- 2006 - Supreme Court orders police reforms in response to the poor human rights record of Indian police.
- 2009 - Delhi High Court delcares that Section 377 of the Indian Penal Code, which outlaws a range of unspecified "unnatural" sex acts, is unconstitutional when applied to homosexual acts between private consenting individuals, effectively decriminalising homosexual relationships in India.

Custodial Deaths

Despite state prohibitions against torture and custodial misconduct by the police, torture is widespread in police custody, which is a major reason behind deaths in custody. The police often torture innocent people until a 'confession' is obtained to save influential and wealthy offenders. G.P. Joshi, the programme coordinator of the Indian branch of the Commonwealth Human Rights Initiative in New Delhi comments that the main issue at hand concerning police violence is a lack of accountability of the police.

In 2006, the Supreme Court of India in a judgement in the *Prakash Singh vs. Union of India* case, ordered central and state governments with seven directives to begin the process of police reform. The main objectives of this set of directives was twofold, providing tenure to and streamlining the appointment/transfer processes of policemen, and increasing the accountability of the police.

Indian Administered Kashmir

Claims of human rights abuses have been made against the Indian Armed Forces and the armed militants operating in Jammu and Kashmir. A 2005 study conducted by Médecins Sans Frontières found that Kashmiri women are among the worst sufferers of sexual violence in the world, with 11.6% of respondents reporting that they had been victims of sexual abuse. Some surveys have found that in the Kashmir region itself (where the bulk of separatist and Indian military activity is concentrated), popular perception holds that the Indian Armed Forces are more to blame for human rights violations than the separatist groups. According to the MORI survey of 2002, in Kashmir only 2% of respondents believed that the militant groups were guilty of widespread human rights abuses, while 64% believed that Indian troops were guilty of the same. This trend was reversed however in other parts of the state. Off late Amnesty International has called on India to "unequivocally condemn enforced disappearances" and to ensure that impartial investigation is conducted on reality of mass graves in its controlled Kashmir region. As the

Indian state police confirms as many as 331 deaths while in custody and 111 enforced disappearances since 1989 . . .

Several international agencies and the UN have reported human rights violations in Indian-administered Kashmir. In a recent press release the OHCHR spokesmen stated "The Office of the High Commissioner for Human Rights is concerned about the recent violent protests in Indian-administered Kashmir that have reportedly led to civilian casualties as well as restrictions to the right to freedom of assembly and expression.". A 1996 Human Rights Watch report accuses the Indian military and Indian-government backed paramilitaries of "committ serious and widespread human rights violations in Kashmir." One such alleged massacre occurred on January 6, 1993 in the town of Sopore. *TIME Magazine* described the incident as such: "In retaliation for the killing of one soldier, paramilitary forces rampaged through Sopore's market setting buildings ablaze and shooting bystanders. The Indian government pronounced the event 'unfortunate' and claimed that an ammunition dump had been hit by gunfire, setting off fires that killed most of the victims." In addition to this, there have been claims of disappearances by the police or the army in Kashmir by several human rights organisations. Jammu and Kashmir Public Safety Act, 1978 : Human rights organisations have also asked Indian government to repeal the Public Safety Act, since "a detainee may be held in administrative detention for a maximum of two years without a court order.".

Many human rights organisations such as Amnesty International and the Human Rights Watch (HRW) have condemned human rights abuses in Kashmir by Indians such as "extra-judicial executions", "disappearances", and torture; the "Armed Forces Special Powers Act", which "provides impunity for human rights abuses and fuels cycles of violence. The Armed Forces Special Powers Act (AFSPA) grants the military wide powers of arrest, the right to shoot to kill, and to occupy or destroy property in counterinsurgency operations. Indian officials claim that troops need such powers because the army is only deployed when national security is at serious risk from armed combatants. Such circumstances, they say, call for extraordinary measures." Human rights organisations have also asked Indian government to repeal the Public Safety Act, since "a detainee may be held in administrative detention for a maximum of two years without a court order." A 2008 report by the United Nations High Commissioner for Refugees determined that Indian Administered Kashmir, was only 'partly Free' .

Press Freedom

According to the estimates of Reporters Without Borders, India ranks 105th worldwide in press freedom index (press freedom index for India is 29.33 for 2009). The Indian Constitution, while not mentioning the word "press", provides for *"the right to freedom of speech and expression"* (Article 19(1) a). However, this right is subject to restrictions under subclause (2), whereby, this freedom can be restricted for reasons of "sovereignty and integrity of India, the security of the State, friendly relations with foreign States, public order, preserving decency, preserving morality, in relation to contempt of court, defamation, or incitement to an offence". Laws such as the Official Secrets Act and Prevention of Terrorism Act (POTA) have been used to limit press freedom. Under POTA, person could be detained for up to six months before the police were required to bring charges on allegations for terrorism-related offenses. POTA was repealed in 2004, but was replaced by amendments to UAPA. The Official Secrets Act 1923 remains in effect.

For the first half-century of independence, media control by the state was the major constraint on press freedom. Indira Gandhi famously stated in 1975 that All India Radio is "a Government organ, it is going to remain a Government organ..." With the liberalisation starting in the 1990s, private control of media has burgeoned, leading to increasing independence and greater scrutiny of government. Organisations like Tehelka and NDTV have been particularly influential, e.g. in bringing about the resignation of powerful Haryana minister Venod Sharma. In addition, laws like Prasar Bharati Act passed in recent years contribute significantly to reducing the control of the press by the government.

LGBT Rights

Homosexuality is criminalised in India by interpretations of the ambiguous Section 377 of the 150 year old Indian Penal Code (IPC). The punishment ranges from ten years to lifelong imprisonment. The law has been used to harass HIV/AIDS prevention efforts, as well as sex workers, men who have sex with men, and other groups at risk of the disease. Scott Long, director of Lesbian, Gay, Bisexual, and Transgender Rights Program at Human Rights Watch sent a letter to Indian Prime Minister Manmohan Singh regarding the arrests of 4 men in 2006 in Lucknow and another 4 in 2001. However, in most areas of India, this law is very rarely enforced. The People's Union for Civil Liberties has published two reports of the rights violations faced by sexual minorities and, in particular, transsexuals (hijras and kothis in India.

On June 2, 2009, the Delhi High Court decriminalised consensual private sexual acts between adults saying

> "We declare that Section 377 IPC, insofar it criminalises consensual sexual acts of adults in private, is violative of Articles 21, 14 and 15 of the Constitution."

Human Trafficking

Human trafficking is a $8 million illegal business in India. Around 10,000 Nepali women are brought to India annually for commercial sexual exploitation. Each year 20,000-25,000 women and children are trafficked from Bangladesh.

Religious Violence

Communal conflicts between religious groups (mostly between Hindus and Muslims) have been prevalent in India since around the time of its independence from British Rule. Among the oldest incidences of communal violence in India was the Moplah rebellion, when Militant Islamists massacred Hindus in Kerala. Irrespective of the bias of British and Hindutva extremists to portray Mappila Lahala as a communal riot, Indian leaders such as Gandhi recognised it as the part of freedom struggle against the British. Communal riots took place during the partition of India between Hindus/Sikhs and Muslims where large numbers of people were killed in large-scale violence.

The 1984 Anti-Sikh Riots was a four-day period during which Sikhs were massacred by members of the secular-centrist Congress Party of India; some estimates state that more than 2,000 were killed. Other incidents include the 1992 Bombay Riots and the 2002 Gujarat violence —in the latter, more than 1,000 Muslims (no citation) were killed following a militant Islamist attack on a train full of Hindu pilgrims in the Godhra Train Burning, where 58 Hindus were killed. Hindutva extremists blames Godhra train tragedy on Muslims, even after a government appointed Committee, lead by a Hindu named Banerjee officially reported the train fire was an accident. Thus in essence for the ethnic cleansing of Muslims in Gujrat, Godhra train accident was used. The news channel 'Tehelka' got it on secret camera the perpetrators claiming the Gujrat massacre was done by the blessing, permission and protection of the Gujrat Chief Minister and Hindutva extremist sympathist Narendra Modi. Lesser incidents plague many towns and villages; representative was the killing of five people in Mau, Uttar Pradesh during Hindu-Muslim rioting, which was triggered by the proposed celebration of a Hindu festival. Other such communal incidents include the 2002 Marad massacre, which occurred after incident in which Muslims were killed and the Hindu community was infiltrated by Hidutva extremist groups, carried out by the militant Islamist group National Development Front, as well as communal riots in Tamil Nadu executed by the Islamist Tamil Nadu Muslim Munnetra Kazagham against Hindus.

Caste related Issues

According to a report by Human Rights Watch, "Dalits and indigenous peoples (known as Scheduled Tribes or adivasis) continue to face discrimination, exclusion, and acts of communal violence. Laws and policies adopted by the Indian government provide a strong basis for protection, but are not being faithfully implemented by local authorities."

Denotified tribes of India, along with many nomadic tribes collectively 60 million in population, continue to face social stigma and economic hardships, despite the fact Criminal Tribes Act 1871, was repealed by the government in 1952 and replaced by Habitual Offenders Act (HOA) (1952), as effectively it only created a new list out of the old list of so-called "criminal tribes. These tribes even today face the consequences of the 'Prevention of Anti-Social Activity Act' (PASA), which only adds to their everyday struggle for existence as most of them live below poverty line. National Human Rights Commission and UN's anti-discrimination body. Committee on the Elimination of Racial Discrimination (CERD) have asked the government to repeal this law as well, as these former "criminalised" tribes continue to suffer oppression and social ostracisation at large and many have been denied SC, ST or OBC status, denying them access to reservations which would elevated their economic and social status.

Other Violence

Invasive methods like 'narcoanalysis' (controlled anesthesia) is now commonly permitted by Indian courts for crime investigation. Even though according to Indian Constitution "nobody may be made a witness against himself", courts have recently proclaimed that even a permission from court is not necessary for conducting this practice. Narcoanalysis is now widely used to replace/circumvent the lack of skill and infrastructure for conducting scientific methods of crime investigation. Narcoanalysis is also alleged as against medical ethics.

It has been found that more than half of the prisoners of the country are detained without adequate evidence. Unlike in other democratic countries, the investigation in India generally commence with the arrest of the accused. As the judicial system is understaffed and sluggish, it is not uncommon to find innocent civilians languishing in jail for many years. For instance, the Bombay high court in September 2009 asked the Maharashtra government to pay Rs 1 lakh as compensation to a 40-year-old man who languished in prison for over 10 years for a crime he didn't commit. ◆

Bibliography

Batra, T.S., *Human Rights: A Critique,* New Delhi, Metropolitan Book Company, 1979.

Bentham, David (ed.), *Politics and Human Rights,* Oxford, Blackwell Publishers, 1995.

Blanc, C. and Breton, T. 1994. l*e lievre et la tortue: Les atouis inattendus des Francais,* Paris, Plon.

Bossuyt, M.J., *Guide to the 'Travaux Preparatoires' of the International Covenant on Civil and Political Rights,* Dordrecht, Boston, Lancaster, Nijhoff Publishers, 1987. p. 851.

Chand, Attar, *Politics of Human Rights and Civil Liberties: A Global Survey,* Delhi, UBH Publishers, 1985.

Chopra, Manika, "Human Rights Commission: Factors behind the Decision", *Mainstream,* October 3, 1992, p. 4.

Commonwealth of Human Rights Initiative, *Newsletter,* vol. 2, no. 5, New Delhi, 1996.

Compliance Manual of Canadian Human Rights Commission, 1994.

Cook, P. and Kirkpatrick, C. 1994. *Social protection in the context of privatisation,* Manchester; mimeographed.

Cranston, Maurice, *What are Human Rights?* London, Bodley Head, 1973. Crowford, James (ed.), The Right of Peoples, New York, Oxford University Press, 1995.

David, Peter, (ed.), *Human Rights,* London, Routledge, 1988.

Davidson, Scott, *Human Rights,* Philadelphia, Open University Press, USA, 1993.

Desai, A.R., *Violation of Democratic Rights in India,* Bombay, Popular Prakashan, 1986.

Devlin, R. 1993. "Privatisation and social welfare", in *CEPAL Review*, No. 49, Santiago, Chile.

Diwan, Paras and Diwan Peeyushi, *Human Rights in India,* New Delhi, Deep and Deep Publications, 1996.

Donnelly, Jack, *The Concept of Human Rights,* London and Sydney, Croom Helm, 1985.

Drury, E. 1993. *Age Discrimination against Older Workers in the European Community,* London, Eurolink Age.

Falk, Richard, *Human Rights and State Sovereignty,* New York, Holmes and Meier Publishers, 1985.

Fashoyin, T. (ed.). 1992, *Industrial Relations and African Development,* New Delhi, South Asian Publishers.

Ferner, Anand Hyman, R. (eds.) 1992. *Industrial Relations in the New Europe,* Oxford.

Flathman, Richard, E., *The Practice of Rights,* Cambridge: Cambridge University Press, 1976.

Gadgil, D. R., *Human Rights in Multi-national Society,* Poona, Gokhale Institute of Politics and Economics, 1986.

Ghosh, Anjan, "Civil Liberties: Uncivil State", *Seminar* (355), March 1989, pp. 24-37.

Gostin, Larry (ed.), *Civil Liberties in Conflict,* London, Routledge, 1988.

Gupta, Vinay, K. (ed.), *Perspectives on Human Rights,* New Delhi, Vikas Publishing House Pvt. Ltd., 1996.

Hariss, Davis (ed.), *International Human Rights Reports,* vol. 2, no. 1, January 1995, University of Nottingham, Nottingham, U.K.

Henkin, L., *The Rights of Man Today,* Colorado, USA, Westview Press, 1978.

Hingurani, R.C., *Human Rights in India,* New Delhi, Oxford and IBH Publishing Co., 1985.

Hoekema, David A., *Rights and Wrong: Coercion, Punishment and the State,* Setingrove, Sesquehanna Press, 1986.

Howard, E. Rhoda, "Cultural Absolution and the Nostalgia to Community", *Human Rights Quarterly,* vol. 15, no. 2, 1993.

Human Rights Manual, Department of Foreign Affairs and Trade, Australian Government Publication Service, Canberra, 1993.

Human Rights News Letters [monthly], Published by the NHRC, New Delhi, vol. 1, nos. 1-3,1994, vol. 2, nos. 1-12, 1995, vol. 3, nos. 1-5, 1996.

Human Rights Terminology in International Law: A Thesaurus, B. Stormorken and L. Zwaak, Dordrecht, Boston, Nijhoff Publishers, 1988, p. 234.

ILO, 1992/93, *Older workers: Conditions of work and transition to retirement,* Conditions of Work and Welfare Facilities Branch Working Papers, country reports on Canada, France, Japan, UK and USA, Geneva.

ILO, 1994, *Freedom of association and collective bargaining,* Report III (4B), International Labour Conference, 81st Session, Geneva.

Iyer, V.R., Krishna, *Human Right and Inhuman Wrongs,* New Delhi, D.K. Publishers and Distributors, 1990.

Jha, R.C. *Resurrecting Human Rights in India,* New Delhi, Sheriden Book Company, 1995.

Johanson, R. 1994. *Retraining Adults in Germany,* Training Policy

Study No. 4, ILO, Geneva.

Khurshid, Salman, *Beyond Terrorism: New Hope for Kashmir,* New Delhi, UBS Publishers Distributors Ltd., 1994.

Livezey, Lowell W., *NGOs and the Idea of Human Rights,* Princeton, Princeton University Press, 1988.

Macfariance, L. J., *The Theory and Practice of Human Rights,* London, Maurice Temple Smith, 1985.

Mallier, A.T. and Shafto, T.A.C. 1992. *The Economics of Flexible Retirement,* London, Academic Press.

Nanda, Scarrih, Shepherd, *Global Human Rights,* Westview Press, USA, 1981.

Narayana, K.R., "Liberal Values and Human Rights", *Mainstream,* vol. XXXIV, No. 21, February 24, 1996, pp. 7-10.

National Commission of Human Rights, Annual Reports, Mexico, May, 1992 and May, 1993.

Nino, Carlos, Sentiago, *The Ethics of Human Rights,* Oxford, Oxford University Press, 1991.

Noorani, A.G., "India's International Accountability on Human Rights", *Economic and Political Weekly,* August 31, 1991, pp. 2035-36.

Paine, Thomas, *Rights of Man,* London, J.M. Dent., 1915.

Ravindran, D.J., "Indivisibility of Human Rights - A Neglected Concept", *Mainstream,* Oct. 15, 1994, pp. 8-10.

Revue Francaise des Affaires Sociales, 1994. *Ages dans J'emploi: Ages dans le travail,* Vol. 48, No. 1, Paris.

Saksena, K.P. (ed.), *Human Rights: Perspectives and Challenges,* New Delhi, Lancers Books, 1994.

Sardar *Vallabhbhai Patel National Police Academy Journal,* volume 46, no. 1, January June, 1994.

Sathe, S.P., "Towards on Effective Human Rights Commission", *Economic and Political Weekly,* October 31, 1992, pp. 2155-56.

Schwab Peter and Adamantia Pollis (ed.), *Toward A Human Rights Framework,* New York, Praeger Publishers, 1982.

Selby, David, *Human Rights,* Cambridge, Cambridge University Press, 1987.

Senegal, E.P. Singh, *Human Rights in India: Problems and Perspectives,* New Delhi, Deep and Deep Publications, 1995.

Singh, Nagendra, *Human Rights and the Future of Mankind,* Delhi, Vanity Books, 1981.

Singh, Prem, "Human Rights Commission: Need for Consensus", *Link,* November 8, 1992, pp. 20-21.

Singvi, L.M., *Horizons of Freedom,* New Delhi, Nation Publication, 1969.

Sohn, L.B., and Buergenthal, T., *The International Protection of Human Rights,* New York, Bobbs Merrill, 1973, p. 1402.

Sorabjee, Soli, J., "State of Human Rights", *Social Action,* vol. 40, January-March 1990, pp. 16-22.

Stanley, Benn, *A Theory, of Rights,* Cambridge, Cambridge University Press, 1988.

State of Human Rights, An Interim Report of the Human Rights Commission of Pakistan, 1993.

Statement of Mr. Virendra Dayal at 52nd session of the United Nations Commission on Human Rights at Geneva, April 10, 1996.

Statistical Office of the European Communities, 1992. *Labour Costs 1988, Volume 1: Principal Results,* Luxembourg. ◆

Index

Other Text Books

1.	Computer Education **(New)**	175/-
2.	Teaching of Physics **(New)**	175/-
3.	Media & Journalism **(New)**	195/-
4.	Modern Education for New Generation **(New)**	175/-
5.	Advanced Education Technology **(New)**	175/-
6.	Comparative Education **(New)**	175/-
7.	Introduction to Educational Research **(New)**	175/-
8.	Advanced Educational Psychology **(New)**	175/-
9.	Educational Administration & Origanisation Management **(New)**	175/-
10.	Social Psychology **(New)**	225/-
11.	Teaching of Commerce **(New)**	175/-
12.	Educational Development & Technology **(New)**	175/-
13.	Disaster Management **(New)**	175/-
14.	Information Technology **(New)**	175/-
15.	Human Resource Development **(New)**	175/-
16.	Mass Media Communication **(New)**	225/-
17.	Adult Education **(New)**	175/-
18.	General Psychology **(New)**	175/-
19.	Distance Education **(New)**	175/-
20.	Teachers Education **(New)**	175/-
21.	Educational Philosophy **(New)**	175/-
22.	Science Teaching in Schools **(New)**	150/-
23.	Indian Polity **(Revised New)**	295/-
24.	New Comparative Government **(Revised New)**	275/-
Advance Study in the History of Modern India (PB)		
25.	(Volume-1: 1707-1803)	225/-
26.	(Volume-2: 1803-1920)	325/-
27.	(Volume-3: 1920-1947)	175/-
28.	Handbook of Nutrition & Dietetics **(New)**	250/-
29.	Development of Education in India	175/-